ECONOMIC ACTIVITY, TRADE, AND INDUSTRY IN THE U.S.-JAPAN-WORLD ECONOMY

ECONOMIC ACTIVITY, TRADE, AND INDUSTRY IN THE U.S.-JAPAN-WORLD ECONOMY

A Macro Model Study of Economic Interactions

F. Gerard Adams, Byron Gangnes, and Shuntaro Shishido

Westport, Connecticut
London

Library of Congress Cataloging-in-Publication Data

Adams, F. Gerard (Francis Gerard)
    Economic activity, trade, and industry in the U.S.-Japan-world
economy : a macro model study of economic interactions / F. Gerard
Adams, Byron Gangnes, and Shuntaro Shishido.
      p. cm.
    Includes bibliographical references and index.
    ISBN 0-275-94488-3 (alk. paper)
    1. United States—Foreign economic relations—Japan—Econometric
models. 2. Japan—Foreign economic relations—United States—
Econometric models. I. Gangnes, Byron. II. Shishido, Shuntaro,
1924- . III. Title.
HF1452.5.J3A3 1993
337.73052—dc20   92-28476

British Library Cataloguing in Publication Data is available.

Library of Congress Catalog Card Number: 92-28476
ISBN: 0-275-94488-3

First published in 1993

Praeger Publishers, 88 Post Road West, Westport, CT 06881
An imprint of Greenwood Publishing Group, Inc.

Printed in the United States of America

The paper used in this book complies with the
Permanent Paper Standard issued by the National
Information Standards Organization (Z39.48-1984).

10 9 8 7 6 5 4 3 2 1

CONTENTS

FIGURES AND TABLES

FIGURES

TABLES

PREFACE

This volume summarizes a unique example of international research cooperation. The study was organized by F. Gerard Adams of the University of Pennsylvania in the United States and by Shuntaro Shishido, then at Tsukuba University in Japan. It drew heavily on the work of Project LINK, an international consortium of model builders directed by Lawrence Klein and Peter Pauly. Its large-scale models for the United States and Japan were, respectively, the Wharton Annual and Industry model, developed at the University of Pennsylvania by Ross Preston and George Schink and maintained by The WEFA Group (Wharton Econometric Forecasting Associates), and the Foundation for the Advancement of International Science (FAIS)/International University of Japan Multisector (originally Tsukuba) Model of Japan, developed for this project by a team at the University of Tsukuba, including S. Shishido, S. Kinoshita, K. Uno, M. Kuroda, K. Harada, Y. Matsumura, and A. Kawakami, and now maintained under auspices of FAIS at the International University of Japan under the direction of Osamu Nakamura.

The project was supported since 1984 by two grants from the National Institute for Research Advancement (NIRA) of Japan to the University of Pennsylvania and the University of Tsukuba for Phase I, and to the FAIS for Phase II. In view of the primary funding, we refer to the system as the NIRA model of the United States and Japan. More recent work on this project has been supported by the International Centre for the Study of East Asian Development (ICSEAD). There was also extensive support through direct financial contributions, and contributions of effort, facilities, and computer time from many sources that aided the development of the LINK Project, the U.S. and Japan models, and the complex computer programs that support the system.

The first phase of the project was initiated and directed by Professors Adams and Shishido. Byron Gangnes served as the principal research assistant. As so often happens in such a project, he did most of the hard work: the estimation of equations, computer programming, and simulations. As much less frequently happens he came to play a far more important role in the project. As a result, he is a full partner in Phase II of the project and in the preparation of this volume. Earlier publications of this project on which we have drawn are Adams and Gangnes (1987), Gangnes (1990), Adams and Shishido (1987), and Adams, Gangnes, and Shishido (1990).

We are grateful to Lynn Costello for a top notch job in the preparation of this book.

We would also like to express our thanks to precursors and collaborators in this work who are too numerous to mention individually.

ECONOMIC ACTIVITY, TRADE, AND INDUSTRY IN THE U.S.-JAPAN-WORLD ECONOMY

1

INTRODUCTION

The trade flows between Japan and the United States represent a significant linkage between these two economies. There are important implications for various dimensions of macroeconomic performance. There are significant impacts on activity in individual industries. The trade disequilibrium between Japan and the United States, amounting to a bilateral trade deficit of some $50 billion, has had implications for overall economic activity and employment in the United States and in Japan, perhaps going part of the way toward explaining the slowdown of the U.S. economy in recent years. An equally important and perhaps politically more important implication, however, has been its unequal impact on industrial sectors and, hence, regions in the two countries. Much of the effect is felt at the level of particular industries. Even a partial redressment of the trade disequilibrium between the two countries could, in addition to its macroeconomic consequences, have significant impact on their respective industries. Changes in the volume and composition of U.S.-Japan trade might further imply significant changes in the trade of each country with the rest of the world.

The issues are not so much conceptual as they are questions of quantity. How sensitive are imports and exports to changes in U.S. and Japanese policies? How great is the impact of the U.S. economy on Japan, and in turn, how much effect does Japan have on the U.S. economy? How much is sectoral output affected? How large an impact does trade adjustment in particular industries—for example, a restriction on exports of Japanese automobiles into the United States or an increase in the purchases of U.S. electronic equipment by Japan—have on the macroeconomies and on the industries of the respective trade partners? How sensitive is the U.S.-Japan economy to economic developments in the rest of the world, including the worldwide repercussion effects of U.S. and Japanese economic policies? These are issues of paramount importance in the current relationship between the two countries; they are central to U.S. and Japanese policy decisions and to the bilateral and multilateral negotiations in which they are involved.

A number of studies have applied econometric methods to measure the quantitative dimensions of the linkage between the economies of Japan and of the United States, for example Adams and Gangnes (1987), Bergsten and Cline (1985), Petri (1984), and Ishii, McKibbin, and Sachs (1985). In each case, macroeconometric models or simulation systems have been used, but in each case the computations have been limited to the macroeconomic dimensions of the issue, or have looked at sectoral behavior without full econometric modeling of the macro economy.

This study is an effort to go a significant step beyond earlier work by explicitly recognizing the sectoral dimension of the U.S.-Japan relationship in a fully specified macroeconomic model. In traditional national macroeconomic models, the sectoral disaggregation does not go beyond national frontiers (except the international input-output studies of Almon and his colleagues). Even in the very large Wharton Annual and Industry Forecasting Model, trade flows have in the past been broken down only into broad final demand and standard international trade classification (SITC) categories; they do not show sectoral disaggregation. Conventional macro models are, therefore, not well suited to handle the sector-specific questions that are central to measuring the trade and industrial implications of alternative macropolicies and, especially, of sectoral policy approaches. To overcome this limitation, the present study disaggregates the trade flows and establishes linkages on the sectoral level. In addition to the built-in input-output system typical of the large macroeconomic models, like the Wharton Annual and Industry Model, this study includes sectoral trade functions, a breakdown of trade between the United States and Japan and with the rest of the world, and linkages between the United States and Japan on the sectoral level.

A second step forward has been to embed the bilaterally linked models of the United States and Japan into a world model system. Since extensive bilateral linkages are empirically burdensome, many bilaterally linked models disregard the rest of the world economy, or they take the external economic environment as exogenous. We were able to embed the linked models of the United States and Japan into the "rest of the world" as seen by Project LINK.[1] As a result, changes in economic conditions in the United States and Japan are communicated to the rest of the world economy through U.S. and Japanese import volumes and export prices. In turn, there is feedback, though not sectorally disaggregated, from the world economy to the United States and Japan. Correspondingly, if there are changes in the economic performance of other countries, these are recognized in the bilateral U.S.-Japan system. The consistency between economic conditions in the United States and Japan and the outside world is maintained.

An additional advantage of the present system is a forecast horizon extending to 1999. The issues to which this work is addressed, questions of international competitiveness and questions of trade and industrial policy on the industry level, call for a longer time horizon than the two or three years usually considered by business cycle models. The large-scale macro models of the United States and Japan used in this study were designed specifically for long-term simulation, permitting us to extend the forecast horizon to an 11-year span, making it possible to study the impact of policies that have long-run effects.

The research effort described in this volume has produced a model of considerable dimension, substantially larger and more detailed than the original Project LINK model because of the very large size of the models of Japan and of the United States that have been included in this model system. This makes possible a highly disaggregated treatment on the industrial level, showing the effect of policies on the competitiveness of particular industries and the ultimate effects on the industrial sector level in each of the partner countries. Yet, even this disaggregation is not sufficient to integrate fully the United States, Japan, and third country markets on the sectoral level. Such a treatment of competitiveness would have required disaggregation on the sectoral level for third countries—Europe, Korea, China, and other developing countries, for example—and would have called for disaggregated macroeconomic models for each of the major country blocks in the world economy. We did not have such a detailed disaggregation to work with, so the present effort carries the sectoral disaggregation only to the borders of the Japan-United States block. However, on the more aggregate level of Project LINK, the linkages between the individual countries and the competitiveness among them are elaborated in consistent world model solutions.

This study is organized as follows: Chapter 1 introduces the problem and lays out the approach. (It includes an executive summary.) Chapter 2 outlines the structure of the two country models, the sectorally disaggregated models of the United States and of Japan. Chapter 3 describes the direct linkages between the country models and their integration into the LINK world model system. Chapter 4 reports the performance characteristics of the two models, their impact on one another, and their interrelation with the rest of the world. Chapter 5 evaluates the impact of changes in exchange rates. Chapter 6 gives some examples of policy simulations, examining alternative scenarios in the context of the linked model system. Chapter 7 summarizes the results, and considers the potential for further research and simulation studies.

EXECUTIVE SUMMARY

This volume summarizes the results of a large-scale study of economic interaction between the economies of the United States and Japan. Such interactions have become increasingly important not only at the macroeconomic level, where they have been recognized for many years, but specifically at the level of individual industries whose activity and employment are influenced by international competition. Policies in either country at the macroeconomic and at the sectoral level potentially have impacts on the trade partner, and these impacts may be direct or through third countries in the comprehensive system that represents the world economy.

To study the questions of international interaction between the United States and Japan, we have elaborated two large-scale models of the United States—the Wharton Annual and Industry Model and the FAIS/International University of Japan (IUJ) Multisector Model—to provide sectorally disaggregated trade flows between the United States and Japan and between these economies and the rest of the world. The two large-scale models have been incorporated into the LINK world model in order to capture their interrelationships with the rest of the world.

Numerous simulations of macroeconomic and sectoral policies and trade and exchange rate policy were carried out. What do these simulations show about the relationship between the economies of the United States and Japan in a world economic setting?

There are strong linkages between the United States and the Japanese economies on the aggregate and on the sectoral levels. These linkages are augmented once the circuits of the "rest of the world" economy, introduced through Project LINK, are brought into play. They reveal strikingly that the impact of the U.S. economy on Japan is many times greater than the effect of a Japanese stimulus on the United States. A 1% aggregate demand stimulus in the United States has a 0.8% effect on Japanese national product. In contrast, a 1% stimulus in Japan has only a 0.1% impact on the United States. This reflects the difference in the size of the two economies, the much greater sensitivity of imports to economic activity in the United States than in Japan, differences in the content of imports of the two countries, and differences in their relationship to the rest of the world economy.

It is not surprising, consequently, that policy simulations designed to bring down the U.S. budget deficit, and that therefore slow down the U.S. economy, also have significant negative effects on the economy of Japan. Even if the U.S. fiscal readjustment is matched by countervailing monetary policy, there is some negative impact on Japan, although the stimulus of monetary policy ultimately offsets domestic U.S. effects and then also those on the Japanese economy. The simulations show the impact on specific industries. Since the United States is primarily an importer of finished products from Japan, specifically from the automobile industry and from electronics and metal product producing sectors, these are the industries most affected.

Macro policy stimulus, amounting to 1% of gross national product (GNP) in the five major industrial economies other than the United States and Japan, has an impact on world GNP of 0.4%. Combining stimulus in these five countries with corresponding stimulus in the United States and Japan yields an increase in world economic activity of 1.3%.

Simulations of alternative exchange rates show that these have considerable impact on industrial sectors as well as on aggregate economic activity. An 8% appreciation of the yen reduces U.S. imports by 1.3%, resulting in a 0.4% positive effect on U.S. GNP and a negative effect of 0.7% on Japanese economic activity.

Industrial policy simulations assuming increased productivity growth in U.S. high-technology industries show complex effects. These policies must be combined with appropriate demand stimulus to avoid an initial increase in excess capacity, but eventually the gain in productivity improves the sectors' competitive position in the domestic and the international economy. It is interesting to note, however, that the impact of such policies on growth in the United States, on trade, and on the Japanese economy is relatively small in the aggregate, though some specific industries are noticeably affected. Long-term projections for the United States and for Japan were also carried out, suggesting growth in the U.S. of 2.9% annually and in Japan of 4.6% per year, in accord with recent trends.

A trade liberalization simulation that removes tariffs on bilateral U.S.-Japan trade has only limited macroeconomic effects because of the low level of existing tariffs. Nevertheless, there are substantial impacts at the level of individual industries.

The model linkage offers substantial possibilities for simulations of macroeconomic trade and industrial policies, including, for example, the Strategic Impediments Initiative or voluntary export restraint arrangements. Even with highly disaggregated models such as the ones included in this study, however, detailed analysis of proposals requires careful integration of real world circumstances into the models to obtain realistic results.

2

STRUCTURE OF THE U.S. AND JAPANESE MODELS

Macroeconometric models, varying widely in size and structure, have been for many years the instrument of choice for economic forecasting and simulation studies. Such models have also been used to study the economic relations between countries, for example Project LINK, and specifically between the United States and Japan (Adams and Gangnes, 1987). This work has, however, focused on broad macroeconomic relationships, since the typical model, like those contained in the LINK system, operates at a high degree of aggregation and emphasizes short-term business cycle phenomena. The challenge of the U.S.-Japan relationship, and for that matter the study of specific trading links between any countries, is that so many of the questions are sector-specific and require a fairly long time perspective. Many of the issues debated in U.S.-Japan trade talks involve specific industries: easing restrictions and duties on specific categories of products, providing industrial policy aid to advanced technology industries, reducing sector-specific structural impediments, and so forth. A long time perspective is required, since adjustments may take many years to become effective. The challenge is not only to observe impacts on the macroeconomy, or even the effects of macroeconomic developments on specific sectors. There is a need to deal with industry-specific actions and their impact on the industries themselves (through changes in trade, production, employment, etc.), on related industries and on the macroeconomy. We have adapted our models, the linkages between them, and their relationships to the LINK world model system to meet these challenges.

What distinguishes the models used here, the Wharton Annual and Industry Model of the United States and the FAIS/IUJ Multisector Model of Japan, is their disaggregation to the industrial sector level for output and trade. Each of these models integrates a flexible input-output production system with a highly detailed macro model. Each model breaks down goods traded into numerous sector categories, distinguishing between Japan-U.S. trade and trade with the rest of the world. Both models are long-run models aiming toward equilibrium growth paths over a long-term perspective. The models have been adapted so that they can be linked to each other through their respective trade flows.

In this chapter, we discuss the structure of the models with particular emphasis on the sectoral output and trade mechanisms.[1] We consider first the structural elements of the econometric model of the United States. Second, we describe the structure of the model of Japan. In Chapter 3, we consider the linkages that tie the two models together and that integrate them into the LINK world model system.

STRUCTURE OF THE U.S. MODEL

The econometric model of the United States used for this project was adapted from the Wharton Annual and Industry Forecasting Model (Wharton Long-Term Model). This model, designed for long run forecasting and simulation of the macroeconomy with detailed industrial disaggregation, was originally developed at the University of Pennsylvania (Preston, 1972) as a sequel to the sectoral disaggregation pioneered by the Brookings Model (Klein, Duesenberry, and Fromm, 1965). The specific feature of these model systems is the integration of a highly detailed macro model, based on traditional neo-Keynesian demand and supply principles, with a flexible input-output system. Over the years, the model has been applied at Wharton Econometrics. It has been revised as new data have become available, and it has been modified to improve the flexibility of the response of the input-output system to relative prices as well as to technological change.

For purposes of this project, it was necessary to make some significant alterations to deal in greater detail with international trade. Specifically, the standard version of the model carries detailed sectoral disaggregation only to the national frontier but not beyond. Import and export flows are modeled in a number of end-use final demand categories and are aggregated to several broad SITC commodity classes for input-output purposes. These are broken down only to broad trade categories: SITC 0 and 1, foods and beverages; SITC 2 and 4, industrial materials; SITC 3, fuels (with some additional disaggregation); and SITC 5 through 9, manufactures. Changes in imports or exports of these categories are translated to the industrial level by fixed share coefficients. As a result, sector-specific shifts in trade would not influence output at the sectoral level through the input-output mechanism beyond what would result from proportional impacts associated with aggregate trade movements. The work carried on here provides a mechanism for linking trade shifts on the industrial-sector level directly to the comparable sectors in the domestic input-output mechanism.

In addition, we added trade equations to measure the responsiveness of U.S. imports of specific categories of manufactures on the sectoral level to income and relative prices in the United States and abroad. This trade disaggregation involved two stages. First, the overall sector imports of the U.S. from all sources were estimated. Then the Japanese share of total U.S. imports was modeled on the basis of relative prices and technological trends. In this section, we provide a brief summary of the structure of the model. Although various revisions of the model have been carried out, its essential character remains as in Preston (1972) and Wharton Econometric Forecasting Associates (1982).

Structural Characteristics: Overview

The Wharton Long-Term Model articulates the structure and interaction of the various sectors of the economy. The model elaborates the traditional Keynesian macro model to the level of individual industrial sectors incorporating a flexible input-output system. It includes the typical structural elements: Demand, Input-Output, Employment, Wage Determination, Prices at the sectoral as well as at the final demand level, Income Flows, and the Financial Sector. The linkages between the sectors are described in Figure 2.1.

The simultaneous dynamic nature of this long-term model must be kept in mind. Solution of the model with the Gauss-Seidel method in the LINK system provides a simultaneous solution for the entire system recognizing the previous path as incorporated in lag adjustments.

Final demand, summing up to real GNP, is disaggregated into ninety end-use categories. These categories include nineteen consumption equations, thirty-four private investment equations, fourteen export and seventeen import equations, and six categories of government expenditures.

The input-output component of the Wharton Long-Term Model provides a bridge between the final expenditure and production sides of the model, converting final expenditures into effective demand for the output of individual producing sectors and converting sectoral prices into implicit deflators for the categories of final expenditure:

$$X - (I - A)^{-1}Hg \qquad\qquad (2.1)$$

where:

H = $(n \times m)$ matrix of final demand coefficients that describe the industrial distribution of the final expenditure components of GNP,

g = (m×1) vector of real final expenditure components of GNP,

A = (n×n) matrix of direct input coefficients describing the delivery of sector i's output required per unit of sector j's output,

X = (n×1) vector of real gross outputs by industries, and

I = (n×n) identity matrix.

This equation describes the relationship between final expenditures (g) and industrial production or gross output (X). The nonzero elements of the $(I-A)^{-1} H$ matrix are determined by behavioral relationships that allow these variables to change in response to relative prices and technological trends. The procedure utilizes an approach similar to that developed by Hickman and Lau (1972) for modeling the changes in the coefficients of international trade matrices.

The labor requirements block is disaggregated to provide employment estimates for thirty-four sectors (which sum to total employment), and man-hour estimates for mining and manufacturing industries disaggregated to the two-digit standard industrial classification (SIC) level.

In the short run, observed factor combinations represent an imperfect adjustment to efficient factor use. Since the capital stock is generally fixed in the short run, any change in output must be achieved by variation of labor inputs. Variations in labor requirements in response to changing sales expectations can take the form of changes in hours worked, employment, or both. Because of fixed costs and time required to hire and fire employees, the short-run adjustment pattern for man-hours is expected to be faster than the short-run adjustment for employment. Different speeds of adjustment imply separate short-run production surfaces for employment and man-hours. However, the long-run characteristics of these surfaces should be identical. The differing speeds of adjustment implied by the coefficients in the employment and manhours equations capture the resulting changes in labor requirements resulting from short-run fluctuations in sales expectations.

In the long run, where the substitution of labor and capital is possible, production decisions in anticipation of sales imply employment decisions based on least-cost factor combinations. The long-run adjustment of factor combinations to changes in factor costs is captured in the lag distribution of the investment functions.

Demographic factors are of major importance in the analysis of long-run economic growth. The size and structure of the population play an influential role on both the supply and demand side of the economy, just as economic factors influence population growth. Current economic conditions influence short-run fertility and immigration trends, and, over the very long run, even mortality. Conversely, short- and long-run changes in the size, age structure, and other characteristics of the population influence consumer demand, the composition of the labor force, and the level of savings. The longer the time frame of the analysis, the more relevant these dynamic relationships become in determining the behavior of the economy. Because of this importance, the model incorporates a version of Wharton's demographic algorithm Popmod designed to permit flexible modeling of the components of demographic growth in the United States: fertility, mortality, both legal and illegal immigration, and changes in the formation of households and families.

Following the level of disaggregation on the production side of the model, the wage sector provides estimates for twenty-eight industrial wage rates. The wage rate equations incorporate both long-run and short-run labor phenomena. The long-run average wage rate follows the classical real-wage model, in which there is no money illusion and nominal wages are fully adjusted for inflation. A considerable lag, however, is permitted before money wages fully adjust for inflation. The wage relationships also incorporate the Phillips curve, sectoral productivity, and wage changes in other sectors.

Three types of industry output prices are identified in the Wharton Long-Term Model. These are: value-added prices, domestic gross output prices, and composite gross output prices. Fifty-six industry prices corresponding to the industries identified in the input-output sector are derived. Industry prices for all sectors except agriculture, coal mining, and crude petroleum and natural gas mining are modeled behaviorally.

The specifications used for the value-added price equations reflect the following hypotheses concerning price determination: (1) industry prices are set by a markup over "normal" costs, that is, cost at normal levels of operation; (2) the size of the markup is affected by demand or capacity conditions; and (3) prices are influenced by productivity trends within the given industry.

Final demand prices are provided for nineteen categories of consumption, three categories of fixed investment, one category of inventories, thirteen export categories, sixteen import categories, and two categories of government expenditure. For each of these final expenditure groups, excluding imports and inventories, the relevant prices are derived as weighted averages of the composite gross output prices with the elements of the endogenous final demand matrix used as weights. Prices for imports are determined in the trade linkage model as trade-weighted averages of Japanese and third country export deflators. International linkages are described below.

The monetary block of the Wharton Long-Term Model determines interest rates and money stock levels using relationships among financial and nonfinancial variables. Government policy parameters are assumed to control the broad money supply (M2), whereas an asset portfolio system determines both the demand for M2 and its composition. Equilibrium in this system sets the key short-term interest rate. A term structure system determines both additional short-term interest rates and long-term interest rates from the equilibrium rate. Key interest rates mark up inflation fully in the long run. This markup results in long-term stability of the real interest rate.

The Trade Sector

The trade block of the model has been adapted to disaggregate imports and exports into industrial-sector categories and to distinguish between trade between the United States and Japan and trade with the rest of the world. In place of the trade sector of the conventional version of the Wharton Long-Term Model, which is modeled on final demand categories, we have developed a sectoral disaggregation based on industrial categories. We use a two-stage procedure. Imports are explained for each of the major industrial categories first as a total. Then relying on the Armington concept (Armington, 1969), imports are divided between imports of the United States from Japan and from the rest of the world. The structure of the equations is as follows:

$$M_i - f\left(\frac{PM_i}{PX_i}, X_i, TIME\right) \tag{2.2}$$

where:

M_i	=	U.S. imports of category i,
PM_i/PX_i	=	relative prices: import prices of category i relative to U.S. output price of category i,
X_i	=	economic activity in category i, and
$TIME$	=	trend.

Lagged relative price terms or lagged dependent variables enter the equations for some industries.

Assuming product differentiation by source of origin, the Japanese share of U.S. imports of category i, M_i^J/M_i, is explained on the basis of relative price and trend,

$$\frac{M_i^J}{M_i} - f\left(\frac{PM_i^J}{PM_i}, \; TREND\right)$$ (2.3)

where PM_i^J and PM_i are, respectively, prices of U.S. category i imports from Japan and from all sources.

Levels of U.S. imports from Japan are then obtained from the identity

$$M_i^J - (\frac{M_i^J}{M_i}) * M_i$$ (2.4)

This system of equations, developed for each manufacturing output category, provides a mechanism for computing the impact of economic activity and prices in the United States on trade with Japan. Nonmanufacturing categories were not required, since there are few significant imports of non-manufactured goods by the United States from Japan. Trade in services is not included in the linkage.

From the perspective of the U.S. model, exports remain exogenous. That is, the exports are established in the outside world, and specifically for purposes of the present project, exports to Japan are determined in the econometric model of Japan, and exports to the rest of the world are determined by rest of the world imports operating through the LINK system. The quantitative flows of imports and exports affect the input-output system of the model directly by altering final demands for each industrial sector category. The trade linkages are described in greater detail in Chapter 3.

The explanation of export prices follows standard macro model methodology for large countries, that is, export prices are principally determined by standard markup mechanisms in the exporting country itself.[2] This is the methodology used by the Wharton model to determine sectoral prices. Since imports are disaggregated by industrial sector, the sectoral gross output prices of the Wharton model were used directly in computing the relative price terms in the import equations. Import prices are exogenous to the U.S. model, being determined in the international linkage system as the weighted average of partner-country export prices. The international price linkages are also discussed in Chapter 3, below.

The exchange rate is exogenous to the U.S. model. This permits adjustment of the exchange rate, or alternatively, change in import and export prices, to test the impact of exchange rate changes in alternative simulations.

Table 2.1 summarizes the results of the estimation of trade equations explaining total U.S. imports (in billions of 1972 U.S. dollars), which were in general regressed on a constant (C), a time trend (65 for the year 1965, 66 for 1966, etc.) (TIME), the contemporaneous and lagged values of the appropriate relative price variable (import price index for the respective sector, 1972 = 100, divided by the price index for the corresponding domestic sector, 1972 = 100) (P), and a domestic activity variable (X). Since appropriate expenditure data were not available, the value of production of the corresponding domestic sector has been chosen. The rate of growth of output (DX) enters some equations. Some equations include a lagged dependent variable (LAG D) as well.

Table 2.2 summarizes the results of the estimation of the equations explaining the share of imports from Japan as part of the total imports for each sector. The independent variable P is the log of the relative price of imports from Japan, where the numerator is the yen price of Japanese exports in the corresponding industry multiplied by the current exchange rate, and the denominator is the dollar import price used in the overall import equation estimation. The variable J appearing in some equations is the log of the yen-dollar exchange rate in dollars per 1000 yen.

Note that the dependent variables here are the shares themselves, not their logarithms. This specification leads to elasticities of import shares with respect to prices that are variable over time and are given by b/s, where b is the estimated coefficient on relative price and s is the share of imports from Japan in the current year.

Direct interpretation of the results in Tables 2.1 and 2.2 is difficult, since there are numerous lags and lagged dependent variables are used in some cases. Table 2.3 summarizes the activity and price elasticities of the overall import equations, and the relative price semielasticities of the import share equations. All of the figures reported are "long-run" elasticities, computed by assuming that current and past values of variables are the same, so that price elasticities are sums of contemporaneous and any lagged coefficients, and the effects of lagged dependent variables are included.

The weighted average activity elasticity for manufacturing imports is 0.57.[3] This is much lower than the estimate of about 1.5 to 2.0 common in the empirical trade literature.[4] In fact, the activity elasticity estimates of the present study are not directly comparable to the income elasticities usually reported. The elasticities given here are of imports with respect to a sectoral output variable, rather than aggregate income. Since manufacturing output rises considerably faster than income during an expansion, the elasticity estimates are lower than in conventional formulations. Numerical estimates of income elasticities for this model yield an overall elasticity for manufactures of 0.98, nearly twice as large as the elasticity reported in Table 2.3. For electrical machinery, the income elasticity is 1.12, and for autos it is 2.41.

The income elasticity estimate of 0.98 is still somewhat lower than those reported in the literature. This is attributable, at least in part, to the use of trend terms or lagged dependent variables in some of the estimated equations. The resulting estimates are appropriate as "long-run" elasticities, but they will be lower than estimates from equations without such trend terms.[5]

Among individual industries, the very large estimates for cement and other transportation equipment stand out. These estimates, which introduce considerable instability into the behavior of these categories, may be unreliable due to the very small trade volumes involved.

The weighted average price elasticity, -1.03, is well within the range of price elasticity estimates of recent studies.[6] There is considerable contrast between the high price elasticities of the transportation categories and some of the metals, and the very low elasticities of textiles and apparel, and nonelectrical machinery. The low price responsiveness of textiles and apparel may be a reflection of the significant barriers to trade in these goods.

The average semielasticity of the Japan import share with respect to the relative price, -0.78, indicates that a 1% increase in Japanese export prices, with overall U.S. import prices unchanged, reduces their share in U.S. imports by slightly less than one percentage point. This average would be considerably lower were it not for the very large estimate for the automobile elasticity. A large elasticity here points toward strong competition between goods of varying source countries, which may not be believable for autos.

The trade equation results are compared in more detail with the results of the Japanese model below.

The other half of the behavioral trade model is the endogenous determination of industry export prices, which contribute to movements in partner-country import prices through the international linkage system. In the U.S. model, export price deflators for traded goods industries are simply defined to move proportionately with changes in composite output deflators.

Applications of the U.S. Model

Versions of this model have been used for numerous applications over many years. The combination of sectoral and aggregate information makes the model suitable for studies that involve industrial development as well as national policy; indeed, one of the important applications of the system was in doing studies of industrial policy (Adams, 1985). The elaboration of the trade sectors is designed to expand the potential of the model to deal with trade policy in general and with the interaction of the economy of the United States with that of Japan. These interactions go well beyond the adjustment of trade, since they involve domestic policies on the sectoral as well as on the national level.

STRUCTURE OF THE JAPANESE MODEL

The Japanese long-term multisector model (Version JLM, F8) used for this project has sixty-four industrial sectors for output, employment, prices, and so forth, containing about 3,400 equations.   The model is designed to analyze structural changes in output, employment, capital, and relative prices, as well as macroeconomic changes in aggregate income, money supply, and interest rates. Thus, changes in medium-term macroeconomic variables can be analyzed in the same context as long-term structural changes, as in the U.S. model.   The analytical framework of the model combines a Leontief-type input-output system with Keynesian-type demand-oriented structural equations.

In order to facilitate the analysis of bilateral dependency, the Japanese model has been made comparable with the U.S. model in a number of ways. The industrial classification system is highly comparable, as shown in Table 2.4. Second, in each sector, output and productive factors, such as raw materials, labor, and capital, are consistently broken down on the same level.   Third, changes in technical relationships between input and output as well as components in final demand are made price-sensitive to permit analysis of structural changes in relation to relative prices, as in the U.S. model.   Fourth, the demographic and labor supply block was estimated and integrated to the economic main block of the model in a similar way to the U.S. model in the revised version of the model, as discussed later.   Finally, there is a detailed demographic sector to track important long-run changes in labor force characteristics.

The Japanese model, however, has distinctive features as compared with its U.S. counterpart and its Japanese predecessors.[7] Interdependence between technical progress and relative prices is more explicitly incorporated than in any other models. This model is a dynamic extension of the previous static version of the model. It is based on 544×409 technology matrices for the past fifteen years.[8] Dynamic RAS algorithms were extensively utilized to make the 64×64 I-O matrices of the present model.   A dynamic version of the static VRAS[9] algorithm D1 was used for updating the input-output matrix; it updates each coefficient in the matrix under a set of technical progress parameters for total factor productivity and primary factor prices, such as wage rate, interest rate, and so forth, and sixty-four sectoral prices for imports.   Unlike conventional input-output models, this model can not only analyze the quantity effect, or backward effect, of final demand on output and employment, but also the forward effect of price or technical changes and their feedback to quantity changes.   The interdependence between forward and backward effects is treated in a consistent input-output framework.   As an important characteristic of the model, it is possible to analyze complex impacts, such as the effects of antipollution policy, which reduce output and employment in the energy sectors through increased energy prices, but also bring about an expansion of output and employment in high technology sectors because of a favorable shift of demand for the latter and a similar expansion of output in anti-pollution equipment and related sectors. The model can produce I-O transaction matrices for each year by updating annually the I-O coefficient matrices.

The second feature of the model relates to investment behavior, which is based on production functions with technical progress. These are based on a Schumpeterian notion that dynamism for capitalistic expansion is based on entrepreneurial innovation seeking higher productivity. Technical progress, as measured in terms of total factor productivity, plays an important role in explaining business investment, together with factor prices. Differences among industries regarding the speed of technical progress are important in determining sectoral growth rates and the comparative advantages of various sectors in international trade.

The model is based on the dual relationship between demand-supply and cost-price linkage systems, and their interaction is regarded as essential in determining all the variables. This notion of a general-equilibrium-type I-O framework, similar to that for the U.S. long-term model, is dynamized by explicitly introducing technical progress, which not only affects both cost-price and demand-supply conditions, but also stimulates sectoral growth rates through sectoral business investment. Higher efficiency provides better profit expectations and greater demand caused by lower output prices, which in turn stimulates investment. An opposite result is likely to occur if the technical factor turns negative, as in some stagnant sectors in Japan. Interestingly, some sectors have continued fairly active investment because of price supports of the government, highlighting the importance of price factors in investment functions.

Trade Equations

Overall real import equations follow a specification similar to equation 2.2 for the U.S. model, but in absolute levels, rather than logarithms. Imports are a function of industry demand, D_i, relative import prices PM_i/PX_i, and in some cases, inventory stocks, IV_i:

$$M_i - \alpha_{1i} + \beta_{1i}D_i + \beta_{2i}\frac{PM_i}{PX_i} + \beta_{3i}IV_i(-1) \tag{2.5}$$

The expected sign of β_3 is negative, reflecting the assumption that Japanese firms will partly draw down existing inventories before increasing imports from abroad. For some industries, equation 2.5 was estimated with a trend variable as well. Imports from the United States are modeled as share equations in log form:

$$\ln\left(\frac{M\$_i^{US}}{M_i \cdot PM\$_i^{US}}\right) = \gamma_{1i} + \beta_{4i} \ln\left(\frac{PM\$_i^{US}}{PM_i \cdot REX}\right) \qquad (2.6)$$

These equations are in dollar terms; $M\$_i^{US}$ is nominal imports from the United States in current dollars, $PM\$_i^{US}$ is the U.S. export price, and REX is a yen exchange rate index.

Import activity and price elasticities, and import share semielasticities are summarized in Table 2.5. These figures have been computed from the estimated coefficients of equations 2.5 and 2.6 and 1983 levels of the various data series. Notice that the weighted average demand elasticity, 1.37, is considerably higher than the average for the U.S. import equations, and is closer to the results of previous studies.[10] A glance down the list suggests this is not just a result of including nonmanufactures in the Japanese average; this is confirmed in Table 2.6, which presents weighted average elasticities for the four broad categories used in Project LINK. The weighted average demand elasticity for Japanese manufacturing imports, 1.53, is larger than the overall average of 1.37. For other broad categories of imports (determined in aggregate equations in the U.S. model), the demand elasticities are closer together, but the Japanese figures are consistently larger than those for the United States.

At least in part, the larger elasticity estimates in the Japan model are a product of the structure of the two models and the specification of import equations. In the Japan model, changes in industry demand do not markedly differ from changes in aggregate income under a fiscal expansion, so there is not the same downward effect on the coefficients observed as a result of the strongly procyclical behavior of the industrial output variables in the U.S. model. The Japan import equations do not employ trend terms or lagged dependent variables, and so will tend to identify more of an import change with changes in current demand.

The responsiveness of Japanese imports to relative import price change is somewhat lower than for the United States. The average price elasticity for manufactured goods imports is -0.89, compared with -1.03 for the United States. The sensitivity of U.S. shares of Japanese manufacturing imports to price changes is much smaller than for the comparable shares in the U.S. market, -0.34 compared with -0.78, but recall that the U.S. average is inflated by the very large share elasticity for automobile imports.

Overall, when one disaggregates by sector, Japanese imports in the model system are significantly more responsive to demand changes than U.S. imports, whereas U.S. imports respond more strongly to price changes, both of imports relative to domestic goods and Japanese goods relative to the goods of other exporting countries.

In the Japan model, export prices, PE_i are tied to output prices, PX_i, but also to the rate of capacity utilization, ROX_i and the exchange rate, REX:

$$\ln(PE_i) = \alpha_i + \beta_{i1}\cdot \ln(PX_i) + \beta_{i2}\cdot \ln(REX) + \beta_{i3}\cdot \ln(ROX_i) \qquad (2.7)$$

The coefficients β_{i2} indicate the extent to which yen fluctuations are "passed through" to dollar export prices. In Chapter 5, we discuss the magnitude of this effect and its implications for the impact of yen appreciation on the economies of Japan, the U.S. and the world.

Applications of the Japanese Model

The Japanese model has many of the features already noted in the U.S. model and, consequently, has much the same application potential. It goes beyond the U.S. model in elaborating the input-output system and investment to incorporate technological developments, an important aspect of Japanese industrial development. It, too, has been elaborated on the trade side to make possible evaluation of trade policies, and to capture the linkages between the economy of Japan and the United States. These linkages make possible studies considering impacts of national policies, trade policies, exchange rate pass-through, and sectoral policies, which are considered in later chapters of this volume.

Figure 2.1
Flow Chart of the Wharton Annual and Industry Forecasting Model

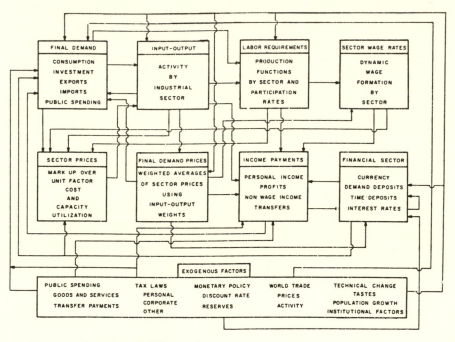

Source: Preston, (1972), p. 4.

Table 2.1
U.S. Manufacturing Industry Import Equations

DEP VAR	SITC#	C	TIME	P	PDL	X	PDL	DX	LAG D	R²/DW
Indus. Chemicals	51-3	-6.93 (-11.0)	0.13 (6.9)	-0.4 (-2.2)	(3,4,2)	-0.52 (-2.9)		0.896 (3.72)		0.97 2.45
				-0.37 (-2.7)						
				-0.3 (-2.0)						
				-0.17 (-1.6)						
Nonind. Chemicals	5OT	-8.04 (-11.0)	0.069 (6.44)	-0.48 (-4.2)	(2,4,2)	0.75 (3.21)				0.97 2.07
				-0.36 (-4.2)						
				-0.24 (-4.2)						
				-0.12 (4.2)						
Leather,	61	-6.22 (-19.0)	0.071 (15.5)	-1.02 (-2.8)						0.94 2.02
Rubber	62	-1.03 (-0.6)	-0.045 (-1.7)	-1.12 (-4.2)		1.37 (1.97)			0.62 (5.65)	0.98 2.02
Lumber	63	-0.33 (-3.1)		-1.36 (-6.5)	(2,3,4)				0.296 (1.38)	0.91 1.89
				-0.44 (-2.6)						
				0.478 (1.88)						
Paper, Pulp	64	-1.76 (-3.8)	0.04 (4.2)			0.607 (3.9)	(2,4,4)			0.87 1.97
						0.148 (1.6)				
						-0.31 (-3.5)				
						-0.77 (-5.4)				
Textiles	65	-0.95 (-1.9)	0.165 (2.47)	-0.54 (-2.9)						0.38 1.39
Cement	661	-4.52 (-4.3)	0.04 (3.75)	-0.88 (-3.0)		3.295 (5.85)			0.491 (4.01)	0.93 1.58
Oth. Stone, Clay, Glass	66OT	-4.53 (-8.5)	0.066 (8.86)	-0.68 (-3.9)	(2,3,2)					0.85 1.25
				-0.45 (-3.9)						
				-0.23 (-3.9)						

Table 2.1—Continued

DEP VAR	SITC#	C	TIME	P	PDL	X	PDL	DX	LAG D	R²/DW
Iron, Steel	67	-6.38 (-3.3)	0.067 (4.8)	-0.68 (-2.2)		0.715 (2.52)				0.7 2.4
Aluminum	684	-8.06 (-9.5)	0.088 (8.64)	-0.99 (-5.7) -0.82 (-5.5) -0.65 (-4.6) -0.47 (-3.1) -0.3 (-1.7)	(2,5,4)					0.87 2.18
Other Nonfer. Metal	68-684	0.099 (0.85)		-0.23 (-2.3) -0.35 (-2.3) -0.35 (-2.3) -0.23 (-2.3)	(3,4,1)	0.523 (2.19)			0.492 (2.44)	0.62 2.05
Fabric. Metal prod.	69, 81	-2.7 (-1.7)		-0.73 (-3.9) -0.59 (-3.9) -0.44 (-3.9) -0.29 (-3.9) -0.15 (-3.9)	(2,5,2)	0.761 (1.83)		-0.53 (-1.4)	0.34 (2.18)	0.97 2.26
Nonelect. Machinery	71	-7.89 (-13.0)	0.082 (8.19)	-0.54 (-4.1)		0.796 (2.81)				0.99 1.28
Electrical Machinery	72	-8.8 (-16.0)	0.138 (18.0)	-0.3 (-2.8) -0.22 (-2.8) -0.15 (-2.8) -0.07 (-2.8)	(2,4,2)					0.99 2.1
Motor Vehicles	732	-5.09 (-7.6)	0.07 (7.69)	-0.44 (-6.5) -0.33 (6.5) -0.22 (-6.4)	(2,4,2)	0.383 (4.15)			0.239 (2.63)	0.96 1.75

Table 2.1—Continued

DEP VAR	SITC#	C	TIME	P	PDL	X	PDL	DX	LAG D	R²/DW
				-0.11 (-6.4)						
Aircraft	734	-10.5 (-3.0)	0.1 (3.3)	-0.59 (-2.4)	(2,4,2)	0.85 (1.7)			0.4 (1.9)	0.85 1.70
				-0.44 (-2.4)						
				-0.3 (-2.4)						
				-0.15 (-2.4)						
Other Transp. Equip.	730T	-5.95 (-3.5)		-0.83 (-2.8)	(2,4,2)	2.088 (3.70)			0.541 (3.75)	0.88 1.82
				-0.62 (-2.8)						
				-0.41 (-2.8)						
				-0.2 (-2.8)						
Furniture	82	-11.3 (-28.0)	0.109 (14.3)	-0.72 (-7.5)	(2,4,2)	0.97 (3.86)				0.99 1.32
				-0.54 (-7.5)						
				-0.36 (-7.5)						
				-0.18 (-7.5)						
Apparel	84	-7.62 (-11.0)	0.09 (6.97)	-0.24 (-1.3)		0.618 (1.64)				0.98 1.49
Instruments	86	-2.96 (-2.7)				1.074 (2.84)			0.53 (3.14)	0.98 2.01
Misc. Manufactures	89	-8.18 (-12.0)	0.088 (6.70)	-1.23 (-3.1)		1.1				0.97 1.76

Notes: Variable abbreviations are defined in the text. R^2 is the adjusted R squared; DW is the Durbin-Watson statistic. Values under the coefficients are t-ratios. Where more than one coefficient is shown, they are lag values in a polynomial distributed lag, the specification of which is given in the column headed "PDL": The first element indicates the number of terms in the estimating polynomial (degree minus one), the second element indicates the number of lags, including the contemporaneous value, and the third element is a code for endpoint restrictions: 2 for far point constraint, 3 for near point constraint, 1 for both, and 4 for neither.

Table 2.2
Share Equations for U.S. Imports from Japan

DEP VAR	SITC#	C	TIME	P	PDL	J	LAG D	DW	R²
Indus. Chemicals	51-3	0.14 (3.50)		-0.07 (-2.1)		-0.07 (-2.7)	0.53 (3.3)	2.3	0.61
Nonind. Chemicals	5OT	0.25 (2.02)		-0.2 (-1.5)		-0.11 (-1.1)	0.56 (3.17)	2.1	0.55
Leather,	61	0.05 (2.44)		-0.017 (-2.45)	(2,4,2)		0.60 (4.0)	1.95	0.91
				-0.013 (-2.45)					
				-0.008 (-2.44)					
				-0.004 (-2.44)					
Rubber†	62	-8.34 (-9.7)	0.082 (7.86)	-0.82 (-5.15)	(3,5,2)			1.66	0.85
				-0.64 (-8.14)					
				-0.47 (-5.5)					
				-0.31 (-3.19)					
				-0.15 (-2.15)					
Lumber†	63	-0.59 (-4.4)		-1.15 (-4.12)			0.76 (11.5)	2.1	0.99
Paper, Pulp	64	0.019 (44.9)		-0.02 (-16.0)	(2,5,2)			2.26	0.94
				-0.017 (-16.0)					
				-0.013 (-16.0)					
				-0.009 (-16.0)					
				-0.004 (-16.0)					
Textiles†	65	0.64 (1.83)	-0.029 (-6.0)	-1.24 (-9.4)				1.36	0.9
Cement	661	0.018 (1.92)					1.04 (4.7)		
							-0.52 (-2.25)	2.23	0.56
Other Stone, Clay, Glass	66OT	0.34 (12.5)	-0.003 (-7.2)	-0.25 (-11.0)				1.84	0.89

Table 2.2 —Continued

DEP VAR	SITC#	C	TIME	P	PDL	J	LAG D	DW	R²
Iron, Steel	67	0.39 (19.6)		-0.06 (-6.0)	(3,5,1)			1.4	0.7
				-0.09 (-6.0)					
				-0.1 (-6.0)					
				-0.09 (-6.0)					
				-0.06 (-6.0)					
Aluminum	684	0.03 (2.03)		-0.018 (-2.1)	(2,4,3)		0.51 (2.2)	1.7	0.55
				-0.036 (-2.1)					
				-0.055 (-2.1)					
				-0.073 (-2.1)					
Other Nonfer.	68-684	0.019 (0.71)		-0.07 (-1.9)		0.014 (0.647)	0.115 (0.5)	1.8	0.24
Fabric. Metal Prod.	69,81	1.13 (6.73)	-0.011 (-4.8)	-0.022 (-3.2)	(2,4,3)			1.8	0.93
				-0.043 (-3.2)					
				-0.065 (-3.2)					
				-0.086 (-3.2)					
Nonelect. Machinery	71	-0.8 (-7.1)	0.015 (7.6)	-0.15 (-4.9)	(2,4,4)	-0.095 (-2.1)		1.7	0.96
				-0.08 (-4.2)					
				0.02 (-0.9)					
				0.05 (2.0)					
Electrical Machinery	72	0.92 (3.6)	-0.009 (-2.9)	-0.3 (-2.3)			0.3 (1.5)	1.4	0.4
Motor Vehicles	732	0.022 (0.88)		-0.47 (-3.6)			0.82 (11.0)	1.32	0.9
Aircraft	734	-0.3 (-2.7)	0.005 (3.2)	-0.16 (-3.2)				1.57	0.45
Other Transp. Equip.*	73OT	-0.64 (-1.9)	0.025 (3.23)			-0.62 (-2.7)	-0.42 (-2.5)	2.11	0.57

Table 2.2 —Continued

DEP VAR	SITC#	C	TIME	P	PDL	J	LAG D	DW	R²
Furniture†	82	-0.82		-1.06			0.74	1.15	0.93
		(-3.3)		(-2.7)			(8.7)		
Apparel†	84	0.74				-1.22	1.2	2.67	0.98
		(2.25)				(-3.13)	(6.68)		
							-0.48		
							(-2.96)		
Instru-ments	86	-0.64	0.014	-0.23				1.65	0.95
		(-11.6)	(18.6)	(-3.65)					
Misc. Manufactures	89	-0.18	0.005	-0.42			0.48	1.52	0.94
		(-1.4)	(3.0)	(-6.8)			(5.0)		

Notes: Variable abbreviations are defined in the text. R² is the adjusted R-squared; DW is the Durbin-Watson statistic. Values under the coefficients are t-ratios. Where more than one coefficient is shown, they are lag values in a polynomial distributed lag, the specification of which is given in the column headed "PDL": The first element indicates the number of terms in the estimating polynomial (degree minus one), the second element indicates the number of lags, including the contemporaneous value, and the third element is a code for endpoint restrictions: 2 for far point constraint, 3 for near point constraint, 1 for both and 4 for neither.

*Includes a dummy variable for a very low share in 1979.

†The dependent variable is the log of the share.

Table 2.3
U.S. Model Import Elasticities

	OVERALL IMPORTS		FROM JAPAN
	DEMAND	REL. PRICE	REL. JA. PRICE
Textiles	——	-0.54	-0.22 †
Apparel	0.62	-0.24	——
Paper, Pulp	-0.33 *	0.00	-0.06 *
Indust. Chemicals	-0.52	-1.24 *	-0.15
Nonind. Chemicals	0.75	-1.20 *	-0.45
Rubber, Plastics	3.61	-2.95	-0.77 †
Leather	——	-1.02	-0.11 *
Lumber, Wood Prod.	——	-1.88 *	-0.13 †
Furniture	0.97	-1.80 *	-0.14 †
Cement	6.47	-1.73	——
Oth. Stone, Clay, Gl.	——	-1.36 *	-0.25
Iron, Steel	0.72	-0.68	-0.40 *
Aluminum	——	-3.23 *	-0.37 *
Oth. Nonfer. Metal	1.03	-2.28 *	-0.07
Fabr. Metal Products	1.15	-3.33 *	-0.22 *
Nonelect. Machinery	0.80	-0.54	-0.16 *
Electrical Machinery	——	-0.74	-0.43
Aircraft	1.42	-2.47 *	-0.16
Oth. Transp. Equip.	4.55	-4.49 *	——
Motor Vehicles	0.50	-1.45 *	-2.61
Instruments	2.29	——	-0.23
Misc. Manufactures	1.10	-1.23	-0.81
Weighted Average:	0.57	-1.03	-0.78

Notes: All elasticities are "long-run" elasticities: Current and lagged values of endogenous variables are assumed to be the same. Dashes indicate the equation was fitted without the indicated income or price term. The numbers in the third column are the semielasticities of shares of imports from Japan with respect to the relative prices of imports from Japan.

*Estimated equation includes lagged independent variables. The elasticity is computed as the sum of the lag coefficients.

†The equation was estimated with the log of the import share as the dependent variable, and the semielasticity was computed using 1984 share data.

Table 2.4
Japan and U.S. Sectoral Classification

JAPAN	UNITED STATES
General Crops	Agriculture, Forestry and Fishing
Industrial Crops	"
Livestock for textiles	"
Other livestock and service	"
Forestry	"
Fishery	"
Coal mining	Coal Mining
Iron Ores	Metal Mining
Nonferrous Metallic Ores	"
Crude Petroleum	Crude Petroleum Extraction
Natural Gas	Natural Gas Extraction
Other Mining	Mining and Quarrying of Nonmetallic Minerals
Meat and Dairy Products	Food and Kindred Products
Grain Products	"
Manufactured Sea Foods	"
Other Foods	"
Beverages	"
Tobacco	Tobacco Manufactures
Natural Textiles	Textile and Mill Products
Chemical Textiles	"
Other Textiles	"
Wearing Apparel	Apparel and Related Products
Wood and Wood Products	Lumber and Wood Products
Furniture	Furniture and Fixtures
Pulp and Paper	Paper and Allied Products
Printing and Publishing	Printing and Publishing
Leather Products	Leather and Leather Products
Rubber Products	Rubber and Miscellaneous Plastic Products
Basic and Intermediate Chemicals	Industrial Chemicals
Final Chemicals	Nonindustrial Chemicals
Petroleum Products	Petroleum Refining and Related Industries
Coal Products	"
Cement	Cement
Other Ceramics	Other Stone, Clay, and Glass
Iron Products	Iron and Steel
Rollings, Castings and Forgings	"
Aluminum (including secondary)	Aluminum
Other non-Metal Products	Other Nonferrous Metals

Table 2.4 —Continued

JAPAN	UNITED STATES
Metal Products	Fabricated Metal Products
Machinery	Machinery, Except Electrical
Electrical Machinery	Electrical Machinery
Automobiles	Motor Vehicles and Parts
Aircraft	Aircraft
Other Transport Equipment	Other Transportation Equipment
Instruments and Related Products	Instruments and Related Products
Miscellaneous Manufacturing	Miscellaneous Manufacturing
Housing Construction	Residential Contract Construction
Industrial Construction	Nonresidential Contract Construction
Public Construction	Other Contract Construction
Other Construction	"
Electric Power	Electric Utilities (Public and Private)
"	Other Federal Enterprises*
"	Other State and Local Enterprises*
Gas	Gas Utilities
Water and Sanitary Service	Sanitary Services
Wholesale and Retail Trade	Wholesale-Retail Trade
Real Estate	Finance, Insurance, and Real Estate
Railways	Railroad Transportation
Trucks and Buses	Local & Highway Passenger Transportation
"	Motor Freight Transport & Warehousing
Other Transportation	Water Transportation
"	Air Transportation
"	Pipeline Transportation
"	Transportation Services
Communications	Communications
Finance and Insurance	Finance, Insurance and Real Estate
Government Services	Government Industry
Public Services	Medical Services*
"	Nonmedical Services*
Other Services	"
Unallocated	———

*Denotes partial correspondence.

Table 2.5
Japan Model Import Elasticities

	OVERALL IMPORTS		FROM U.S.
	DEMAND*	REL. PRICE	REL. U.S. PRICE†
General Crops	1.36	-0.33	-0.38
Industrial Crops	0.92	-0.12	-0.19
Livestock, Textiles	1.06	——	-0.01
Livestock	2.65	-0.09	-0.17
Forestry	3.35	-1.16	-0.21
Fisheries	5.04	-0.44	-1.17
Iron Ores	1.03	-1.00	——
Nonfer. Metal Ore	1.10	-0.11	-0.34
Coal Mining	0.98	——	-0.11
Crude Petroleum	0.95	-0.58	——
Natural Gas	0.80	——	——
Other Mining	0.19	-1.53	-0.13
Meat, Dairy	1.29	-0.78	-0.19
Grain Products	1.00 ‡	-0.44	-0.23
Manuf. Sea Food	1.87	-0.41	-0.13
Other Foods	1.00 ‡	-0.25	-0.15
Beverages	2.55	-0.38	——
Tobacco	3.29	-1.01	——
Natural Textiles	1.15	-1.64	-0.01
Chemical Textiles	1.00	-3.61	-0.74
Other Textiles	4.51	-0.92	-0.09
Wearing Apparel	1.57	-1.00	-0.09
Paper, Pulp	0.86	-1.13	-0.58
Basic, Int. Chems.	1.13	-1.27	-0.33
Final Chemicals	1.73	-0.32	-0.19
Petroleum Prods.	1.87	-0.96	-0.01
Coal Products	7.83	-1.15	-0.68
Rubber Products	2.01	-1.87	——
Leather Products	2.79	-1.09	-0.11
Wood Products	0.87	——	-0.27
Furniture	3.52	-0.49	-0.07
Cement	1.00	-1.27	-0.97
Other Ceramics	2.60	——	——
Iron Products	0.60	-0.27	-0.12
Roll., Cast., Forg.	4.99	-0.48	-0.07
Aluminum	1.18	-1.38	-0.35
Oth. Nonfer. Metal	1.38	——	-0.13
Metal Products	1.27	-0.25	-0.38
Nonelect. Machinery	1.00 ‡	-0.63	-0.25
Electrical Machinery	0.95	-0.94	-0.35
Aircraft	1.09	-0.60	-0.91
Oth. Transp. Equip.	1.00 ‡	-1.54	-0.43
Automobiles	2.00	-2.52	-0.48

Table 2.5 —Continued

| | OVERALL IMPORTS | | FROM U.S. |
	DEMAND*	REL. PRICE	REL. U.S. PRICE†
Instruments	1.98	-1.85	-0.31
Misc. Manufactures	0.99	-2.41	-0.08
Weighted Average:	1.37	-0.64	-0.25

Notes: Dashes indicate the equation was fitted without the indicated price term.

*Overall import equations were estimated in levels; approximate elasticities were computed using 1983 quanties of imports and demands.

†Figures are semielasticities of the share of imports from the U.S. with respect to the relative price of imports from the U.S. The equations for imports from the U.S. were estimated with the log of the share as the dependent variables; semielasticities were computed using 1983 import share data.

‡Constrained to equal 1.00.

Table 2.6
Comparison of Semiaggregate Import Elasticities
in the U.S. and Japan Models

		OVERALL IMPORTS		FROM PARTNER
		DEMAND	REL. PRICE	REL. PRICE

United States:

SITC	0, 1 Food & Bev.	1.17	-0.16	—— *
	2, 4 Raw Materials	1.07	-0.52	—— *
	3 Energy †	2.68	-0.15	—— *
	5-9 Manufactures	0.57	-1.03	-0.78
	Total	0.70	-0.93	-0.68

Japan:

SITC	0, 1 Food & Bev.	1.76	-0.43	-0.33
	2, 4 Raw Materials	1.55	-0.63	-0.22
	3 Energy	1.12	-0.56	-0.09
	5-9 Manufactures	1.53	-0.89	-0.34
	Total	1.37	-0.64	-0.29

*Bilateral linkaged are not modeled for U.S. imports from Japan in this category.

†Computed numerically from simulations of an increase in government spending and an increase in energy import prices.

TRADE LINKAGES OF THE U.S. AND JAPAN MODELS IN THE LINK SYSTEM

Trade volumes and prices form a network for international transmission of economic events. The linkages among countries determine how much economic events in one country affect other countries and, in turn, how much feedback there is and the equilibrium outcome to which the world economy settles. In this chapter, we explore the links between the economies. First we consider how the trade impacts are introduced into the detailed models of the United States and Japan. Then we outline the LINK world model system, and we explain how the models have been integrated into LINK. This was one of the objectives of this research; it permits us to draw on the structure of LINK to deal with the "rest of the world". The advantages of using LINK were, however, somewhat offset by the fact that LINK uses only a four-category disaggregation of world trade: SITC 0,1 (food products); SITC 2,4 (other raw materials); SITC 3 (fuels); and SITC 5-9 (manufactures). This means that special linkages between these broad categories and the detailed trade categories of the U.S. and Japanese models are necessary. It also means, unfortunately, that competition between the United States and Japan and third countries is only imperfectly captured at the sectoral level.

TRADE LINKAGES OF THE U.S. AND JAPAN MODELS

The dominant linkage between the U.S. and the Japan models is through real trade flows. As we have noted in the previous chapter, the special character of the present models is the representation of sectoral import functions, so that imports for each of the principal industrial categories are determined on the basis of economic activity in the sector and relative prices. In turn, the share of Japanese imports in overall U.S. imports for each sector is determined in the

U.S. model. Similarly, the Japanese model determines total Japanese imports for each sector and the share of the sectoral imports originating in the United States. This offers the opportunity for sector-specific linkages from the United States to Japan and from Japan to the United States. The sectoral trade flow linkages are determined with U.S. imports from Japan representing an exogenous input into the Japanese model and Japanese imports from the United States similarly treated as an input into the U.S. system.

The export and import flows at the sector level are introduced into the input-output identities to affect domestic gross output as follows:

$$X_i - X_i^I + F_i + E_i - M_i \tag{3.1}$$

where:

X_i = total output of sector i,

X_i^I = intermediate demand for sector i,

F_i = final domestic demand for sector i,

E_i = exports from sector i, and

M_i = imports into sector i.

Sector outputs are thus determined by direct recognition of the exports and imports of each sector in the input-output mechanism. Each of the export and import categories consists of two components E_i^J and E_i^{ROW}, and M_i^J and M_i^{ROW} respectively, where the components designated J represent the endogenous U.S./Japan trade flows of the bilateral model system, and rest of the world flows (ROW) are determined by the LINK system as described below.

$$X_i - X_i^I + F_i + E_i^J + E_i^{ROW} - M_i^J - M_i^{ROW} \tag{3.2}$$

In addition to trade flows, the model includes industry-level trade price linkages. The import price in an industry, PM_i, is a trade-weighted average of export prices of the partner country, PE_i^J, and of the rest of the world, PE_i^{ROW}, from the LINK model:

$$PM_i - \alpha_i \cdot PE_i^J + (1 - \alpha_i) \cdot PE_i^{ROW} \tag{3.3}$$

In this example, α_i is the share of Japanese imports in total U.S. imports of industry i. Changes in import prices affect the domestic economy through the behavioral import demand equations described above. They also feed directly into industry prices by altering the composite price, P_i, of industry output,

$$P_i - \mu_i \cdot PM_i + (1 - \mu_i) \cdot PX_i \qquad\qquad (3.4)$$

where μ_i is the share of imports in industry sales. Changes in foreign export prices therefore alter the cost of intermediate products for domestic producers, in addition to their more obvious effect on competitiveness between domestic and imported final goods.

A difficulty with modeling international price linkages is the degree of uncertainty surrounding the extent to which changing domestic prices or exchange rates are "passed through" as changes in export prices.[1] We discuss the implications of limited pass-through by Japanese exporters in Chapter 5 below. A second problem with prices lies in the domestic country models themselves. Foreign prices on the broad international level and in specific trading partners potentially impact the level of prices in competing domestic industries. For example, an increase in the price of cars imported into the United States from Japan potentially impacts directly on the price of American cars through a competitive response by U.S. producers. Neither of the models incorporates direct competitive price adjustments of this type at the industry level.

INTEGRATION INTO PROJECT LINK

The Structure of Project LINK

Project LINK is the premier econometric model of the world economy.[2] It encompasses seventy-nine separate country models and the trade linkages among them.   The purpose of Project LINK is to tie together major macroeconometric models being used in each of the main countries or regions of the world, and to generate a consistent model system for studying the world economy.

The LINK approach is to accept models from each country or area as they are designed by resident model builders for their own use, based on the assumption that each model builder knows his own country or area best. The technical linkages in trade volumes and prices, explained below, impose only a small degree of homogeneity across the models. The LINK system includes a broad range of different models containing from 30 to more than 1,000 equations per country. The major industrial countries account for the larger models. There are significant differences in the amount of detail implemented in these models with regard to the level of disaggregation, the representation of channels for transmitting economic policy, the simultaneous determination of certain variables, and the relative importance of demand and supply and other characteristics. The LINK system includes twenty-six models for industrial economies, seven models for centrally planned economies, thirty-eight models for individual developing countries, and seven regional models for groups of developing countries. The system is completed by a residual category for the rest of the world.

By far, the most important mechanism linking different economies is the international flow of merchandise exports and imports. The centerpiece of linkage and the technique by which consistency is maintained is the world trade matrix, an accounting design that lays out the intercountry and interregional trade flows on a bilateral basis. Consistency is achieved by requiring that the exports of each country or region be estimated as a weighted sum of the imports of its trading partners using the latest available trade matrix as a source of the appropriate weights. There is a corresponding linkage with respect to prices; each country or area model generates export prices, and the linkage procedure computes import prices for each importing country as a weighted average of the supplier export prices. A consistent set of export and import volumes and prices is obtained by iterations of the model.

The common agreement within LINK is to disaggregate foreign trade into four SITC subgroups: SITC 0, 1 (food, beverages, and tobacco), SITC 2, 4 (industrial materials), SITC 3 (mineral fuels), and SITC 5 to SITC 9 (manufactures and other). For LINK purposes, the trade and price relations in these variables are estimated in U.S. dollars, the numeraire of the system.

No comparable linkage mechanism is available for service flows. Although individual country models generally provide a fair amount of detail for service flows vis-a-vis the rest of the world, the lack of bilateral data makes it impossible to provide a direct linkage or to enforce consistency; the latter problem is particularly troublesome, since, even in the underlying data sets, consistency is usually not enforced for the service trade imports and exports.

For many of the countries, other linkages are also modeled, including, for example, commodity prices, interest rates, and exchange rates. It has not been possible to model capital flows on a bilateral basis. Most of the models contain a certain amount of information with regard to capital flows, but, so far, this has not been used to establish linkages. This does not, however, mean that there are no monetary linkages. Rather, they assume the form of direct linkage via interest rates and exchange rates. The exchange rate submodel is designed to provide a consistent set of exchange rate equations for the big ten industrial countries. In addition, countries with some sort of pegging scheme are represented in the system. In long-term solutions, an effort is made to force the exchange rates of each of the country economies toward a purchasing power parity path. A linkage submodel deals with commodity prices determined on worldwide markets.

Models for basic commodities are used to generate price forecasts. These common commodity prices then determine relevant export prices in commodity-exporting developing countries. Finally, a mechanism is provided for implementing specific direct linkages that are required by individual country models. The Canadian model, for example, accesses many variables in the U.S. model, such as automobile demand and investment.

Solution and Simulation of Project LINK

An extensive set of computer programs has been developed to maintain the LINK system and to provide a consistent solution among the various models. The model solution algorithm solves each country model sequentially and then enters the information obtained from the solution as exogenous information in the next model. This method, which is very much like the Gauss-Seidel procedure used within the solution for each country model, proceeds in a blockwise fashion. Each country model is solved in turn, and once a complete solution for the world system has been obtained, a new sequence of country solutions is carried out. This procedure continues until successive solutions yield approximately equivalent values for world trade and economic activity.

In practice, the solution process begins by entering realistic forecast solutions of each of the models prepared by the country forecast groups without linkage. These are called the prelinkage solutions. From this starting point, the program proceeds interactively, by introducing the material from the other models—imports, export prices, commodity prices, and some other systemwide variables—into each country model to generate the postlinkage solution which fulfills the world consistency requirements. Postlinkage solutions for the individual countries are often different for the prelinkage solution, since the original foreign trade assumptions may differ from those obtained in a linked solution. Similarly, the consistent world solution for the trade aggregates and prices may also be different on a postlinkage basis from that obtained by aggregation prior to linkage (though the latter aggregation is not, of course, consistent).

Initially, we develop a base solution that represents a consistent forecast based on current conditions in each country and a reasonable set of assumptions about fiscal, monetary, and trade policies. For long-run forecasts, trend assumptions are often imposed on the forecast to assure that the long-run outcomes are reasonable. Simulation exercises are then run as alternatives to the base solution. In each formulation, we hold policy assumptions and other exogenous variables fixed to their baseline values, except for the particular changes required to achieve the objectives of the alternative solution.

LINK has been the basis for numerous simulation studies, including the regular forecasting exercises, testing the price and activity multiplier interrelationships between countries (Hickman, 1975), examining the impact of alternative policy scenarios (Klein, 1988), recent concerns with macro policy coordination (Klein, 1989), evaluating the impact of protectionism (Klein et al. 1987), investigating the effect of industrial incentive policies (Klein et al. 1985), evaluating the shocks from high oil prices, dealing with varied assumptions about exchange rates, studying arms reduction proposals, viewing perspectives for world agricultural markets, and performing many other analyses.

The Industrially Disaggregated Models in LINK

One of the principal targets of this project was to integrate the industrially disaggregated models of Japan and of the United States into the model of Project LINK. LINK normally uses the Wharton Quarterly Model of the United States and the Kyoto Model (Moriguchi) of Japan. Both of these are business-cycle-oriented forecasting models, but neither has significant sectoral disaggregation, and both organize their trade disaggregation in the traditional grouping of Project LINK. Since bilateral trade flows in LINK are based on fixed base year share coefficients, there is no mechanism by which changes in relative prices or competitiveness alter the allocation of a country's import demand across its trading partners. Finally, neither of these models provides sectorally disaggregated linkages from trade categories into production sectors.

As discussed above, both the disaggregated models we use—the Wharton Annual and Industry Model of the United States and the FAIS/IUJ Multisector Model for Japan—contain a detailed breakdown of production activity by sector. Both largely match this breakdown in the trade block, and both link what happens in trade with production activity on a sectoral basis. Moreover, they are able to deal with bilateral flows among the United States, Japan, and the rest of the world.

Our task, consequently, was begun by substituting into LINK the Wharton Annual and Industry Model for the Wharton Quarterly Model, and the FAIS/IUJ Multisector Model for the Kyoto Model. We will refer to the merged system as the NIRA-LINK system. In this section, we discuss how this task was accomplished. The issue is that the two models contain a highly detailed sectoral disaggregation, whereas the LINK system does not. How have these two systems been linked?

The objective of our approach is to make use of the sectorally disaggregated import flows into the United States and into Japan, as determined in the disaggregated models. Where available, this information is dominant. On the other hand, where such disaggregation is not available, for the other countries of the world, we use the more broadly aggregated information available from LINK.

Figures 3.1 and 3.2 contrast, in broad terms, the trade circuits as treated in LINK and in the NIRA-LINK system. The LINK version shows solutions for each of the country models, and then processing of the information in the trade, exchange rates, direct linkage, and world commodity market blocks. Feedback from these blocks goes back to the country models, and solution rounds continue until a convergence criterion is satisfied. The NIRA-LINK algorithm separates out Japan and the United States for treatment on a bilateral and disaggregated basis, but retains the countries in the LINK system for trade and other variables relating these countries with the rest of the world. A consistent solution for the Japan and U.S. models and for their linkage is obtained first. This information is introduced into LINK, and solutions are obtained for the LINK system models. The information from the full LINK solution then enters the Japan-U.S. system and modifies that solution. This process proceeds through several solution rounds until convergence is obtained. In this way, the detailed models are made an integral part of LINK.

The detailed structure of these linkages is illustrated in Figures 3.3 to 3.7. Equation specifications for the United States and the Japan models are described in Tables 3.1 and 3.2. Figure 3.3 describes the nominal flows of imports into the United States, considering manufactures only. On the top of the chart are shown the nominal import flows, divided into twenty-two manufacturing sectors. Imports from Japan by sectors (TMJUGT$$_k$) are shown as a subset of overall U.S. imports by sectors (TMUGT$$_k$). The multiple lines signify the sectoral breakdown. The import flows into the United States from Japan become the disaggregated export flows from Japan. We note that U.S. imports from the rest of the world are also originally sectorally disaggregated but are reaggregated when they enter the LINK system.

The introduction of the flows into the LINK trade matrix is shown in the center of the page. In order to use the bilateral Japan-U.S. trade estimates and to use the trade matrix for all other flows, we adjust the coefficients on the U.S. import column of the trade matrix. U.S. imports from Japan are directly determined by the aggregation of the sectoral U.S. model import equations. The entries in the matrix for U.S. imports from other countries as a share of total U.S. imports are then adjusted proportionally to preserve a unit column sum. The effect of this procedure is to enforce the U.S.-Japan model's prediction for Japan's share in U.S. imports, and to assure that any difference between this and the LINK trade matrix values can be allocated evenly across other U.S. trading partners.

On the right-hand side of Figure 3.3, we show that imports of "rest of the world" (ROW) countries are accepted from LINK on the standard highly aggregated basis, but are disaggregated on the basis of historical patterns into the more detailed breakdown of the U.S. and Japan models. There are both advantages and disadvantages to this scheme. Economic activity is transmitted among the U.S., Japan, and "rest of the world" countries. In the case of the

United States and Japan, direct bilateral linkages on the sectoral level prevail. For other countries, activity feeds through on the aggregate level, though not on the sectoral level. The aggregate feedthroughs are translated, on a proportional basis in correspondence to the base year nominal breakdown by sector, into sectoral feedback to the United States and to Japan. This means that there is no explicit treatment of competition between the United States and Japan on the sectoral level in third countries in this model—though there is competition on a more aggregate level. Unfortunately, it also limits the sectoral treatment of exports from the United States and Japan to the ROW sector since these categories too are dealt with at a broader level of aggregation. However, in the absence of sectoral modeling of the ROW region, it would not be possible to provide a more detailed treatment. Such an extension of the model would represent a major additional research effort, since it would call for a sectorally detailed trade matrix and disaggregation of the other country models.

An equally detailed bilateral trade disaggregation is not necessary for the nonmanufactured goods components of U.S. imports, since almost all U.S. imports from Japan are in the SITC 5-9 category. Quantitatively, U.S. imports from Japan in the other trade categories are very small, so that these categories have been handled without a detailed breakdown on the U.S. import side, though they must be allocated to different sectors when they enter the Japan model. This treatment is shown in Figure 3.4.

The corresponding diagram for Japan is shown in Figure 3.5. In this case, all Japanese imports are maintained on a sectoral basis, not just imports of manufactures. These are then split through equations influenced by relative competitiveness into imports from the United States and from the rest of the world, as we did with manufactures in the case of U.S. imports. As above, the trade matrix is adjusted to allow Japanese imports from the United States to be determined by the Japan model, and proportional adjustments are made to the trade matrix coefficients of other countries, in the Japan import column.

With respect to prices, somewhat analogous procedures have been followed. These are summarized in Figures 3.6 and 3.7. Domestic industry price indexes computed by each model are translated on a sectoral basis into export prices and used directly to determine import prices faced by the partner country (the United States for imports from Japan and Japan for imports from the United States). To provide export prices faced by the rest of the world, the sector prices are used to move export prices for the broad LINK product aggregates. This is essentially the procedure that would be used by LINK, which determines export prices for broad aggregates within the exporting country and uses trade matrix weights to derive the appropriate import prices faced by each LINK country.

As we have noted above, there are a number of other linkage variables that are carried from one country to others within the LINK system. These variables are particularly important in the case of the United States, whose interest rates play an important role in interest-related phenomena throughout the world. These linkages have been maintained in the present system as they are in LINK, with appropriate linkages from variables in our U.S. model and, where necessary, from the Japan model to the LINK direct linkage block.

Figure 3.1
World Model Solution—LINK Algorithm

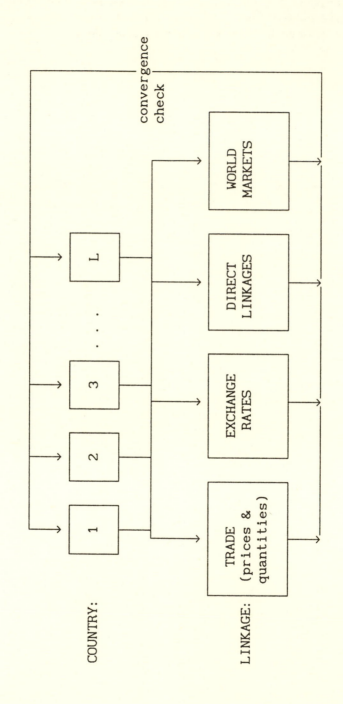

Figure 3.2
World Model Solution—NIRA–LINK Algorithm

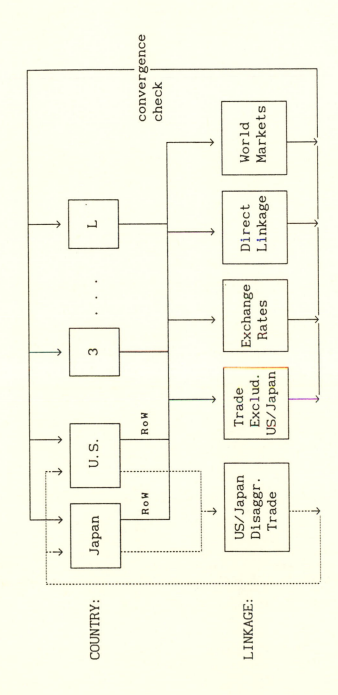

Figure 3.3
Trade Linkages: U.S. Manufacturing Imports, Japan Exports, LINK

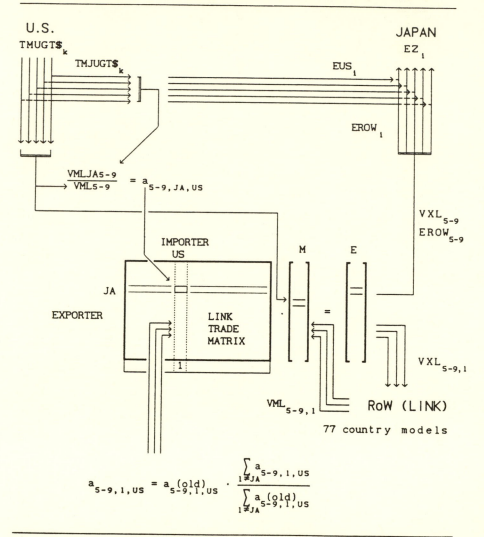

$$a_{5-9,1,US} = a_{5-9,1,US}(old) \cdot \frac{\sum_{1 \neq JA} a_{5-9,1,US}}{\sum_{1 \neq JA} a_{5-9,1,US}(old)}$$

Note: There are 22 U.S. manufacturing industries, k = 1-22, corresponding to the LINK trade category SITC 5-9; 25 Japanese manufacturing industries, i = 19-25, 27-30, 33-46; and 79 countries in LINK, including U.S. and Japan, l = 1-79.

Figure 3.4
Trade Linkages: U.S. Nonmanufacturing Imports, Japan Exports, LINK

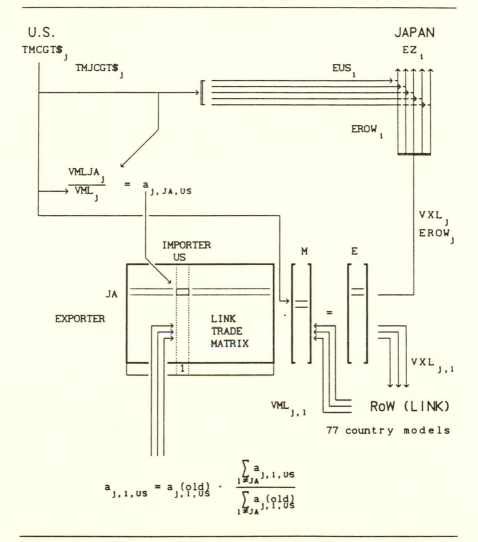

$$a_{J,1,US} = a_{J,1,US}(old) \cdot \frac{\sum\limits_{1 \neq JA} a_{J,1,US}}{\sum\limits_{1 \neq JA} a_{J,1,US}(old)}$$

Note: There are 3 nonmanufacturing U.S. trade sectors: $j = 01, 24$, and 3 (aggregated from five detailed energy categories); 21 Japanese nonmanufacturing industries, $i = 1-18, 31, 32, 64$; and 79 countries in LINK, including U.S. and Japan, $l=1-79$.

Figure 3.5
Trade Linkages: Japan Imports, U.S. Exports, LINK

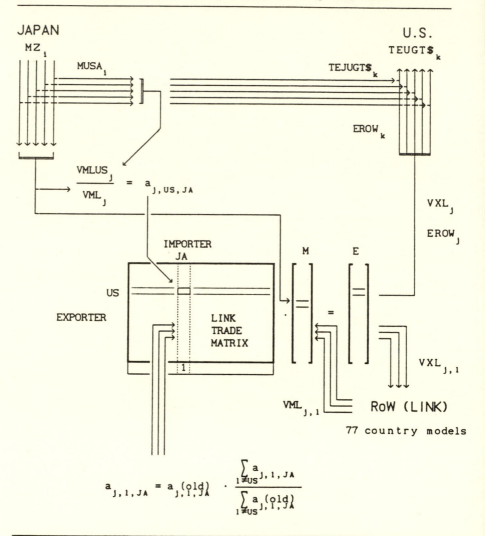

Note: There are four LINK trade categories, j = 0&1, 2&4, 3, 5-9; 47 Japanese industries, i = 1-46, 64; 30 U.S. industries, k = 1-30; and 79 countries in LINK, including U.S. and Japan, l = 1-79.

Figure 3.6
Trade Price Linkages: U.S. Exports, Japan Imports, LINK

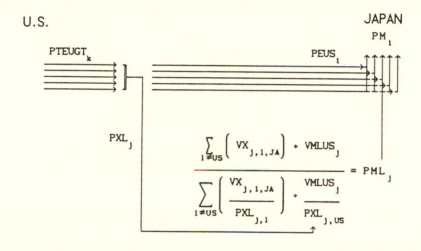

Note: There are four LINK trade categories, j = 0&1, 2&4, 3, 5-9, 30 U.S. manufacturing industries, k = 1-30; 47 Japanese manufacturing industries, i = 1-46, 64; and 79 countries in LINK, including U.S. and Japan, l = 1-79.

Figure 3.7
Trade Price Linkages: Japan Exports, U.S. Manufacturing Imports, LINK

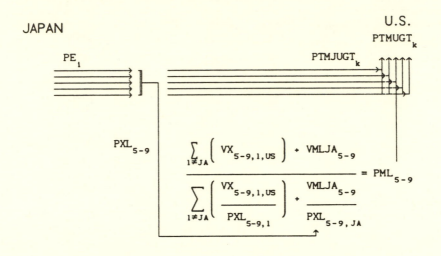

Note: There are 22 U.S. manufacturing industries, k = 1-22, corresponding to the LINK trade category SITC 5-9; 25 Japanese manufacturing
industries, i = 19-25, 27-30, 33-46; and 79 countries in LINK, including
U.S. and Japan, l = 1-79.

Table 3.1
Trade Linkage Equations for the U.S. Model

U.S. IMPORTS:

Imports by industry:

$$TMUGT_k = f(\ . \ ) , \qquad k=1-22$$
$$\text{(manufactures)}$$
$$TMCGT_j = f(\ . \ ) , \qquad j=01,24,3(\text{several})$$

Nominals:

$$TMUGT\$_k = TMUGT_k \cdot PTMUGT_k / 100$$
$$TMCGT\$_j = TMCGT_j \cdot PTMEGT_k / 100$$

Imports in LINK catgs.:

$$VML_{5-9} = \left(\sum_{k=1}^{22} TMUGT_k \right) \cdot FOBCIF_{5-9} \cdot PMC_{5-9}$$

$$VML_j = TMCGT_j \cdot FOBCIF_j \cdot PMC_j, \quad j=01,24,3$$

Imports from Japan:

$$TMJUGT_k = f(\ . \ ) , \qquad k=1-22$$
$$TMJCGT_j = \gamma_j \cdot TMCGT_j , \qquad j=01,24,3$$

(γ_j is the baseyear proportion imported from Japan.)

Nominals:

$$TMJUGT\$_k = TMJUGT_k \cdot PTMJUGT_k / 100$$
$$TMJCGT\$_j = TMJCGT_j \cdot PTMEGT_j / 100$$

Imports from Japan in LINK categories:

$$VMLJA_{5-9} = \left(\sum_{k=1}^{22} TMJUGT\$_k \right) \cdot FOBCIFJ_{5-9}$$

$$VMLJA_j = TMJUGT\$_j \cdot FOBCIFJ_j , \qquad j=01,24,3$$

U.S. EXPORTS:

Exports to Japan:

$$TEJUGT\$_k = \left(\sum_{i \in k} MUSA_i \right) \cdot FOBCIF_k , \qquad k=1-30$$

($i \in k$ are the more detailed Japan I-O categories corresponding to U.S. I-O category k.)

Total exports in LINK catgs.:

$$VXL_j = \sum_{1 \neq JA} VML_{j,1} \cdot \alpha_{j,1,US} + JAVMLUS_j$$
$$1=\text{countrs. in LINK}$$
$$j=01,24,3,59$$

(Computed in LINK; $\alpha_{j,1,US}$ are elements of the LINK trade matrix.)

Total exports to other countries:

$$EROW_j = VXL_j - JAVMLUS_j$$

Table 3.1—Continued

Total exports to other countries
in industry k:

$$EROW_k = \beta_{j,k} \cdot EROW_j , \quad k=1\text{-}30$$

($\beta_{j,k}$ are baseyear industry shares
in total exports to RoW.)

Total exports in industry k: $TEUGT\$_k = TEJUGT\$_k + EROW_k$

Total real exports in k: $TEUGT_k = TEUGT\$_k / PTEUGT_k \cdot 100$

U.S. EXPORT PRICES:

Export price in industry i: $PTEUGT_k = f(.),$ $k=1\text{-}30$

                                 $PTEEGT_j = f(.),$ $j=01,24,3,59$

LINK category export prices: $\%\Delta\ PXL_j = \%\Delta\ PTEEGT_j,$ $j=01,24,3,59$

U.S. IMPORT PRICES:

Import prices from Japan: $\%\Delta\ PTMJUGT_k = \underset{i \varepsilon k}{AVE}\left(\%\Delta\ JAPE_i\right) - \%\Delta\ JAREXL$

                                                i=Japan industry,
                                                k=U.S. industry
                          (JAREXL is the yen/dollar exchange rate.)

Import prices from world:

Import prices in LINK catgs. (computed in LINK):

$$PML_j = \frac{\sum\limits_{l \ne JA}\left(VX_{j,1,US}\right) + VMLJA_j}{\sum\limits_{l \ne JA}\left(\dfrac{VX_{j,1,US}}{PXL_{j,1}}\right) + \dfrac{VMLJA_j}{PXL_{j,JA}}} \quad , \qquad \begin{array}{l} \text{l=LINK countries,} \\ \text{j=01,24,3,59} \end{array}$$

$PMC_j = PML_j$

Import Prices in industries:

$$\%\Delta\ PTMUGT_k = \delta_k \cdot \%\Delta\ PTMJUGT_k + (1-\delta_k) \cdot \%\Delta\ PMC_{5-9},$$
                                                k=1-22 (Manufs.)

(δ_k is the baseyear Japanese share in industry imports.)

$$\%\Delta\ PTMEGT_j = \%\Delta\ PMC_j,$$ $j=01,24,3$

Table 3.2
Trade Linkage Equations for the Japan Model

JAPAN IMPORTS:

Imports by industry: $MM_i = f(\ .\ )$, $i=1\text{-}46; 64$

Nominals: $MZ_i = MM_i \cdot PM_i\ /\ 100$

Imports in LINK catgs: $VML_j = \left(\sum_{i \in j} MM_i\right) \cdot FOBCIF_j \cdot PMC_j / REXL$

$$j=01, 24, 3, 59$$

Nominal Imports from US: $MUSA_i = f(\ .\ )$, $i=1\text{-}46, 64$

Imports from U.S. in: $VMLUS_j = \left(\sum_{i \in j} MUSA_i\right) \cdot FOBCIF_j$,
LINK categories
$$j=01, 24, 3, 59$$

JAPAN EXPORTS:

Exports to U.S.: $EUS_i = \rho_{i,k} \cdot USMJ\$_k \cdot REXL \cdot FOBCIF_i$,
$$i=19\text{-}25, 27\text{-}30, 33\text{-}46$$
($\rho_{i,k}$ allocates broader U.S. import catgs.;
REXL is the yen/dollar exchange rate.)

Total Exports in LINK catgs: $VXL_j = \sum_{1 \neq US} VML_{j,1} \cdot \alpha_{j,1,JA} + USVMLJA_j$

l=countries in LINK
j=01, 24, 3, 59
(Computed in LINK system; $\alpha_{j,1,JA}$ are
elements of the LINK trade matrix.)

Total Exports to Other Countries: $EROW_j = VXL_j - USVMLJA_j$

Total Exports to Other Countries: $EROW_i = \beta_{j,i} \cdot EROW_j \cdot REXL$,
in industry i
$$i=1\text{-}46, 64$$
($\beta_{j,i}$ are baseyear industry shares
in total exports to RoW.)

Total Exports in industry i: $EZ_i = EUS_i + EROW_{1,}$ $i=1\text{-}46, 64$

Total Real Exports in i: $ER_i = EZ_i\ /\ PE_i \cdot 100$

Table 3.2—Continued

Japan Export Prices:

Export Price in industry i: $PE_i = f(\; . \;)$, $i=1\text{-}46,64$

LINK Category Export Prices: $PXL_j = \dfrac{\displaystyle\sum_{i \varepsilon j} EZ_i}{\displaystyle\sum_{i \varepsilon j} ER_i} \cdot 100 \cdot REXL(70)/REXL,$

$j=01,24,3,59$

Japan Import Prices:

Import Prices from the US: $\%\Delta\ PEUS_i = \%\Delta\ USPE_k$,

$i = JA$ industry,
$k = US$ industry

Import Prices from the World:

Import Prices in LINK catgs (computed in LINK):

$$PML_j = \frac{\displaystyle\sum_{l \neq US}\left(VX_{j,1,JA}\right) + VMLUS_j}{\displaystyle\sum_{l \neq US}\left(\dfrac{VX_{j,1,JA}}{PXL_{j,1}}\right) + \dfrac{VMLUS_j}{PXL_{j,US}}} \quad , \qquad \begin{array}{l} l = \text{link countries,} \\ j = 01,24,3,59 \end{array}$$

$PMC_j = PML_j \cdot REXL/REXL(1970)$

Import Prices in industries:

$$\%\Delta\ PMDOL_i = \delta_i \cdot \%\Delta\ PEUS_i + (1-\delta_i)\cdot\Big[\ \%\Delta\ PMC_i - \%\Delta\ REXL\ \Big],$$

$i = 1\text{-}46,64$
$j=01,24,3,59$

(δ_i is the baseyear U.S. share in industry imports)

$PM_i = PMDOL_i \cdot REXL/REXL(1980)$

INTERDEPENDENCE IN THE U.S.-JAPAN-WORLD ECONOMY

Real trade flows provide a channel for international transmission of aggregate demand shocks. The influence of such transmission on a partner country depends on the impact of the shock on the source country (multiplier effects), the extent to which the change in source-country economic activity is reflected in changing trade volumes (import propensities), and the relative size of the national economies. At the industry level, international transmission will vary with activity and import responsiveness across categories of goods and patterns of interindustry demand.

In this chapter, we compare the transmission of aggregate demand shocks originating in the United States, Japan, and the rest of the world, and look for structural explanations for differences that are observed. We report on simulations carried out with the combined NIRA-LINK model system. First, we present a discussion of the methodology. Then, we provide a detailed description of medium-term baseline forecasts. Finally, we present alternative multiplier simulations.

ESTABLISHING THE BASE SIMULATION

The objective of this study is to establish a view of the macroeconomy and of sectoral trade relations among the United States, Japan, and the rest of the world. We begin in this section with a discussion of forecast procedures, first for the short and medium term and then for the longer term. Then, we discuss the main features of the base solutions.

As the starting point for our short- and medium-term baseline solution, we used the Spring 1989 forecast of Project LINK. The exogenous inputs into the models of Japan and of the United States correspond approximately to those used in the LINK solutions. Similarly, we have used the exogenous assumptions for the models of the "rest of the world" exactly as these models appear in the Project LINK forecast. It should be noted, however, that the results obtained will not be the same as those of the Japan and U.S. models operated in a free-standing unlinked mode, nor will they match precisely what was obtained with Project LINK using the normal LINK models of the United States and Japan. Our Japan and U.S. models are considerably different from the models currently in the ordinary forecasting version of LINK. These models call not only for somewhat different exogenous input variables, but would produce different results even if the inputs could be made precisely the same. The linkage of the models also affects the solution. Indeed, it was our experience that the linked solutions produced rather different results than the original unlinked solutions. This is because the trade prices of the unlinked solution turned out to be rather different from those that had been assumed in each of the separate unlinked solutions. Some adjustments were necessary to bring both models in line with actual economic conditions in a linked solution. These adjustments are carried forward to all the alternative solutions so that, although they are important in influencing the base solution, they do not affect the differences between the base solution and the alternatives. Our aim was to produce a realistic short- and medium-term view of the Japanese and U.S. economies in the context of the world economy. We aimed for a base solution that was in line with recent thinking by business cycle analysts in the various countries at the time the calculations were made.

For long-term forecasting, to be considered at greater length below, one approach would be to depict the economy simply on its potential growth path. This is not possible or desirable here. Econometric models incorporate both cyclical and long-term elements, and feedback effects operating in the models cannot be ignored for purposes of long-term forecasting. Our desire for consistent solutions also stands in the way of such a procedure, since there is no assurance that both countries could be on their full employment growth paths and still maintain internal and external consistency. Finally, there are political obstacles with respect to the full employment path, since each country has a variety of objectives, including the balance of payments, that clearly cannot all be met at the same time. The policy maker seeking an optimum solution must weight the objectives and must recognize the tradeoffs between them. Formal procedures, like optimal control (Kendrick, 1981; Petersen, 1988), could be used to achieve the best solution, but such an effort is beyond the scope of this project. The procedure used here was in line with that typically used by forecasters for long-term forecasts. The initial period of the forecast until 1992 was largely determined on the basis of known business cycle trends and policy pronouncements. Beyond this initial period, the problem is that policy becomes in effect an endogenous variable. Policy parameters were moved in order to bring the economy toward what appeared to the forecaster to be a reasonable full employment growth path. For the United States this was a path that maintained the economy near a 7% unemployment rate, reasonable inflation, and led to gradual return to equilibrium in the balance of payments. This long-term path corresponds closely to the estimates produced by Wharton Econometric Forecasting Associates in their Spring 1989 forecast (The WEFA Group, 1989). A similar effort was used by the Japanese forecasting group to produce a Japan base solution. Together, these forecasts represent a prelinkage base solution.

Second, we linked the two models, Japan and the United States, in a bilateral linkage. Potentially, the linkages could affect the growth path, yielding a solution significantly different from the one obtained by an unlinked solution. In practice, the difference between the linked and unlinked solution is not large, except for some specific sectors, since the unlinked solutions were designed with a realistic appraisal of the likely impact of the external environment and since the linkage effects themselves are not extremely large. Where the linkage has introduced impacts that were deemed unreasonable, some adjustments have been made, and similarly where the unlinked solution produced results, particularly on the industry level, that appeared unreasonable, some further modifications have been introduced. These adjustments, however, are very few and of moderate size.

Finally, we have introduced the two models into the LINK environment, allowing for the full feedbacks from the rest of the world. Again, there is the possibility of changes in the base path. In practice, the feedback effects turned out to be very small, again because the base solutions were made with realistic assumptions about the world environment.

Perspective on the Short- and Medium-Term Base Simulation

In this section, we evaluate the short- and medium-term base simulation to the year 1992. (The long-term baseline is discussed in Chapter 6, below.) This is a linked simulation that describes the outlook for the United States and Japan in the context of the entire world (LINK) economy. Summary statistics for the base solution are shown in Tables 4.1 to 4.6. In the summary below, we point out some changes that have emerged since the Spring 1989 forecasting exercise.

For the United States:

- After the rapid growth of the U.S. economy during 1988 (3.8%), economic activity slows to 2.0% in 1989 and to 1.5% in 1990 with a strong cyclical recovery in 1991 and 1992. Although the annual statistics do not quite show a recession, these slow growth figures are not inconsistent with a brief period of recession in quarterly statistics during 1990. Of course, the recession in the United States has turned out to be somewhat later and more severe, with a slow recovery beginning in mid 1991.

- The inflation experience of this base forecast is also consistent with current appraisals, with an acceleration of inflation in 1989 and 1990 to between 5% and 6% annual and then a return to slower inflation with the cyclical recovery in the early 1990s. The employment and unemployment rate statistics are slightly more pessimistic than more recent forecasts showing rates in the upper 6% range by 1992. (The actual rate exceeded 7%).

- The major imbalances continue to affect the U.S. economy. The federal deficit rises to over $200 billion during the slowdown in 1990, and remains in the $160 billion range in subsequent years. The trade deficit (current account) remains close to the $150 billion deficit mark throughout the medium-term forecast period. Recent data suggest a federal government deficit of $250 billion in 1991. Extraordinary costs have caused the deficit to deteriorate further since then. Trade balance improvement has occurred at a faster pace than our baseline suggests, but deficit remains large particularly with respect to Japan.

- The patterns of demand follow closely cyclical expectations, with decline in real fixed investment (business and residential) and a significant inventory swing in the 1989 to 1991 period.

- The United States exchange rate shows some further decline during 1989 and 1990 and then stabilizes during the remainder of the forecast period.

For Japan:

- Only moderate slowdown of real economic activity to the 3% to 4% level during 1989 to 1990 with recovery to more rapid growth averaging 5% per year in the early 1990s. Since this baseline was prepared, a slowdown has occurred in 1991-1992.

- Inflation in the 1% to 2% per year range over the medium-term forecast period. This is somewhat higher than the negatives recorded earlier but remains a very low inflation performance.

- A continued trade surplus running around $70 billion annually throughout the entire medium-term forecast period.

- Nevertheless, considerable readjustment of real trade with growth of imports from the United States broadening to a number of important manufactured products categories—for example, wearing apparel, wood products and furniture, and metal products.

For the World Economy:

- The LINK system shows a pattern of slower growth in 1989 to 1992, and then a cyclical revival not surprisingly as in the United States and Japan. The recession recovery is now forecast to appear in 1993.

- A similar overall pattern of world trade with slower growth of exports and imports for the 1989 to 1990 period. A significant deceleration of the exports of the developing countries in Asia is shown, and there is some deterioration of their trade balances.

This base solution deserves considerably more detailed discussion, but that is beyond the scope of this volume. We use the base solution as a starting point for our simulations, assuming in every alternative that the base solution would prevail in the absence of the specific changes introduced in the alternative simulation. In order to simplify the presentation, most of the results of the alternative simulations will be summarized as deviations from the results of the base simulation.

MULTIPLIER SIMULATIONS

The purpose of multiplier simulations is to evaluate the performance of the model in response to some specific changes in the exogenous inputs. In this way, we can compare the performance of this model to other models on a comprehensive basis. The simulations carried out here match simulations carried out in recent years for models of the U.S. economy in the extensive model comparison projects headquarters at the University of Pennsylvania (Adams and Klein, 1991) and in the international model comparisons completed in a recent Brookings Institution project (Bryant et al., 1988).

Expansion in the United States and Japan:
Macroeconomic Effects

Fiscal stimulus simulations were performed individually on the U.S. and Japanese economies. In each case, domestic government spending was increased 1% of base year GNP, with this absolute increase in spending sustained over the forecast horizon (1987-1992).

These simulations should be viewed as debt-financed fiscal expansions. No accommodative monetary policy, however, was undertaken (aside from an endogenous monetary policy reaction built into the U.S. model).

Demand Stimulus in the United States

The impact of a 1% of GNP increase in U.S. defense spending is summarized in Table 4.7. The effect on key macro variables and components of GNP is given in Table 4.8 for the United States and Table 4.9 for Japan. Effects on world trade and activity are summarized by region in Tables 4.10 and 4.11. All tables, except the world GNP table, report results as differences (and percent differences) from the baseline model solution.

The 1% of GNP increase in U.S. government spending raises U.S. real output by 2.8% in the first year. This is a rather large multiplier compared with those of other major econometric models (see the comparison of major model multipliers in Table 4.12), although the multiplier declines to 1.0 six years out. The strong economic expansion reduces the U.S. unemployment rate by nearly two percentage points on impact, and substantially raises consumer prices and short-term interest rates. Aggregate real imports grow 2% above base, initially, and 6.8% above base by 1992. The combination of surging imports and crowding out of investment combine to pull the multiplier down sharply after the first several years.

The strong rise in imports translates into a measurable impact on the economies of Japan and the rest of the world. Real Japan exports rise 1% on impact and 2.8% in six years, to raise Japanese output nearly a percentage point. The effect on Japanese prices and interest rates is negligible. As a result of the increased U.S. demand, world activity rises 0.8% in the first year, declining to 0.6% above base by 1992.

Feedback effects from expansion in third countries play an important role in bilateral U.S.-Japan transmission. As Table 4.11 shows, in 1987, U.S. growth accounted for 1970$ 45.5 billion of the total world activity increase of 1970$ 50.0 billion, so that the bulk of Japanese expansion in this first year is directly attributable to increased U.S. demand for Japanese exports. By 1992, however, contemporaneous U.S. expansion represents just 1970$ 15.3 billion of the overall world expansion of 1970$ 40.4 billion, and other country import growth represents a larger share of Japan's export gains.

Table 4.13 illustrates this point more directly by splitting U.S.-Japan bilateral trade out of total world trade. In 1987, U.S. imports represented $2.92 billion of the total Japan export rise of $3.41 billion. By 1992, U.S. imports from Japan are still a substantial part of the Japanese gains of $14.7 billion, but now one-third ($5.1 billion) goes to other countries. Canada is shown separately, since it is the only country of roughly equal importance in U.S. imports. Canada gains slightly more than Japan from the U.S. expansion.[1] These considerations highlight the importance of viewing the U.S.-Japan bilateral relationship in a global context.

Demand Stimulus in Japan

Tables 4.14 to 4.18 report a similar fiscal policy simulation for the Japanese economy. The simulation performed is a sustained 1% of gross national expenditure (GNE) increase in Japan government investment.[2] Table 4.14 summarizes the domestic and international transmission effects of the policy, with details for the Japan economy given in Table 4.15, the U.S. economy in Table 4.16, and the world economy in Tables 4.17 and 4.18.

The domestic economy effects of the Japanese fiscal expansion are a substantial rise in GNE initially (1.7%) with very little crowding out over the forecast horizon, so that GNE is still 1.4% above base in 1992. The money and price sectors of the Japan economy show very little response to the fiscal shock—in fact we have a deflation initially—so that all components of national expenditure are above base in 1992. The multipliers for the FAIS/IUJ model and other major models of the Japan economy are summarized along with those for U.S. models in Table 4.12, above. Note that although the multiplier is somewhat smaller than that of the U.S. Long-Term Model, it is the highest of the Japanese models reported.

Although the domestic activity response of the Japan model is fairly substantial, the extent of transmission to partner countries is much smaller than for the similar U.S. fiscal exercise. Whereas U.S. fiscal expansion raises real imports by 2.2% initially and 6.8% by 1992, the Japanese expansion results in just 1.1% higher imports on impact and 1.3% after six years. (Compare Tables 4.7 and 4.14.) U.S. exports to Japan rise only 0.15% and U.S. activity just 0.06% above base in response to the Japanese fiscal expansion. Compared with the 0.8% of GNE impact on Japan of a U.S. expansion, Japan's policy impact on the United States is about 1/10th as large.[3] Figure 4.1 illustrates graphically the impact of U.S. and Japan fiscal expansion on the domestic and partner-country economies. The almost negligible impact of Japanese activity on the United States is striking. The impact of Japanese expansion on the world economy as a whole (Table 4.18) is similarly limited, with world activity rising 0.13 to 0.16% above base as a result of the Japanese fiscal expansion.

The very small effect of Japanese expansion on the United States follows directly from the relatively smaller size of the Japan economy, the somewhat smaller fiscal multiplier, and the more limited responsiveness of Japanese import demand to the fiscal shock. Given the weighted average import demand elasticity of 1.37 (see Table 2.5), the 1.4% rise in gross national expenditure in 1992 should raise imports about 1.9% above their baseline level. The actual increase is a somewhat smaller 1.3%. This 1.3% increase in real imports represents an increase in nominal imports of 584 billion yen, about $4.8 billion, of which about twenty-five percent are increases in U.S. exports. So the 1.4% increase in Japanese output results in just over one billion dollars more of U.S. exports; this is just 0.2% of baseline U.S. exports and 0.02% of U.S. GNP. The U.S. multiplier effect and some expansion in the Rest of the World increase this stimulus to 0.06%. Unless Japanese import demand responds much more dramatically to increased domestic demand, we simply should not expect to see appreciable transmission of Japanese fiscal policy to the United States.[4]

Transmission of U.S. and Japanese activity would be somewhat more similar were it not for the surprisingly large increase in U.S. imports that occurs with a U.S. fiscal expansion. The high responsiveness of U.S. imports is explained in part by price effects in the U.S. economy. There are also some sectors with high import coefficients.[5]

Taking the latter point first, the first pair of columns in Table 4.19 give 1992 changes and percent changes from base for industry-level U.S. manufacturing imports under the expansionary U.S. fiscal policy. Four industries stand out with substantially greater than average increases relative to the baseline: industrial chemicals, other nonferrous metals, aircraft, and other transportation equipment. The behavior of these four categories can be traced to special features of the estimated equations: industrial chemicals was fitted with a negative activity elasticity that causes imports to increase even with negative output growth in 1992; the other three categories combine relatively large income and price elasticities with a lagged dependent variable to generate extraordinarily large responses to rising activity and falling relative import prices.

Although these categories account for less than 10% of baseline U.S. imports, their very large increases contribute a significant portion of the overall import rise. Exogenizing the four import equations reduces the increase in aggregate imports from 6.9% to 4.6%, as shown in the second two columns of Table 4.19.[6]

The remaining 4.6% increase is still nearly four times as large as that experienced in Japan. A good part of this difference can be explained by the very different price experience of the two economies under the fiscal expansions, and by the differences in responsiveness of imports in the two economies to these relative price changes.

Unlike the Japanese experience, fiscal expansion in the United States produces substantial inflation; the GNP deflator is up 4.4% by 1992. Since import prices rise only 1.1% over the period, relative import prices are reduced by 3.3%. With a weighted average import price elasticity for manufactures of -1.03 (see Table 2.3), this should contribute roughly three percentage points to the rise in real manufacturing imports. This is indeed the case, as the final column of Table 4.19 illustrates. With relative price elasticity coefficients set to zero in the import equations, the increase in manufacturing imports falls from 6.2% to

2.8%; for aggregate imports, the reduction is from 4.6% to 2.8%. Removing price effects on imports would therefore reduce the impact on Japan of U.S. fiscal stimulus by about one-half, to about 0.4% of Japanese GNE.[7]

An important reason to expect somewhat less responsive imports in Japan than in the United States involves the relative composition of trade of the two economies. On the basis of previous trade studies, one would expect the U.S. economy, which increasingly imports manufactured goods, to experience greater import response, since income elasticity estimates for manufactures tend to be higher than for the raw material goods that make up a substantial portion of Japanese imports.

The strong asymmetry found in this study, as well as the almost negligible impact of Japan on the United States, is not unique to this model. The absolute and relative impacts found here are well within the range of estimates of previous analyses. Two recent studies, Bryant et al. (1988) and Helliwell (1988), provide an opportunity to compare our international transmission results with comparable forecasts of a number of other major econometric models. Bryant et al. (1988) reports the result of a comparison of ten international models participating in a Brookings Institution project in 1985. The year-by-year impact on Japan of a 1% of GNP U.S. fiscal expansion for the ten models is given in Table 4.20. The average transmission for the ten models over the six-year period is very similar to the results for the present model.[8]

Helliwell (1988) compares bilateral transmission under both U.S. and Japanese fiscal expansions for the Japan Economic Planning Agency Model (EPA), the Federal Reserve Board MultiCountry Model (MCM), and the OECD Interlink Model (OECD). In Figures 4.2 and 4.3, we combine his graphical results for the three models with the results of the present analysis. All four models clearly agree on the very limited effect of Japanese fiscal expansion on the United States, although giving somewhat more varying results for the extent of transmission of the U.S. fiscal shock to Japan.

Table 4.21, adapted from Tables 5 and 6 in Oudiz and Sachs (1984), permits a comparison of our and others' estimates for transmission of activity, as well as price and current account balance effects. The table reports short-run activity and price response in the originating and partner country, and the effect on the ratio of current account to GNP. The effects are average effects for the first two simulation years. Note that the bilateral transmission multiplier for Japan on the United States (0.06) is within the range of estimates of the other models. The U.S. effect on Japan (0.37) is slightly larger than the other models but of comparable magnitude when adjustment is made for the large domestic multiplier.

The effect of the U.S. expansion on deteriorating the U.S. current account balance is somewhat smaller than for other models, and the initial deflation in Japan of our model is unique. Both of these effects may be attributable to our exogenous treatment of exchange rates, which are determined endogenously in the other models. Since the U.S. economy tends to experience an appreciation following a fiscal expansion, the current account would be expected to deteriorate further.[9] Japan, on the other hand, generally experiences a yen depreciation following a fiscal expansion, which would tend to offset the deflationary tendency we observed.[10]

The asymmetry of economic transmission between the United States and Japan is a common result of this and a number of other models. The result has important implications for evaluating the relative merits of policies that might be undertaken to redress the U.S.-Japan trade imbalance. Clearly, demand policies originating in the United States will have a much larger impact than similar policies in Japan. This does not apply to policies that directly restrict or expand trade, and thereby bypass the link between economic expansion and trade volumes.

Expansion in the United States and Japan: Industry-Level Effects

In the previous section, we have shown that changes in U.S. aggregate demand can have significant effects on the Japanese macroeconomy. However, the distribution of these effects will not be uniform across industries. The change in activity in individual Japanese industries depends on the initial allocation of spending in the U.S. economy, the responsiveness of U.S. industry imports, and the structure of interindustry demand in both economies. Japanese gains will be concentrated in industries that experience strong U.S. demand (and import) expansion, that are heavily dependent on U.S. trade, or that supply industries of this kind.

Following the discussion in Chapter 3, Japanese industry output is given by:

$$X_i - F_i + E_i - M_i + X_i^I + IV_i \qquad (4.1)$$

where:

X_i is output,

F_i is final demand for output of industry i,

E_i and M_i are exports and imports, respectively,

IV_i is the change in inventories, and

X_i^I is the indirect demand of other industries for industry i output.

Expanding the term for indirect demand, we have:

$$X_i = F_i + E_i - M_i + \sum_{j \neq i} a_{ij} X_j + IV_i \qquad (4.2)$$

Abstracting from the inventory change term, this can be rewritten to highlight the dependence of industry output on trade of this and other industries:

$$X_i = (E_i - M_i) + \sum_{j \neq i} a_{ij} (E_j - M_j) + F_i + \sum_{j \neq i} a_{ij} F_j + \sum_{j \neq i} a_{ij} \sum_{k \neq j} a_{kj} X_k \qquad (4.3)$$

With a U.S. expansion, output in Japanese industry i will increase directly if U.S. imports $(M_i^{US} = E_i)$ increase, but also if U.S. imports in client industries (E_j) increase or if there are induced rises in direct or indirect final demands (F_i, F_j).[11] The increase in U.S. imports itself depends on direct and indirect demands through the input-output structure of the U.S. economy:

$$M_i^{US} = f \left(F_i^{US} + E_i^{US} + \sum_{j \neq i} a_{ij}^{US} X_j^{US}, \text{ relative prices} \right) \qquad (4.4)$$

Finally, in addition to thse numerous quantity effects, relative price changes may alter final demands, import demands, and, through changes in the factor mix, the composition of intermediate demands. As we saw above, these latter effects are not of negligible importance in the U.S. fiscal policy simulation.

Table 4.22 summarizes industry-level effects of the U.S. fiscal policy simulation. For each industry, first year and sixth year percent changes from base in U.S. output and real imports from Japan are given, as well as the resulting change in Japanese output. On average, manufacturing gross output in the United States rises 5.1% above base in the first year, and imports rise 2.7%. Aluminum, iron and steel, aircraft, and other transportation equipment show the largest output gains, which translate into larger-than-average rises in imports. Over six years, import gains are substantial, contributing to output declines in about half of the industries. The huge increases in basic chemicals, other nonferrous metals, aircraft, and other transportation equipment may be attributable to extreme estimated coefficient values.

In Japan, industry output gains range from 0.1% to 5.5% in the first year and 0.4% to 13.5% in year six. In percentage terms, the most affected industries are textiles, basic chemicals, rubber products, iron products, other nonferrous metals, nonelectrical and electrical machinery, other transportation equipment, autos, and instruments. These percentage changes do not indicate the absolute magnitude of the industry impacts, a perhaps better measure of the importance of the industry changes in the overall Japanese economy. Table 4.23 provides this information, giving changes for the sixth year in output in the industries as level differences from baseline output and as a percentage of baseline output. On this basis, it is easy to see that most of the "action" is in the machinery and transportation sectors, metals, and chemicals. Many of the other sectors show negligible effects.[12]

We have argued that the output effects in Japan should depend not just on direct trade linkage equations, but also the entire input-output structure of both economies. Are such interindustry relationships of quantitative importance? To assess this, Table 4.24 decomposes, for several of the more affected industries, the absolute change in Japanese output into the portions attributable to domestic final demand, exports, imports (with a minus sign), indirect demands, and inventory change. As expected, there is a marked difference between intermediate goods and final goods industries in the proportion of the change in output attributable to final demand $(F + E - M)$ and intermediate demand (X^I). Increases in output in the chemical and iron industries are dominated by increases in indirect demand, whereas the other industries are primarily influenced by direct final demands.

Because of the importance of indirect demand, the increase in exports is not a very good indicator of output gains in an industry. In the iron products industry, exports change almost not at all, but increasing indirect demand (primarily from the steel industry) raises output substantially. Basic chemicals experience an export decline in the second year, but still post strong output gains.

The importance of factors other than exports can be seen in the final goods industries also. There is nearly as much first-year increase in output in electrical machinery as in autos, even though exports in electrical machinery are up only $1/6^{th}$ as much. Additionally, the composition of changes in industry expenditure can shift over the course of the simulation. In the first year, more than a third of the increased steel shipments go to other industries, but by year six, indirect demand is actually down slightly from base levels.

Another way to see the importance of industrial structure for international transmission is to look at the impact of a U.S. shock on nontraded Japanese industries.[13] Table 4.25 gives output changes for construction, utilities, and other service industries. Many of the changes are substantial; note especially the rise in wholesale and retail trade. These effects are the result of interindustry linkages and of macroeconomic feedbacks that affect housing and industrial construction, for example.

Although we have seen that effects of a Japanese fiscal expansion on the U.S. economy are very small, for the sake of completeness, Table 4.26 shows the transmission of a Japan fiscal expansion to U.S. industries. As before, the table gives Japanese output changes, changes in Japan's imports from the United States, and the resulting change in U.S. outputs (all in percent differences from the baseline simulation). In percentage terms, the domestic (Japanese) industries most affected by the fiscal stimulus are intermediate goods, such as coal products, wood products, cement, and metal products, although many industries are up by more than 1%. Japan's imports rise much less than their American counterparts, and there is much less variation across industries. The effects on U.S. industries are very small, with basic chemicals, aluminum, and autos most affected in percentage terms.

The macroeconomic and input-output structures are clearly crucial for determining the transmission of activity at the industrial level. An analysis of empirical trade equations will provide only a partial picture of industrial response without reference to a complete model.

The Impact of Rest of the World Expansion

The Rest of the World is important as a mechanism for propagating a demand stimulus originating in the United States. Similarly, the United States. and Japan are clearly vulnerable to disturbances arising in third countries. To assess the extent of this multilateral interdependence, we have simulated a 1% of GNP increase in government spending in each of the other Big Seven countries, with unchanged policies in the United States, and Japan.[14] The macroeconomic impact of this Rest of the World expansion is summarized in Tables 4.27 and 4.28, with world effects in Tables 4.29 and 4.30.

Looking first at the overall world effects, we see that increased demand raises world real output 0.3% in the first year (1988), and 0.4% in the following year. The effect on the European Community (EC) is, of course, much larger at 0.8% in 1988 and over 1% above base in 1989. It is noteworthy that the developing countries are little affected by the expansion, with output rising just 0.1% above baseline levels. This stands in sharp contrast to the U.S. fiscal expansion where developing country gains were roughly half as large (in percentage terms) as developed country gains. This difference is due to the greater responsiveness of U.S. import demand and the larger share of the less developed country (LDC) exports in U.S. imports. The first point can be seen by comparing Tables 4.29 and 4.30 with Tables 4.10 and 4.11. In the ROW expansion, EC imports rise just 1.5% for a 1% rise in output; in the U.S. expansion (Tables 4.10 and 4.11), U.S. imports rise over 8% for a 2-3% increase in GNP. As for trade composition, just 10% of EC imports come from developing countries, compared with 36% for the United States. Overall, 60% of EC trade is with other EC countries.

The effects on the United States and Japan of the expansion in the other Big Seven countries are rather small. Both the United States and Japan experience increases in activity of 0.1% above base, with real exports up about 0.4% to

0.5%. The small effect on Japan is particularly interesting, in light of the substantial effects of a U.S. fiscal expansion on Japan. Again, the reason is the insular nature of this group of European countries; just 3.6% of EC imports are from Japan in the 1988 baseline solution.

CONCLUSIONS

In this chapter, we have presented model simulations of U.S., Japan, and ROW demand expansion. These calculations have assumed a simple fiscal demand stimulus. Other policy approaches will be considered in succeeding chapters. These results illustrate the operation of each domestic economy, and quantify the extent of interdependence among the U.S., Japan, and world economies with regard to changes in economic activity. Several general results emerge from these analyses.

First, transmission of economic activity is highly asymmetric. The impacts of a U.S. expansion on the Japan economy are much larger than the effect on the United States of Japanese expansion. A 1% of GNP increase in U.S. fiscal expenditure raises Japanese output about 1% after six years; the corresponding Japan fiscal expansion raises U.S. GNP just 0.06%. Even after accounting for differences in country size, the U.S. economy exerts twice as great an impact on Japan as Japan does on the United States. This difference is due to Japan's somewhat lower fiscal multiplier and the smaller induced rise in imports in Japan.

In addition, U.S. expansion exerts a much larger impact on the world economy than a similar expansion in other Big Seven countries. Again the large U.S. multiplier is one source of this dominance, but the rather insular pattern of EC trade is also important. The U.S. expansion raises output worldwide, whereas the EC expansion is limited mostly to the industrialized world.

Other-country trade has important effects on the bilateral transmission of economic activity. Within several years of a U.S. fiscal shock, a significant portion of the additional stimulus to Japan is due to increased import demand in countries other than the U.S.

At the industry level, trade responses play a central role in determining international transmission. Although macroeconomic multipliers and input-output structure are important elements of trade interdependence at the industry level, the most important determinants of transmission remain the marginal propensities to import and import price elasticities of the trade equations.

The industrial structure of national economies is crucial as well to determining industry-level transmission of activity and prices. Clearly, industry import demand depends on interindustry input requirements as well as on final demand; similarly, ultimate impacts on foreign industries depend on their direct exports and on the exports of other industries consuming their output as intermediate inputs. Similar relationships govern transmission of industry prices internationally.

Figure 4.1
Domestic and Partner-Country Effects of Fiscal Expansion

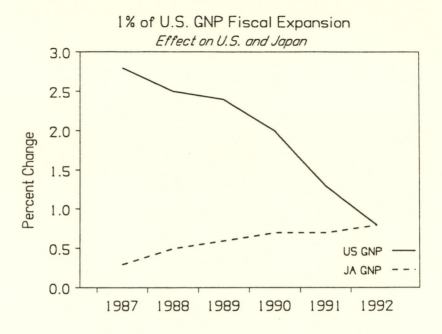

1% of U.S. GNP Fiscal Expansion
Effect on U.S. and Japan

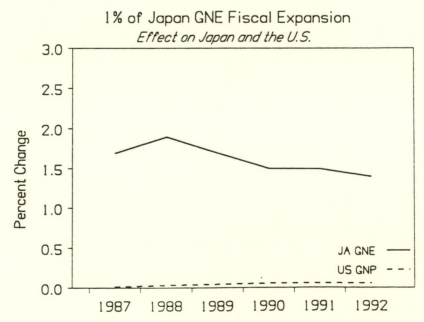

1% of Japan GNE Fiscal Expansion
Effect on Japan and the U.S.

Figure 4.2

Transmission from the U.S. to Japan in Several Models

Source: EPA, MCM, OECD results are from Helliwell (1988).

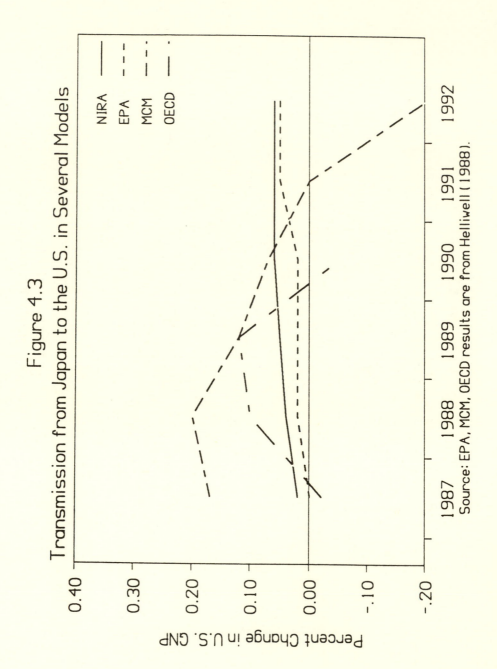

Figure 4.3

Transmission from Japan to the U.S. in Several Models

Source: EPA, MCM, OECD results are from Helliwell (1988).

Table 4.1
Baseline Simulation: U.S. Macro Summary

	1987	%CHG	1988	%CHG	1989	%CHG	1990	%CHG	1991	%CHG	1992	%CHG
Selected Economic Indicators												
GNP (72$ billion)	1785.1	3.6	1852.6	3.8	1890.5	2.0	1919.4	1.5	1977.5	3.0	2030.9	2.7
Nominal GNP ($b)	4466.9	8.0	4850.8	8.6	5225.0	7.7	5606.7	7.3	6018.4	7.3	6396.3	6.3
GNP Deflator	250.2	4.2	261.8	4.6	276.4	5.6	292.1	5.7	304.4	4.2	315.0	3.5
Consumer Prices	350.4	4.3	368.2	5.1	389.0	5.6	410.8	5.6	427.9	4.2	443.2	3.6
Employment (mil.)	111.0	2.2	113.2	1.9	114.8	1.5	115.2	0.3	117.7	2.2	118.9	1.0
Unemployment Rate (%)	6.9	-7.8	6.5	-5.2	6.4	-1.2	7.4	15.7	6.7	-9.7	6.8	1.7
3-Month CD Rate (%)	8.2	9.4	9.3	12.4	10.9	18.1	10.1	-7.8	8.9	-11.7	8.2	-8.2
M2 ($b)	2816.3	6.8	2990.5	6.2	3168.8	6.0	3357.9	6.0	3569.0	6.3	3792.9	6.3
Federal Surplus ($b)	-147.4	17.5	-148.4	-0.7	-171.6	-15.6	-204.7	-19.3	-171.4	16.3	-168.4	1.7
Current Account ($b)	-146.4	6.0	-146.9	-0.3	-153.2	-4.3	-142.6	6.9	-151.8	-6.5	-155.9	-2.6
W.A. $ Exchange Rate	90.2	11.8	95.6	6.0	97.5	2.0	98.8	1.4	98.2	-0.7	97.8	-0.4
Real Gross National Product by Category (72$ billion)												
Personal Consumption	1161.4	2.8	1201.5	3.4	1236.9	2.9	1273.0	2.9	1299.2	2.1	1329.1	2.3
Durable Goods	201.3	3.9	212.6	5.6	217.7	2.4	224.6	3.2	228.2	1.6	230.9	1.2
Nondurable Goods	422.3	2.4	433.4	2.6	443.8	2.4	455.0	2.5	459.7	1.0	469.4	2.1
Services	537.9	2.8	555.4	3.3	575.4	3.6	593.4	3.1	611.3	3.0	628.9	2.9
Gross Private Investment	322.5	7.1	337.7	4.7	334.4	-1.0	315.7	-5.6	344.6	9.2	361.7	5.0
Fixed Investment	308.8	6.0	322.3	4.4	320.8	-0.4	314.6	-1.9	329.8	4.8	347.0	5.2
Nonresidential	241.2	5.8	250.9	4.0	255.9	2.0	252.0	-1.5	266.0	5.5	282.3	6.1
Residential	67.6	7.1	71.4	5.5	64.9	-9.1	62.6	-3.6	63.8	2.0	64.7	1.3
Change in Bus. Inventories	13.7	36.8	15.4	12.9	13.5	-12.3	1.1	-91.8	14.8	999.9	14.7	-0.6
Net Exports, Goods and Srvcs.	-25.8	21.9	-20.8	19.4	-23.3	-12.0	-20.5	12.0	-26.7	-30.4	-29.4	-10.0
Exports	157.1	7.2	166.7	6.1	169.6	1.7	177.1	4.5	183.5	3.6	194.2	5.8
Imports	182.9	1.9	187.5	2.5	192.8	2.9	197.6	2.5	210.2	6.4	223.6	6.4
Government Purchases	326.9	0.6	334.2	2.2	342.6	2.5	351.2	2.5	360.4	2.6	369.6	2.5

Note: Figures are billions of 1972 dollars and annual growth rates, unless otherwise noted.

Table 4.2
Baseline Simulation: U.S. Gross Output by Industry

	1987	%CHG	1988	%CHG	1989	%CHG	1990	%CHG	1991	%CHG	1992	%CHG
Agric., For., Fish.	108.6	-1.2	111.0	2.3	112.6	1.4	112.3	-0.3	116.7	3.9	117.5	0.8
Metal Mining	4.5	8.2	4.7	4.7	4.7	-0.5	4.4	-6.2	4.6	6.4	4.7	1.3
Coal Mining	7.9	3.6	8.1	3.6	8.1	-0.6	7.9	-2.7	8.1	3.2	8.3	2.0
Oil Extraction	12.1	-1.5	11.9	-1.4	11.7	-2.1	11.5	-1.9	11.2	-1.9	11.1	-1.6
Natural Gas Extract.	3.3	0.6	3.3	-1.1	3.3	-1.1	3.2	-1.1	3.2	-1.1	3.2	-1.1
Nonmetal Mining	4.5	6.1	4.7	3.2	4.6	-1.1	4.5	-3.1	4.6	3.9	4.7	1.9
Resid. Construction	54.0	8.4	57.2	6.0	51.8	-9.4	49.9	-3.7	51.2	2.6	52.1	1.7
Nonres. Construction	51.1	2.9	52.5	2.8	53.1	1.2	52.6	-1.0	54.2	3.1	56.4	4.0
Other Construction	38.6	4.1	40.1	4.0	41.1	2.3	41.1	0.1	42.6	3.5	44.3	4.1
Food and Beverages	133.2	3.0	136.4	2.4	140.0	2.6	142.4	1.7	146.9	3.2	149.6	1.8
Tobacco	6.4	-1.6	6.6	2.7	6.6	0.4	6.4	-3.3	6.6	3.2	6.6	0.3
Textiles	36.7	3.8	38.5	4.9	38.9	1.1	39.5	1.5	38.7	-2.1	39.2	1.5
Apparel	25.0	3.2	26.2	4.9	27.1	3.4	28.2	4.0	27.5	-2.5	28.1	2.2
Paper, Pulp	47.8	3.3	49.7	4.0	50.7	2.0	50.9	0.4	52.9	3.9	54.1	2.3
Printing, Publish.	44.9	3.5	46.3	3.2	47.4	2.3	47.9	1.1	49.7	3.7	50.7	2.1
Industrial Chemicals	22.5	5.0	23.2	3.4	23.3	0.3	23.0	-1.4	23.9	4.3	24.1	0.7
Nonind. Chemicals	77.5	4.2	81.2	4.7	83.0	2.2	84.1	1.4	87.2	3.6	89.5	2.7
Petr., Coal Refining	32.6	0.6	33.2	1.9	33.5	1.0	33.8	0.6	34.5	2.1	34.8	0.9
Rubber, Plastics	32.3	4.2	33.9	5.0	34.7	2.3	35.1	1.2	36.4	3.6	37.4	2.9
Leather	4.1	1.5	4.2	2.9	4.2	0.2	4.2	0.9	4.0	-5.0	4.1	2.2
Lumber, Wood Prod.	29.0	1.7	31.2	7.7	30.2	-3.2	29.6	-2.2	30.8	4.0	31.4	2.1
Furniture	14.4	4.1	15.0	4.0	15.2	1.7	15.2	-0.3	15.9	4.6	16.3	2.8
Cement	1.4	6.3	1.5	4.9	1.5	-1.0	1.5	-1.9	1.5	3.7	1.6	2.5
Oth. Stone, Clay, Gl.	21.9	3.4	23.1	5.4	23.0	-0.2	22.9	-0.5	23.7	3.6	24.2	2.2
Iron, Steel	30.4	3.2	30.7	1.1	28.4	-7.5	26.2	-7.9	25.7	-1.8	26.2	1.8
Aluminum	2.2	18.0	2.4	10.1	2.3	-2.0	2.2	-5.3	2.2	-1.9	2.2	-0.7
Oth. Nonfer. Metal	45.5	3.4	46.7	2.6	44.5	-4.7	42.1	-5.3	43.3	2.8	43.4	0.3
Fabr. Metal Products	65.5	2.4	68.7	4.9	69.0	0.5	68.3	-1.0	70.7	3.5	72.8	2.9
Nonelect. Machinery	122.4	6.1	131.0	7.0	134.4	2.6	134.8	0.3	144.6	7.3	154.2	6.7
Electrical Machinery	98.6	6.3	105.0	6.5	107.9	2.8	109.2	1.2	113.5	3.9	116.2	2.4
Aircraft	25.0	4.4	25.3	1.5	24.3	-4.1	22.6	-7.0	22.6	0.1	23.2	2.8

Oth. Transp. Equip.	25.0	4.3	26.0	3.9	25.2	-2.9	25.6	1.6	25.3	-1.3	26.5	4.7
Motor Vehicles	95.0	3.8	102.0	7.3	100.7	-1.3	98.6	-2.1	99.2	0.6	100.3	1.1
Instruments	30.0	3.6	31.6	5.5	32.7	3.4	33.3	1.8	35.2	5.7	36.6	4.1
Misc. Manufactures	15.0	6.2	15.8	5.4	16.0	1.3	16.0	-0.1	16.7	4.5	16.9	1.3
Rail Transportation	14.0	6.9	14.7	5.5	14.9	0.9	14.8	-0.3	15.5	4.7	16.0	3.1
Passenger Transport.	4.3	2.9	4.5	3.2	4.6	2.2	4.6	1.5	4.7	2.4	4.8	1.9
Truck Transport.	39.9	4.9	41.8	4.6	42.7	2.4	43.4	1.5	45.1	3.9	46.5	3.1
Water Transport.	7.1	4.1	7.2	1.1	7.2	0.3	7.2	0.6	7.3	1.2	7.4	1.5
Air Transport.	20.9	6.0	21.9	4.9	22.9	4.5	23.8	4.0	24.8	4.0	25.7	3.7
Pipeline Transport.	2.0	1.5	2.1	1.1	2.1	0.8	2.1	-0.1	2.1	1.5	2.1	0.5
Transport. Services	3.1	3.6	3.2	2.7	3.3	2.1	3.3	1.8	3.4	2.5	3.5	2.3
Communications	93.6	6.4	98.8	5.6	103.7	4.9	108.2	4.3	113.4	4.8	118.2	4.3
Electrical Utilities	48.0	2.5	49.6	3.4	50.8	2.4	51.4	1.0	52.9	2.9	54.3	2.7
Water, Sewer	13.9	4.2	14.4	3.6	14.9	3.3	15.3	2.9	15.8	2.7	16.1	2.4
Wholesale, Retail	440.5	3.9	455.6	3.4	466.1	2.3	475.1	1.9	486.9	2.5	499.3	2.5
Fin., Ins., Real Estate	421.7	3.2	434.4	3.0	447.9	3.1	459.1	2.5	474.5	3.4	489.0	3.1
Oth. Nonmed. Servs.	290.7	3.7	300.5	3.4	309.1	2.9	316.5	2.4	325.4	2.8	333.7	2.5
Medical Services	99.7	4.1	103.4	3.7	107.6	4.0	111.6	3.7	116.3	4.2	119.6	2.8
Federal Enterprise	14.7	6.8	15.2	3.5	15.6	2.7	16.0	1.9	16.4	2.5	16.7	2.3
St., Local Enterprise	15.4	2.8	15.9	3.7	16.5	3.2	16.9	2.9	17.4	3.0	17.9	2.6

Note: Baseline output levels in billions of 1972 dollars and annual growth rates. Includes indirect business taxes.

Table 4.3
Baseline Simulation: Japan Macro Summary

	1987	%CHG	1988	%CHG	1989	%CHG	1990	%CHG	1991	%CHG	1992	%CHG
					Selected Economic Indicators							
GNE (80¥ billion)	307756.0	5.7	325068.0	5.6	337150.0	3.7	349974.0	3.8	366573.0	4.7	385555.0	5.2
Nominal GNE (¥b)	327826.0	4.4	347747.0	6.1	367014.0	5.5	386355.0	5.3	409141.0	5.9	434903.0	6.3
GNE Deflator	114.9	-0.1	116.4	1.3	119.0	2.3	121.2	1.8	123.0	1.4	124.7	1.4
Pers. Cons. Deflator	106.2	-1.1	106.3	0.1	108.5	2.1	110.6	2.0	113.0	2.2	115.5	2.2
Employment (mil.)	57.8	0.4	58.2	0.6	58.7	0.8	59.0	0.7	59.5	0.8	60.0	0.9
Unemployment Rate (%)	2.7	1.8	2.7	0.5	2.8	1.0	2.8	1.3	2.8	1.0	2.9	0.8
Bank Lending Rate (%)	5.8	0.1	5.8	0.0	5.9	1.2	5.9	0.3	5.9	-0.4	5.8	-0.2
Govt. Surplus (¥b)	-20279.0	-19.7	-22923.0	-13.0	-24323.0	-6.1	-25882.0	-6.4	-27540.0	-6.4	-29043.0	-5.5
Current Account ($b)	52.1	45.1	81.0	55.4	77.9	-3.8	76.1	-2.3	73.2	-3.8	71.1	-3.0
¥/$ Exchange Rate	144.6	-14.2	128.8	-11.0	123.8	-3.9	121.4	-2.0	121.5	0.1	121.8	0.3
					Real Gross National Expenditure by Category (80¥ billion)							
Private Consumption	175287.0	4.2	183084.0	4.4	190214.0	3.9	197147.0	3.6	204267.0	3.6	211702.0	3.6
Nonprofit Consumption	1643.9	0.3	1649.3	0.3	1654.7	0.3	1660.2	0.3	1665.6	0.3	1671.1	0.3
Government Consumption	28807.0	3.0	29672.0	3.0	30562.0	3.0	31479.0	3.0	32423.0	3.0	33396.0	3.0
Business Investment	47133.0	2.5	49246.0	4.5	52224.0	6.0	54832.0	5.0	58604.0	6.9	63335.0	8.1
Residential Investment	22513.0	4.1	23774.0	5.6	24272.0	2.1	24220.0	-0.2	24728.0	2.1	25552.0	3.3
Government Investment	27342.0	12.0	30569.0	11.8	31990.0	4.6	33467.0	4.6	35003.0	4.6	36600.0	4.6
Priv. Inventory Invest.	2569.1	999.9	3133.5	22.0	2989.6	-4.6	2891.8	-3.3	3453.2	19.4	4204.9	21.8
Govt. Inventory Invest.	305.9	0.0	305.9	0.0	305.9	0.0	305.9	0.0	305.9	0.0	305.9	0.0
Net Exports	2154.6	184.3	3635.2	68.7	2938.9	-19.2	3972.5	35.2	6123.2	54.1	8787.8	43.5
Exports	52078.0	11.4	57633.0	10.7	60464.0	4.9	63691.0	5.3	68148.0	7.0	73421.0	7.7
Imports	49923.0	8.5	53998.0	8.2	57525.0	6.5	59718.0	3.8	62025.0	3.9	64633.0	4.2

Note: Figures are billions of 1980 yen and annual growth rates, unless otherwise noted.

Table 4.4
Baseline Simulation: Japan Gross Output by Industry

	1987	%CHG	1988	%CHG	1989	%CHG	1990	%CHG	1991	%CHG	1992	%CHG
General Crops	8824.1	1.0	8801.0	-0.3	8651.0	-1.7	8357.5	-3.4	8207.6	-1.8	7978.5	-2.8
Industrial Crops	558.3	8.9	587.4	5.2	601.8	2.4	633.0	5.2	663.1	4.8	686.7	3.6
Livestock,Textiles	0.4	-8.4	0.4	-8.4	0.3	-8.4	0.3	-8.4	0.3	-8.4	0.3	-8.4
Livestock	4406.1	3.0	4474.7	1.6	4509.6	0.8	4477.8	-0.7	4515.5	0.8	4533.3	0.4
Forestry	1471.9	-3.6	1430.7	-2.8	1385.2	-3.2	1348.6	-2.6	1323.8	-1.8	1298.3	-1.9
Fisheries	2985.6	-0.4	2988.3	0.1	2983.2	-0.2	3034.0	1.7	3031.5	-0.1	3050.3	0.6
Coal Mining	254.5	3.4	274.4	7.8	270.8	-1.3	270.7	-0.1	266.1	-1.7	263.9	-0.8
Iron Ores	1.2	-10.2	1.1	-10.2	1.0	-10.2	0.9	-10.2	0.8	-10.2	0.7	-10.2
Nonfer. Metal Ore	101.9	-4.4	97.4	-4.4	93.1	-4.4	89.0	-4.4	85.1	-4.4	81.3	-4.4
Crude Petroleum	18.7	-3.7	18.0	-3.7	17.3	-3.7	16.7	-3.7	16.1	-3.7	15.5	-3.7
Natural Gas	74.3	0.0	74.3	0.0	74.3	0.0	74.3	0.0	74.3	0.0	74.3	0.0
Other Mining	1989.1	4.8	2116.4	6.4	2171.4	2.6	2236.6	3.0	2338.3	4.5	2454.0	5.0
Meat, Dairy	5347.5	4.0	5491.0	2.7	5563.4	1.3	5540.4	-0.4	5582.9	0.8	5610.2	0.5
Grain Products	4042.2	-1.0	4010.0	-0.8	3974.1	-0.9	3925.5	-1.2	3887.7	-1.0	3843.9	-1.1
Manuf. Sea Food	2957.3	0.2	3023.6	2.2	3063.1	1.3	3221.3	5.2	3273.5	1.6	3343.1	2.1
Other Foods	11838.0	7.4	11966.0	1.1	12676.0	5.9	12407.0	-2.1	12706.0	2.4	12606.0	-0.8
Beverages	4908.7	-2.8	5304.3	8.1	5215.4	-1.7	5561.2	6.6	5575.6	0.3	5831.7	4.6
Tobacco	2634.7	-1.9	2763.6	4.9	2724.5	-1.4	2827.4	3.8	2820.1	-0.3	2885.9	2.3
Natural Textiles	877.4	8.5	875.6	-0.2	898.0	2.6	907.2	1.0	940.7	3.7	971.9	3.3
Chemical Textiles	395.8	7.8	396.4	0.2	409.7	3.3	410.0	0.1	424.5	3.5	437.4	3.0
Other Textiles	6306.4	9.0	6315.0	0.1	6464.5	2.4	6511.3	0.7	6737.5	3.5	6921.0	2.7
Wearing Apparel	5828.1	2.2	6027.6	3.4	6262.0	3.9	6425.4	2.6	6653.6	3.6	6881.4	3.4
Wood, Products	5272.2	0.9	5637.2	6.9	5808.9	3.0	5955.1	2.5	6256.7	5.1	6583.6	5.2
Furniture	3717.8	5.0	3837.7	3.2	3929.5	2.4	4011.6	2.1	4142.0	3.3	4293.6	3.7
Pulp, Paper	7762.1	1.3	7968.1	2.7	8033.5	0.8	8144.8	1.4	8201.9	0.7	8462.5	3.2
Print, Publish.	7696.1	2.1	7902.1	2.7	8049.9	1.9	8211.6	2.0	8008.4	-2.5	8257.4	3.1
Leather Products	520.4	2.6	526.3	1.1	533.4	1.4	540.0	1.2	550.5	1.9	559.7	1.7
Rubber Products	2545.7	8.5	2624.3	3.1	2740.3	4.4	2846.3	3.9	3008.9	5.7	3186.1	5.9
Basic, Int. Chems.	14834.0	5.7	15653.0	5.5	16266.0	3.9	16805.0	3.3	17489.0	4.1	18316.0	4.7
Final Chemicals	10485.0	4.2	11066.0	5.5	11604.0	4.9	12163.0	4.8	12812.0	5.3	13568.0	5.9
Petroleum Prods.	16434.0	10.7	17550.0	6.8	19007.0	8.3	19615.0	3.2	20394.0	4.0	21108.0	3.5
Coal Products	2117.0	1.6	2389.6	12.9	2348.7	-1.7	2445.0	4.1	2503.9	2.4	2626.7	4.9
Cement	968.2	8.7	1045.5	8.0	1118.9	7.0	1161.1	3.8	1215.6	4.7	1281.6	5.4

Table 4.4—Continued

	1987	%CHG	1988	%CHG	1989	%CHG	1990	%CHG	1991	%CHG	1992	%CHG
Other Ceramics	7703.5	6.0	8159.4	5.9	8434.7	3.4	8696.6	3.1	9066.5	4.3	9504.2	4.8
Iron Products	7908.0	0.4	9320.0	17.9	9074.0	-2.6	9425.0	3.9	9560.0	1.4	10028.0	4.9
Roll., Cast., Forg.	16789.0	2.1	17774.0	5.9	18329.0	3.1	18688.0	2.0	19235.0	2.9	19870.0	3.3
Aluminum	1351.2	6.9	1444.2	6.9	1543.7	6.9	1650.0	6.9	1763.6	6.9	1885.1	6.9
Oth. Nonfer. Met.	6660.0	-6.3	7060.7	6.0	7328.4	3.8	7494.2	2.3	7772.6	3.7	8187.9	5.3
Metal Products	13309.0	5.5	14095.0	5.9	14814.0	5.1	15529.0	4.8	16445.0	5.9	17497.0	6.4
Machinery	29097.0	2.9	29908.0	2.8	31230.0	4.4	32704.0	4.7	34961.0	6.9	37795.0	8.1
Electr. Machinery	41626.0	23.2	46241.0	11.1	49742.0	7.6	53633.0	7.8	59171.0	10.3	65681.0	11.0
Automobiles	25260.0	0.9	27042.0	7.1	28904.0	6.9	30698.0	6.2	32955.0	7.4	35270.0	7.0
Aircraft	678.0	7.7	730.6	7.7	787.2	7.7	848.2	7.7	913.9	7.7	984.7	7.7
Oth. Transportation	3513.9	6.1	3733.7	6.3	4031.9	8.0	4335.2	7.5	4687.4	8.1	5154.8	10.0
Instruments	4391.5	-4.7	4440.4	1.1	4542.8	2.3	4695.2	3.4	4983.3	6.1	5316.1	6.7
Misc. Manufs.	11127.0	3.6	11692.0	5.1	12157.0	4.0	12579.0	3.5	13177.0	4.8	13871.0	5.3
Housing	20986.0	4.1	22130.0	5.4	22586.0	2.1	22587.0	0.0	23055.0	2.1	23787.0	3.2
Indus. Construction	20165.0	2.8	21067.0	4.5	21970.0	4.3	22804.0	3.8	23863.0	4.6	25145.0	5.4
Public Construction	14409.0	8.3	15632.0	8.5	16191.0	3.6	16768.0	3.6	17377.0	3.6	18018.0	3.7
Oth. Construction	15281.0	3.3	15945.0	4.3	16488.0	3.4	16999.0	3.1	17638.0	3.8	18407.0	4.4
Electric Power	10912.0	1.9	11180.0	2.5	11417.0	2.1	11792.0	3.3	12272.0	4.1	12866.0	4.8
Gas	1468.7	-0.8	1467.9	-0.1	1494.6	1.8	1531.9	2.5	1585.7	3.5	1647.0	3.9
Water, Sanitary	3817.1	1.3	3874.8	1.5	3926.3	1.3	3981.4	1.4	4050.9	1.7	4129.3	1.9
Whlsle., Retail	63730.0	3.6	65943.0	3.5	67609.0	2.5	69110.0	2.2	70852.0	2.5	72787.0	2.7
Real Estate	31956.0	4.8	33547.0	5.0	35130.0	4.7	36554.0	4.1	38070.0	4.1	39650.0	4.1
Railways	3405.6	-0.2	3421.6	0.5	3444.3	0.7	3459.1	0.4	3482.5	0.7	3510.4	0.8
Trucks, Buses	10304.0	1.9	10533.0	2.2	10706.0	1.6	10833.0	1.2	11025.0	1.8	11249.0	2.0
Oth. Transportation	7263.2	2.3	7457.0	2.7	7584.0	1.7	7689.5	1.4	7825.1	1.8	7973.8	1.9
Communications	6299.5	2.6	6441.2	2.3	6575.3	2.1	6689.7	1.7	6868.4	2.7	7072.7	3.0
Finance, Insurance	21990.0	4.7	23041.0	4.8	23921.0	3.8	24626.0	2.9	25441.0	3.3	26308.0	3.4
Govt. Services	17479.0	1.6	17761.0	1.6	18049.0	1.6	18342.0	1.6	18640.0	1.6	18944.0	1.6
Public Services	38009.0	3.5	39147.0	3.0	40568.0	3.6	42143.0	3.9	43983.0	4.4	45855.0	4.3
Other Services	48277.0	2.6	50158.0	3.9	51448.0	2.6	52979.0	3.0	54790.0	3.4	56776.0	3.6
Unallocated	9618.0	6.4	10251.0	6.6	10728.0	4.7	11182.0	4.2	11729.0	4.9	12367.0	5.4
TOTAL	652957.0	4.4	683872.0	4.7	708202.0	3.6	731217.0	3.2	760944.0	4.1	795548.0	4.5

Note: Baseline output levels in billions of 1980 yen and annual growth rates.

Table 4.5

Baseline Simulation: World Trade by Region (f.o.b.)

	1987	1988	%CHG	1989	%CHG	1990	%CHG	1991	%CHG	1992	%CHG
United States											
Exports	249.3	312.5	25.4	340.5	9.0	372.6	9.4	405.3	8.8	444.2	9.6
Imports	410.9	436.5	6.2	464.8	6.5	486.5	4.7	538.5	10.7	601.1	11.6
Balance	-161.6	-123.9		-124.3		-113.9		-133.3		-156.9	
Japan											
Exports	224.8	259.8	15.6	283.2	9.0	304.2	7.4	330.1	8.5	360.5	9.2
Imports	129.3	145.3	12.4	158.8	9.3	171.9	8.2	188.0	9.4	206.5	9.8
Balance	95.5	114.5		124.3		132.3		142.0		154.0	
Other Industr. Countries											
Exports	1265.4	1409.2	11.4	1536.1	9.0	1665.6	8.4	1816.9	9.1	1994.0	9.7
Imports	1239.8	1388.7	12.0	1516.4	9.2	1655.2	9.2	1799.1	8.7	1970.4	9.5
Balance	25.5	20.4		19.7		10.3		17.9		23.6	
EC											
Exports	937.7	1039.3	10.8	1134.0	9.1	1230.3	8.5	1338.5	8.8	1464.3	9.4
Imports	918.7	1028.5	12.0	1134.8	10.3	1242.5	9.5	1357.9	9.3	1494.7	10.1
Balance	19.0	10.8		-0.8		-12.2		-19.5		-30.4	
Developing Countries											
Exports	513.8	578.8	12.6	626.1	8.2	674.7	7.8	741.9	10.0	819.9	10.5
Imports	470.8	547.8	16.4	603.1	10.1	661.7	9.7	728.2	10.1	801.8	10.1
Balance	43.0	30.9		23.1		13.1		13.7		18.2	
Asia Including China											
Exports	271.7	332.0	22.2	356.8	7.5	380.7	6.7	412.6	8.4	450.2	9.1
Imports	253.5	314.7	24.1	352.6	12.0	388.7	10.2	426.0	9.6	472.1	10.8
Balance	18.2	17.3		4.2		-8.0		-13.4		-22.0	
Asian NIEs											
Exports	175.6	219.4	24.9	233.9	6.6	247.6	5.9	266.3	7.6	288.8	8.5
Imports	149.2	195.5	31.0	222.0	13.5	245.2	10.5	269.1	9.7	300.1	11.5
Balance	26.4	23.8		11.9		2.4		-2.8		-11.3	
CPEs Excluding China											
Exports	202.7	215.8	6.4	230.1	6.7	248.7	8.1	268.8	8.1	292.2	8.7
Imports	193.9	207.6	7.1	223.1	7.5	241.1	8.1	260.2	7.9	282.4	8.5
Balance	8.9	8.1		7.0		7.6		8.7		9.8	
World Exports	2455.9	2776.0	13.0	3016.0	8.6	3265.8	8.3	3563.0	9.1	3910.7	9.8
World Export Price	3.4	3.5	4.4	3.6	3.8	3.8	3.4	3.9	3.1	4.0	3.2
World Exports Real (70$b.)	733.0	793.2	8.2	830.3	4.7	869.1	4.7	919.3	5.8	978.0	6.4

Note: Figures are billions of U.S. dollars and annual growth rates. NIEs are newly industrializing economies; CPE refers to the centrally-planned economies.

Table 4.6
Baseline Simulation: World GNP Growth by Region

	1987	1988	1989	1990	1991	1992	Mean
U.S.	3.6	3.8	2.0	1.5	3.0	2.7	2.8
Japan	5.7	5.6	3.7	3.8	4.7	5.2	4.8
Other Industr. Countries	2.3	3.2	2.5	2.5	2.8	2.8	2.7
Canada	5.5	4.5	2.0	2.4	3.9	6.1	4.1
Australia, N.Z.	1.7	2.5	2.0	2.9	2.7	1.4	2.2
EC	2.1	3.2	2.6	2.4	2.7	2.7	2.6
Rest of Industrialized	1.9	2.6	2.2	3.2	3.2	1.3	2.4
Developing Countries	4.8	4.7	4.7	5.4	5.8	5.9	5.2
OPEC	0.7	2.3	2.1	3.5	4.4	4.7	2.9
Africa	2.7	3.1	4.2	3.7	3.4	2.9	3.3
Asia Including China	7.6	8.6	6.7	6.7	7.0	7.0	7.3
Asian NIEs	12.6	9.9	4.5	6.6	6.7	8.1	8.0
Middle East Nonoil	3.2	3.3	4.5	4.5	4.7	4.7	4.2
Western Hemisphere	2.4	-0.8	1.9	4.1	4.4	4.7	2.8
C.P.E. Excluding China	2.6	3.1	2.8	3.1	3.3	3.3	3.0
World Total	3.0	3.5	3.1	3.4	3.7	3.8	3.4

Note: Figures are annual growth rates of real GNP, 1970 U.S. dollar basis. NIEs are newly industrializing economies; CPE refers to the centrally-planned economies.

Table 4.7
U.S. Government Defense Expenditure Increased by 1% of GNP

	1987	1988	1989	1990	1991	1992
United States:						
Govt. Defense Expend.	17.9	17.9	17.9	17.9	17.9	17.9
Gross National Product	50.4	45.8	46.0	38.4	25.3	16.9
Percent Difference	2.8	2.5	2.4	2.0	1.3	0.8
Multiplier	2.8	2.6	2.6	2.2	1.4	1.0
Imports (%Dif.)	2.2	3.0	4.2	5.3	6.0	6.8
Current Account ($b)	-14.3	-18.5	-24.6	-29.4	-34.4	-42.3
Japan:						
Gross National Expend.	875.0	1505.0	1958.0	2372.0	2727.0	3275.0
Percent Difference	0.3	0.5	0.6	0.7	0.7	0.8
Exports (%Dif.)	0.9	1.3	1.7	2.2	2.5	2.8
Current Account ($b)	2.1	3.6	5.0	6.3	7.3	8.9
World:						
World Exports	5.1	7.1	9.8	12.7	15.8	19.4
Percent Difference	0.7	0.9	1.2	1.5	1.7	2.0
World GNP	50.1	49.4	53.3	50.6	43.4	40.5
Percent Difference	0.8	0.8	0.8	0.8	0.6	0.6

Notes: Figures are absolute and percent differences from the baseline simulation.
Unless otherwise indicated, U.S. figures are in billions of 1972 dollars, Japanese
figures are in billions of 1980 yen, and world figures are in billions of 1970
dollars.

Table 4.8
U.S. Fiscal Expansion: U.S. Macro Summary

	1987	%DIF	1988	%DIF	1989	%DIF	1990	%DIF	1991	%DIF	1992	%DIF
					Selected Economic Indicators							
GNP (72$ billion)	50.4	2.8	45.8	2.5	46.0	2.4	38.4	2.0	25.3	1.3	16.9	0.8
Nominal GNP ($b)	139.5	3.1	189.3	3.9	267.2	5.1	325.9	5.8	335.7	5.6	335.6	5.2
GNP Deflator	0.7	0.3	3.6	1.4	7.2	2.6	10.9	3.7	12.9	4.2	13.8	4.4
Consumer Prices	1.4	0.4	5.1	1.4	9.5	2.4	13.7	3.3	15.9	3.7	16.8	3.8
Employment (mil.)	1.7	1.5	2.3	2.0	2.6	2.3	2.6	2.3	2.4	2.0	2.0	1.7
Unemployment Rate (%)	-1.4	-20.2	-1.7	-26.5	-1.9	-29.1	-1.7	-23.5	-1.4	-21.1	-1.1	-15.6
3-Month CD Rate (%)	0.7	7.9	0.8	9.0	1.3	11.6	1.4	13.5	0.9	10.3	0.5	6.0
M2 ($b)	63.9	2.3	103.4	3.5	144.1	4.5	181.8	5.4	198.9	5.6	203.3	5.4
Federal Surplus ($b)	-12.8	8.7	-13.7	9.2	-14.3	8.3	-26.5	13.0	-40.3	23.5	-53.3	31.7
Current Account ($b)	-14.3	9.8	-18.5	12.6	-24.6	16.1	-29.4	20.6	-34.4	22.7	-42.3	27.1
W.A. $ Exchange Rate	0.0	0.0	0.0	0.0	0.0	0.0	0.0	0.0	0.0	0.0	0.0	0.0
					Real Gross National Product by Category (72$ billion)							
Personal Consumption	20.2	1.7	25.0	2.1	30.0	2.4	29.5	2.3	25.8	2.0	22.1	1.7
Durable Goods	11.2	5.5	12.5	5.9	12.8	5.9	10.2	4.5	7.5	3.3	5.3	2.3
Nondurable Goods	5.9	1.4	6.7	1.5	8.6	1.9	9.1	2.0	7.9	1.7	6.9	1.5
Services	3.2	0.6	5.8	1.0	8.6	1.5	10.2	1.7	10.4	1.7	9.8	1.6
Gross Private Investment	15.8	4.9	8.5	2.5	6.6	2.0	2.2	0.7	-4.8	-1.4	-6.9	-1.9
Fixed Investment	10.5	3.4	4.4	1.4	4.1	1.3	1.5	0.5	-2.3	-0.7	-4.0	-1.1
Nonresidential	4.6	1.9	3.9	1.6	5.3	2.1	4.4	1.7	2.3	0.9	0.2	0.1
Residential	5.9	8.8	0.4	0.6	-1.1	-1.8	-2.8	-4.5	-4.6	-7.2	-4.2	-6.5
Change in Bus. Inventories	5.2	38.4	4.1	26.6	2.4	18.0	0.7	59.3	-2.5	-16.7	-2.9	-19.9
Net Exports, Goods and Srvcs.	-3.5	13.4	-5.5	26.6	-8.4	35.9	-11.2	54.5	-13.6	51.0	-16.1	54.9
Exports	0.6	0.4	0.2	0.1	-0.2	-0.1	-0.7	-0.4	-0.9	-0.5	-0.9	-0.5
Imports	4.0	2.2	5.7	3.0	8.1	4.2	10.4	5.3	12.7	6.0	15.2	6.8
Government Purchases	17.9	5.5	17.9	5.3	17.9	5.2	17.9	5.1	17.9	5.0	17.9	4.8

Note: Figures are differences and percent differences from the baseline solution in billions of 1972 dollars, unless otherwise noted.

Table 4.9

U.S. Fiscal Expansion: Japan Macro Summary

	1987	%DIF	1988	%DIF	1989	%DIF	1990	%DIF	1991	%DIF	1992	%DIF
						Selected Economic Indicators						
GNE (80¥ billion)	874.5	0.3	1505.2	0.5	1958.0	0.6	2371.9	0.7	2727.4	0.7	3275.3	0.8
Nominal GNE (¥b)	712.6	0.2	1462.2	0.4	2099.1	0.6	2718.6	0.7	3315.1	0.8	4074.2	0.9
GNE Deflator	-0.1	-0.1	-0.1	-0.1	-0.1	0.0	0.0	0.0	0.0	0.0	0.0	0.0
Pers. Cons. Deflator	-0.1	-0.1	0.0	0.0	0.1	0.1	0.2	0.1	0.2	0.2	0.3	0.3
Employment (thous.)	19.8	0.0	46.7	0.1	71.5	0.1	93.8	0.2	111.1	0.2	128.6	0.2
Unemployment Rate (%)	0.0	-0.2	0.0	-0.4	0.0	-0.5	0.0	-0.6	0.0	-0.6	0.0	-0.7
Bank Lending Rate (%)	0.0	0.0	0.0	0.0	0.0	0.0	0.0	0.0	0.0	0.0	0.0	0.0
Govt. Surplus (¥b)	75.4	-0.4	167.4	-0.7	244.4	-1.0	327.9	-1.3	391.1	-1.4	469.7	-1.6
Current Account ($b)	2.1	4.1	3.6	4.5	5.0	6.4	6.3	8.2	7.3	10.0	8.9	12.5
¥/$ Exchange Rate	0.0	0.0	0.0	0.0	0.0	0.0	0.0	0.0	0.0	0.0	0.0	0.0
					Real Gross National Expenditure by Category (80¥ billion)							
Private Consumption	126.6	0.1	281.3	0.2	399.6	0.2	505.7	0.3	605.4	0.3	725.8	0.3
Nonprofit Consumption	0.0	0.0	0.0	0.0	0.0	0.0	0.0	0.0	0.0	0.0	0.0	0.0
Government Consumption	0.0	0.0	0.0	0.0	0.0	0.0	0.0	0.0	0.0	0.0	0.0	0.0
Business Investment	178.7	0.4	352.1	0.7	435.3	0.8	492.5	0.9	522.9	0.9	604.3	1.0
Residential Investment	87.6	0.4	191.0	0.8	189.1	0.8	166.3	0.7	164.8	0.7	186.6	0.7
Government Investment	0.0	0.0	0.0	0.0	0.0	0.0	0.0	0.0	0.0	0.0	0.0	0.0
Priv. Inventory Invest.	163.8	6.4	199.9	6.4	197.4	6.6	186.9	6.5	181.1	5.2	219.9	5.2
Govt. Inventory Invest.	0.0	0.0	0.0	0.0	0.0	0.0	0.0	0.0	0.0	0.0	0.0	0.0
Net Exports	317.8	14.7	480.2	13.2	735.9	25.0	1020.7	25.7	1253.4	20.5	1538.9	17.5
Exports	475.4	0.9	723.4	1.3	1046.4	1.7	1377.9	2.2	1679.7	2.5	2076.9	2.8
Imports	157.6	0.3	243.1	0.5	310.5	0.5	357.2	0.6	426.4	0.7	538.1	0.8

Note: Figures are differences and percent differences from the baseline solution in billions of 1980 yen, unless otherwise noted.

Table 4.10
U.S. Fiscal Expansion: World Trade by Region (f.o.b.)

	1987	%DIF	1988	%DIF	1989	%DIF	1990	%DIF	1991	%DIF	1992	%DIF
United States												
Exports	0.9	0.4	2.0	0.6	3.5	1.0	5.3	1.4	6.6	1.6	7.6	1.7
Imports	13.0	3.2	19.1	4.4	28.4	6.1	38.0	7.8	47.9	8.9	59.6	9.9
Balance	-12.1		-17.1		-24.9		-32.6		-41.3		-52.0	
Japan												
Exports	3.4	1.5	6.1	2.3	8.6	3.1	10.9	3.6	12.6	3.8	14.7	4.1
Imports	0.5	0.4	1.1	0.7	1.7	1.1	2.3	1.3	2.9	1.6	3.7	1.8
Balance	2.9		5.0		6.9		8.6		9.7		11.1	
Other Industr. Countries												
Exports	6.9	0.5	12.7	0.9	20.8	1.4	30.0	1.8	39.4	2.2	49.2	2.5
Imports	2.1	0.2	5.6	0.4	9.7	0.6	14.6	0.9	18.3	1.0	21.0	1.1
Balance	4.9		7.1		11.1		15.4		21.0		28.2	
EC												
Exports	3.5	0.4	7.1	0.7	11.9	1.0	17.5	1.4	22.9	1.7	28.3	1.9
Imports	1.3	0.1	4.0	0.4	6.9	0.6	10.2	0.8	13.5	1.0	16.1	1.1
Balance	2.2		3.1		5.0		7.2		9.4		12.3	
Developing Countries												
Exports	5.5	1.1	8.1	1.4	12.4	2.0	17.0	2.5	21.8	2.9	27.2	3.3
Imports	1.3	0.3	3.4	0.6	6.0	1.0	9.2	1.4	12.2	1.7	15.7	2.0
Balance	4.2		4.7		6.4		7.8		9.6		11.6	
Asia Including China												
Exports	2.3	0.9	4.1	1.2	6.6	1.9	9.6	2.5	12.8	3.1	16.4	3.7
Imports	0.9	0.3	2.2	0.7	4.0	1.1	6.1	1.6	8.2	1.9	10.7	2.3
Balance	1.5		1.9		2.7		3.5		4.6		5.8	
Asian NIEs												
Exports	1.7	1.0	2.9	1.3	4.8	2.1	7.0	2.8	9.4	3.5	12.1	4.2
Imports	0.8	0.6	2.0	1.0	3.5	1.6	5.4	2.2	7.1	2.6	9.1	3.0
Balance	0.9		1.0		1.4		1.6		2.3		3.0	
CPEs Excluding China												
Exports	0.2	0.1	0.4	0.2	0.7	0.3	1.1	0.4	1.4	0.5	1.7	0.6
Imports	0.0	0.0	0.1	0.0	0.2	0.1	0.3	0.1	0.4	0.2	0.5	0.2
Balance	0.2		0.4		0.6		0.8		1.0		1.1	
World Exports	16.8	0.7	29.3	1.1	46.0	1.5	64.4	2.0	81.7	2.3	100.5	2.6
World Export Price	0.0	0.0	0.0	0.2	0.0	0.3	0.0	0.5	0.0	0.6	0.0	0.6
World Exports Real (705b.)	5.1	0.7	7.1	0.9	9.8	1.2	12.7	1.5	15.8	1.7	19.4	2.0

Notes: Figures are differences from the baseline simulation in billions of U.S. dollars and percent. NIEs are newly industrializing economies; CPE refers to the centrally-planned economies.

Table 4.11
U.S. Fiscal Expansion: World Real GNP by Region

	1987	%DIF	1988	%DIF	1989	%DIF	1990	%DIF	1991	%DIF	1992	%DIF
U.S.	45.5	2.8	41.4	2.5	41.6	2.4	34.7	2.0	22.8	1.3	15.3	0.8
Japan	1.2	0.3	2.0	0.5	2.6	0.6	3.2	0.7	3.6	0.7	4.4	0.9
Other Industr. Countries	2.3	0.1	4.4	0.2	6.9	0.3	9.9	0.5	13.1	0.6	16.0	0.7
Canada	1.4	0.9	2.8	1.7	4.8	2.9	6.9	4.0	9.3	5.2	11.8	6.2
Australia, N.Z.	0.1	0.1	0.1	0.1	0.1	0.2	0.2	0.2	0.2	0.3	0.2	0.3
EC	0.7	0.1	1.1	0.1	1.4	0.1	1.9	0.1	2.6	0.2	2.9	0.2
Rest of Industrialized	0.1	0.1	0.3	0.1	0.6	0.2	0.9	0.4	1.0	0.4	1.1	0.4
Developing Countries	1.1	0.1	1.6	0.2	2.2	0.2	2.9	0.3	3.7	0.3	4.7	0.4
OPEC	0.2	0.2	0.3	0.3	0.4	0.4	0.4	0.4	0.4	0.4	0.5	0.4
Africa	0.0	0.1	0.1	0.1	0.1	0.2	0.1	0.3	0.2	0.3	0.2	0.3
Asia Including China	0.6	0.1	0.9	0.2	1.3	0.2	2.0	0.3	2.5	0.4	3.0	0.4
Asian NIEs	0.4	0.5	0.5	0.6	0.7	0.7	1.0	1.0	1.2	1.2	1.5	1.4
Middle East Nonoil	0.0	0.0	0.1	0.1	0.1	0.1	0.1	0.2	0.2	0.3	0.2	0.3
Western Hemisphere	0.2	0.1	0.3	0.1	0.3	0.1	0.3	0.1	0.5	0.2	0.9	0.3
C.P.E. Excluding China	0.0	0.0	0.0	0.0	0.0	0.0	0.1	0.0	0.1	0.0	0.2	0.0
World Total	50.0	0.8	49.4	0.8	53.3	0.8	50.6	0.8	43.4	0.6	40.4	0.6

Note: Figures are differences and percent differences from the baseline solution in billions of 1970 dollars. NIEs are newly industrializing economies; CPE refers to the centrally-planned economies.

Table 4.12
Fiscal Multiplier Comparisons

	YEAR 1	YEAR 2	YEAR 3
United States:			
NIRA	2.8	2.6	1.4
A&G(87)	1.3	1.8	0.8
EPA	2.0	1.9	—
MCM	1.5	0.8	—
IMS(85)	1.0	1.0	0.9
A&K(91)	1.6	0.7	-0.4
Japan:			
NIRA	1.7	1.9	1.8
A&G(87)	1.7	1.5	1.2
EPA	1.1	1.5	—
MCM	1.2	1.4	—
IMS(85)	0.6	0.7	0.7

Sources: A&G(87) is from Adams and Gangnes (1987). EPA, MCM, and
IMS(85) are from Ishii, McKibben, and Sachs (1985); EPA is Japan
Economic Planning Agency model, MCM is Federal Reserve Board
MultiCountry Model. A&K(91) is an average of ten model multipliers
from the Model Comparison Project, reported in Adams and Klein (1991).

Table 4.13
U.S. Fiscal Expansion: Changes in Bilateral Merchandise Trade Flows

Year: 1987

EXP\IMP	U.S.	Japan	Canada	RoW	Total
U.S.	——	0.127	0.377	0.376	0.88
Japan	2.921	——	0.027	0.459	3.407
Canada	2.437	0.013	——	0.091	2.541
RoW	7.661	0.33	0.127	1.886	10.005
Total	13.02	0.47	0.531	2.813	16.833

Year: 1992

EXP\IMP	U.S.	Japan	Canada	RoW	Total
U.S.	——	1.046	1.285	5.302	7.634
Japan	9.547	——	0.114	5.07	14.732
Canada	13.121	0.132	——	0.663	13.917
Row	36.918	2.474	0.384	24.43	64.206
Total	59.587	3.653	1.784	35.466	100.49

Note: Cell entries give changes from baseline levels for trade flowing from exporters (rows) to importers (columns) in billions of U.S. dollars.

Table 4.14
Japan Government Investment Increased by 1% of GNE

	1987	1988	1989	1990	1991	1992
Japan:						
Government Investment	3078	3078	3078	3078	3078	3078
Gross National Expend.	5166	6283	5830	5400	5433	5577
Percent Difference	1.7	1.9	1.7	1.5	1.5	1.4
Multiplier	1.7	2.0	1.9	1.8	1.8	1.8
Imports (%Dif.)	1.1	1.5	1.3	1.3	1.3	1.3
Current Account ($b)	-2.6	-3.7	-3.6	-3.8	-4.1	-4.5
United States:						
Gross National Product	0.35	0.81	1.01	1.19	1.23	1.27
Percent Difference	0.02	0.04	0.05	0.06	0.06	0.06
Exports (%Dif.)	0.10	0.15	0.15	0.13	0.12	0.11
Current Account ($b)	0.4	0.5	0.6	0.7	1.0	1.1
World:						
World Exports	0.6	0.6	0.4	0.4	0.4	0.4
Percent Difference	0.1	0.1	0.1	0.0	0.0	0.0
World GNP	7.7	9.9	9.5	9.1	9.2	9.5
Percent Difference	0.13	0.16	0.15	0.14	0.13	0.13

Notes: Figures are absolute and percent differences from the baseline simulation. Unless otherwise indicated, U.S. figures are in billions of 1972 dollars, Japanese figures are in billions of 1980 yen, and world figures are in billions of 1970 dollars.

Table 4.15
Japan Fiscal Expansion: Japan Macro Summary

	1987	%DIF	1988	%DIF	1989	%DIF	1990	%DIF	1991	%DIF	1992	%DIF
					Selected Economic Indicators							
GNE (80¥ billion)	5166.4	1.7	6283.2	1.9	5830.1	1.7	5399.7	1.5	5432.9	1.5	5576.7	1.4
Nominal GNE (¥b)	4883.6	1.5	6935.9	2.0	7589.9	2.1	7976.5	2.1	8577.6	2.1	9315.7	2.1
GNE Deflator	-0.7	-0.6	-0.2	-0.2	0.2	0.1	0.4	0.3	0.5	0.4	0.7	0.5
Pers. Cons. Deflator	-0.2	-0.2	0.0	0.0	0.3	0.3	0.5	0.4	0.6	0.5	0.7	0.6
Employment (thous.)	130.3	0.2	219.9	0.4	262.4	0.4	284.7	0.5	300.0	0.5	313.4	0.5
Unemployment Rate (%)	0.0	-1.0	0.0	-1.7	0.0	-1.8	0.0	-1.5	0.0	-1.2	0.0	-1.0
Bank Lending Rate (%)	0.0	-0.3	0.0	-0.1	0.0	0.4	0.0	0.3	0.0	0.2	0.0	0.2
Govt. Surplus (¥b)	-2711.0	13.4	-2287.0	10.0	-2174.0	8.9	-2060.0	8.0	-2063.0	7.5	-2065.0	7.1
Current Account ($b)	-2.6	-4.9	-3.7	-4.6	-3.6	-4.7	-3.8	-4.9	-4.1	-5.6	-4.5	-6.3
¥/$ Exchange Rate	0.0	0.0	0.0	0.0	0.0	0.0	0.0	0.0	0.0	0.0	0.0	0.0
					Real Gross National Expenditure by Category (80¥ billion)							
Private Consumption	825.6	0.5	1470.9	0.8	1680.4	0.9	1804.6	0.9	1945.1	1.0	2088.3	1.0
Nonprofit Consumption	0.0	0.0	0.0	0.0	0.0	0.0	0.0	0.0	0.0	0.0	0.0	0.0
Government Consumption	0.0	0.0	0.0	0.0	0.0	0.0	0.0	0.0	0.0	0.0	0.0	0.0
Business Investment	785.2	1.7	1361.6	2.8	1316.3	2.5	1116.3	2.0	1041.4	1.8	1054.8	1.7
Residential Investment	572.4	2.5	1018.6	4.3	641.2	2.6	350.7	1.4	346.7	1.4	384.1	1.5
Government Investment	3077.5	11.3	3077.5	10.1	3077.5	9.6	3077.5	9.2	3077.5	8.8	3077.5	8.4
Priv. Inventory Invest.	501.6	19.5	338.4	10.8	71.1	2.4	14.7	0.5	24.0	0.7	47.6	1.1
Govt. Inventory Invest.	0.0	0.0	0.0	0.0	0.0	0.0	0.0	0.0	0.0	0.0	0.0	0.0
Net Exports	-596.0	-27.7	-984.0	-27.1	-957.0	-32.6	-964.0	-24.3	-1002.0	-16.4	-1076.0	-12.2
Exports	-33.9	-0.1	-159.9	-0.3	-195.8	-0.3	-202.8	-0.3	-207.4	-0.3	-230.9	-0.3
Imports	562.4	1.1	823.9	1.5	760.9	1.3	760.8	1.3	794.3	1.3	844.8	1.3

Note: Figures are differences and percent differences from the baseline solution in billions of 1980 yen, unless otherwise noted.

Table 4.16
Japan Fiscal Expansion: U.S. Macro Summary

	1987	%DIF	1988	%DIF	1989	%DIF	1990	%DIF	1991	%DIF	1992	%DIF
Selected Economic Indicators												
GNP (72$ billion)	0.35	0.0	0.81	0.0	1.01	0.1	1.19	0.1	1.23	0.1	1.27	0.1
Nominal GNP ($b)	0.91	0.0	2.57	0.1	4.20	0.1	6.35	0.1	8.38	0.1	10.37	0.2
GNP Deflator	0.00	0.0	0.02	0.0	0.07	0.0	0.15	0.1	0.23	0.1	0.31	0.1
Consumer Prices	0.00	0.0	0.06	0.0	0.14	0.0	0.24	0.1	0.35	0.1	0.45	0.1
Employment (mil.)	0.01	0.0	0.02	0.0	0.04	0.0	0.05	0.0	0.06	0.0	0.06	0.1
Unemployment Rate (%)	-0.01	-0.1	-0.02	-0.3	-0.03	-0.4	-0.04	-0.5	-0.04	-0.6	-0.04	-0.6
3-Month CD Rate (%)	0.00	0.0	0.01	0.1	0.02	0.2	0.03	0.3	0.03	0.3	0.03	0.4
M2 ($b)	0.42	0.0	1.29	0.0	2.22	0.1	3.37	0.1	4.57	0.1	5.79	0.2
Federal Surplus ($b)	0.25	-0.2	0.55	-0.4	0.81	-0.5	1.06	-0.5	1.29	-0.8	1.42	-0.8
Current Account ($b)	0.38	-0.3	0.45	-0.3	0.56	-0.4	0.74	-0.5	0.97	-0.6	1.12	-0.7
W.A. $ Exchange Rate	0.00	0.0	0.00	0.0	0.00	0.0	0.00	0.0	0.00	0.0	0.00	0.0
$/Y Exchange Rate	0.00	0.0	0.00	0.0	0.00	0.0	0.00	0.0	0.00	0.0	0.00	0.0
Real Gross National Product by Category (72$ billion)												
Personal Consumption	0.10	0.0	0.26	0.0	0.40	0.0	0.53	0.0	0.62	0.0	0.67	0.1
Durable Goods	0.05	0.0	0.14	0.1	0.19	0.1	0.22	0.1	0.23	0.1	0.23	0.1
Nondurable Goods	0.03	0.0	0.07	0.0	0.11	0.0	0.15	0.0	0.18	0.0	0.20	0.0
Services	0.02	0.0	0.05	0.0	0.10	0.0	0.16	0.0	0.20	0.0	0.24	0.0
Gross Private Investment	0.09	0.0	0.20	0.1	0.22	0.1	0.24	0.1	0.17	0.1	0.14	0.0
Fixed Investment	0.06	0.0	0.12	0.0	0.13	0.0	0.16	0.1	0.12	0.0	0.11	0.0
Nonresidential	0.03	0.0	0.08	0.0	0.12	0.0	0.15	0.1	0.17	0.1	0.17	0.1
Residential	0.03	0.0	0.04	0.1	0.01	0.0	0.01	0.0	-0.04	-0.1	-0.06	-0.1
Change in Bus. Inventories	0.03	0.2	0.08	0.5	0.09	0.6	0.08	7.1	0.05	0.3	0.03	0.2
Net Exports, Goods and Srvcs.	0.16	-0.6	0.35	-1.7	0.40	-1.7	0.42	-2.1	0.44	-1.6	0.47	-1.6
Exports	0.16	0.1	0.25	0.2	0.25	0.1	0.23	0.1	0.21	0.1	0.20	0.1
Imports	0.00	0.0	-0.10	-0.1	-0.15	-0.1	-0.19	-0.1	-0.23	-0.1	-0.26	-0.1
Government Purchases	0.00	0.0	0.00	0.0	0.00	0.0	0.00	0.0	0.00	0.0	0.00	0.0

Note: Figures are differences and percent differences from the baseline solution in billions of 1972 dollars, unless otherwise noted.

Table 4.17
Japan Fiscal Expansion: World Trade by Region (f.o.b.)

	1987	%DIF	1988	%DIF	1989	%DIF	1990	%DIF	1991	%DIF	1992	%DIF
United States												
Exports	0.55	0.2	0.91	0.3	0.85	0.3	0.91	0.2	0.99	0.2	1.10	0.2
Imports	0.09	0.0	0.20	0.0	0.12	0.0	0.02	0.0	-0.07	0.0	-0.09	0.0
Balance	0.46		0.71		0.73		0.89		1.06		1.19	
Japan												
Exports	0.06	0.0	0.28	0.1	0.22	0.1	0.18	0.1	0.20	0.1	0.28	0.1
Imports	1.71	1.3	2.60	1.8	2.37	1.5	2.40	1.4	2.61	1.4	2.88	1.4
Balance	-1.65		-2.31		-2.16		-2.22		-2.41		-2.60	
Other Industr. Countries												
Exports	0.75	0.1	1.59	0.1	1.66	0.1	1.69	0.1	1.84	0.1	2.14	0.1
Imports	0.26	0.0	0.80	0.1	0.87	0.1	0.88	0.1	0.99	0.1	1.21	0.1
Balance	0.49		0.79		0.79		0.80		0.85		0.93	
EC												
Exports	0.38	0.0	0.92	0.1	1.02	0.1	1.05	0.1	1.17	0.1	1.38	0.1
Imports	0.18	0.0	0.57	0.1	0.60	0.1	0.59	0.0	0.70	0.1	0.91	0.1
Balance	0.20		0.35		0.42		0.46		0.46		0.47	
Developing Countries												
Exports	0.99	0.2	1.58	0.3	1.59	0.3	1.68	0.2	1.84	0.2	2.11	0.3
Imports	0.35	0.1	0.86	0.2	1.06	0.2	1.21	0.2	1.41	0.2	1.76	0.2
Balance	0.64		0.72		0.53		0.47		0.43		0.35	
Asia Including China												
Exports	0.48	0.2	0.84	0.3	0.84	0.2	0.86	0.2	0.92	0.2	1.04	0.2
Imports	0.19	0.1	0.50	0.2	0.63	0.2	0.68	0.2	0.80	0.2	1.02	0.2
Balance	0.28		0.34		0.21		0.18		0.12		0.02	
Asian NIEs												
Exports	0.21	0.1	0.40	0.2	0.42	0.2	0.43	0.2	0.45	0.2	0.50	0.2
Imports	0.15	0.1	0.42	0.2	0.51	0.2	0.54	0.2	0.56	0.2	0.66	0.2
Balance	0.05		-0.02		-0.09		-0.12		-0.12		-0.16	
CPEs Excluding China												
Exports	0.05	0.0	0.12	0.1	0.13	0.1	0.13	0.1	0.15	0.1	0.17	0.1
Imports	0.00	0.0	0.03	0.0	0.04	0.0	0.05	0.0	0.06	0.0	0.07	0.1
Balance	0.05		0.09		0.08		0.08		0.09		0.11	
World Exports	2.40	0.1	4.48	0.2	4.45	0.1	4.59	0.1	5.02	0.1	5.81	0.1
World Export Price	0.00	0.0	0.00	0.1	0.00	0.1	0.00	0.1	0.00	0.1	0.00	0.1
World Exports Real (70Sb.)	0.56	0.1	0.64	0.1	0.43	0.1	0.36	0.0	0.35	0.0	0.35	0.0

Notes: Figures are differences from the baseline simulation in billions of U.S. dollars and percent. NIEs are newly industrializing economies; CPE refers to the centrally-planned economies.

Table 4.18
Japan Fiscal Expansion: World Real GNP by Region

	1987	%DIF	1988	%DIF	1989	%DIF	1990	%DIF	1991	%DIF	1992	%DIF
U.S.	0.31	0.0	0.73	0.0	0.92	0.1	1.08	0.1	1.11	0.1	1.15	0.1
Japan	6.90	1.7	8.39	1.9	7.79	1.7	7.21	1.5	7.26	1.5	7.45	1.5
Other Industr. Countries	0.19	0.0	0.37	0.0	0.37	0.0	0.38	0.0	0.48	0.0	0.52	0.0
Canada	0.06	0.0	0.12	0.1	0.15	0.1	0.17	0.1	0.20	0.1	0.22	0.1
Australia, N.Z.	0.05	0.1	0.06	0.1	0.05	0.1	0.05	0.1	0.05	0.1	0.05	0.1
EC	0.07	0.0	0.13	0.0	0.09	0.0	0.05	0.0	0.08	0.0	0.10	0.0
Rest of Industrialized	0.02	0.0	0.05	0.0	0.08	0.0	0.10	0.0	0.14	0.1	0.14	0.1
Developing Countries	0.25	0.0	0.38	0.0	0.40	0.0	0.42	0.0	0.38	0.0	0.34	0.0
OPEC	0.07	0.1	0.10	0.1	0.10	0.1	0.11	0.1	0.11	0.1	0.12	0.1
Africa	0.00	0.0	0.01	0.0	0.01	0.0	0.01	0.0	0.01	0.0	0.01	0.0
Asia Including China	0.14	0.0	0.21	0.0	0.24	0.0	0.25	0.0	0.23	0.0	0.19	0.0
Asian NIEs	0.04	0.1	0.03	0.0	0.02	0.0	0.02	0.0	0.01	0.0	0.00	0.0
Middle East Nonoil	0.00	0.0	0.01	0.0	0.01	0.0	0.01	0.0	0.01	0.0	0.01	0.0
Western Hemisphere	0.03	0.0	0.05	0.0	0.04	0.0	0.03	0.0	0.02	0.0	0.01	0.0
C.P.E. Excluding China	0.00	0.0	0.00	0.0	0.00	0.0	0.01	0.0	0.01	0.0	0.01	0.0
World Total	7.65	0.13	9.87	0.16	9.46	0.15	9.09	0.14	9.24	0.13	9.48	0.13

Note: Figures are differences and percent differences from the baseline solution in billions of 1970 dollars. NIEs are newly industrializing economies; CPE refers to the centrally-planned economies.

Table 4.19
U.S. Fiscal Expansion: Decomposition of U.S. Real Import Effects

	STANDARD SIMULATION		FOUR INDS. EXOGENIXED		PRICE EFFECTS REMOVED	
	1992	%DIF	1992	%DIF	1992	%DIF
Textiles	0.03	0.9	0.04	1.1	0.00	0.0
Apparel	0.32	2.2	0.45	3.1	0.42	2.9
Paper, Pulp	-0.04	-1.8	-0.04	-1.6	-0.03	-1.4
Indust. Chemicals	1.02	29.7	0.00	0.0	0.00	0.0
Nonind. Chemicals	0.16	5.6	0.21	7.2	0.08	2.8
Rubber, Plastics	0.13	10.0	0.17	13.0	0.08	6.3
Leather	0.04	4.2	0.04	4.8	0.00	0.0
Lumber, Wood Prod.	0.16	13.4	0.18	15.1	0.00	0.0
Furniture	0.39	15.7	0.47	19.1	0.11	4.3
Cement	0.00	0.0	0.00	0.0	0.00	0.0
Oth. Stone, Clay, Gl.	0.21	7.0	0.23	7.8	0.00	0.0
Iron, Steel	0.23	4.2	0.48	8.7	0.33	6.0
Aluminum	0.15	14.0	0.17	15.4	0.00	0.0
Oth. Nonfer. Metal	4.72	70.3	0.00	0.0	0.00	0.0
Fabr. Metal Products	0.72	13.1	0.85	15.6	0.08	1.5
Nonelect. Machinery	1.09	4.0	1.55	5.7	0.82	3.0
Electrical Machinery	1.98	5.0	2.18	5.5	0.00	0.0
Aircraft	2.65	111.0	0.00	0.0	0.00	0.0
Oth. Transp. Equip.	1.53	98.7	0.00	0.0	0.00	0.0
Motor Vehicles	1.58	6.3	2.14	8.6	1.73	7.0
Instruments	0.31	5.7	0.40	7.4	0.45	8.4
Misc. Manufactures	0.72	6.5	1.03	9.2	0.71	6.3
Total	18.10	10.6	10.55	6.2	4.78	2.8
Macro Tot. Imports		6.9		4.6		2.8

Notes: From fiscal policy simulations of the U.S. model with Japan and the rest of the world exogenous. Figures are absolute and percentage differences from the baseline simulation in billions of 1972 dollars.

Table 4.20
U.S. Fiscal Policy Transmission in Other International Models

	SIMULATION YEAR					
	1	2	3	4	5	6
DRI	0.6	1.3	1.3	1.2	1.5	2.3
EPA	0.3	0.9	1.6	2.4	3.4	4.9
LINK	0.1	0.1	0.1	0.1	0.0	0.0
LIVERPL	0.0	0.1	0.2	0.2	0.2	0.2
MCM	0.4	1.1	1.4	1.4	1.4	1.5
MCKIBB	0.5	0.3	0.2	0.1	0.1	0.1
OECD	0.6	0.6	0.4	0.4	0.3	0.1
TAYLOR	0.3	0.8	1.2	1.4	1.4	1.3
VAR	0.0	0.0	0.0	0.0	0.0	0.0
WEFA	0.4	0.2	0.0	-0.4	-0.9	-1.4
AVERAGE	0.32	0.54	0.64	0.68	0.74	0.90

Source: Bryant et al. (1988).

Notes: Figures are percent differences from baseline Japanese GNP under a a 1% of GNP U.S. fiscal expansion. The simulations performed were actually reductions in U.S. government spending, and signs have been reversed for this table. The simulations differ from the present study by holding monetary aggregates unchanged at baseline levels in all countries, rather than permitting endogenous monetary policy response. The fiscal shock employed is somewhat larger than that of the present study, since spending is increased in each year of the simulation by 1% of current year baseline GNP, rather than applying an increase of 1% of first year GNP in each of the simulation years.

Models included are DRI International Model (DRI); Japanese Economic Planning Agency World Econometric Model (EPA); world model of Project LINK (LINK); Liverpool Model, University of Liverpool, P. Minford and Associates (LIVERPL); U.S. Federal Reserve Board MultiCountry Model (MCM); McKibben-Sachs Global Model (MCKIBB); OECD Interlink Model (OECD); John Taylor's model, Stanford University (TAYLOR); Minneapolis World VAR Model, R. Litterman and C. Sims (VAR); World Model of the WEFA Group (WEFA).

Table 4.21
U.S. and Japanese Fiscal Policy Transmission in Other International Models

| | U.S. Fiscal Expansion | | | | | |
| | Domestic Effect | | | Effect on Japan | | |
	GNP	INFL	CA/GNP	GNP	INFL	CA/GNP
NIRA	2.64	0.69	-0.23	0.37	-0.0003	0.11
MCM	1.20	0.14	-0.48	0.20	0.01	0.02
EPA	2.08	0.08	-0.33	0.29	0.00	0.08
A&G(87)	1.54	0.43		0.11	-0.14	

| | Japan Fiscal Expansion | | | | | |
| | Domestic Effect | | | Effect on the U.S. | | |
	GNP	INFL	CA/GNP	GNP	INFL	CA/GNP
NIRA	1.81	-0.11	-0.16	0.06	0.02	0.0002
MCM	1.41	0.16	-0.13	0.10	0.00	0.04
EPA	1.56	0.28	-0.20	0.00	0.02	0.02
A&G(87)	1.74	-0.07		-0.02*	0.03	

Sources: MCM, EPA figures from Oudiz and Sachs (1984): MCM is Federal Reserve Board MultiCountry Model; EPA is Japan Economic Planning Agency Model; A&G(87) is from Adams and Gangnes (1987).

Notes: Figures for GNP and inflation are average percent differences from the baseline solution over the first two simulation years. CA/GNP reports the two-year average absolute difference in the Current Account-to-GNP ratio.

*Becomes positive by year 3.

Table 4.22
U.S. Fiscal Expansion: Industry-Level Effects in the U.S. and Japan

	U.S.				JAPAN	
	OUTPUT		IMP. FR. JAPAN		OUTPUT	
	YR. 1	YR. 6	YR. 1	YR. 6	YR. 1	YR. 6
General Crops	2.6	0.9				
Industrial Crops						
Livestock,Textiles						
Livestock						
Forestry						
Fisheries						
Coal Mining	5.4	1.4				
Iron Ores	2.3	-1.1		NOT		
Nonfer. Metal Ore				BILATERALLY		
Crude Petroleum	0.0	0.0		LINKED		
Natural Gas						
Other Mining	4.2	-1.5				
Meat, Dairy	1.9	1.2				
Grain Products						
Manuf. Sea Food						
Other Foods						
Beverages						
Tobacco	5.0	0.5				
Natural Textiles	4.4	1.2	-0.1	0.9	0.4	1.2
Chemical Textiles					0.3	1.3
Other Textiles					0.3	0.8
Wearing Apparel	4.6	1.8	2.0	2.0	0.1	0.4
Wood, Products	7.1	-3.9	-0.3	14.7	0.5	0.7
Furniture	3.0	-0.5	4.1	15.7	0.3	0.6
Pulp, Paper	3.0	0.4	-0.1	-3.9	0.3	0.7
Leather Products	4.5	2.6	0.0	4.0	0.1	0.4
Rubber Products	3.9	0.9	5.2	6.8	1.3	1.9
Basic, Int. Chems.	3.2	-2.5	5.6	23.3	0.4	1.1
Final Chemicals	2.7	0.2	2.3	3.9	0.2	0.7
Petroleum Prods.	2.9	2.3	2.9	2.3	0.2	0.6
Coal Products					0.9	0.5
Cement	5.2	-1.3	—	—	0.3	0.8
Other Ceramics	5.1	-1.3	0.0	6.8	0.2	0.7
Iron Products	9.2	-2.1	8.7	3.6	1.3	0.4
Roll., Cast., Forg.					0.7	0.6
Aluminum	8.5	-15.8	0.3	13.8	—	—
Oth. Nonfer. Met.	4.3	-13.7	8.5	78.4	0.5	3.6
Metal Products	5.0	-0.9	1.4	15.6	0.3	0.9
Nonel. Machinery	4.1	0.1	3.2	3.4	0.8	1.5
Electr. Machinery	7.3	2.2	-0.1	5.4	0.3	1.5
Automobiles	9.1	0.2	3.7	4.2	0.6	1.4
Aircraft	14.2	-2.3	26.5	106.3	—	—
Oth. Transp. Equip.	11.1	2.2	45.7	101.3	5.5	13.5
Instruments	4.1	1.4	4.3	5.4	0.8	1.7
Misc. Manufs.	3.1	0.0	—	—	0.3	0.8
Total	5.1	-0.1	2.7	6.7	0.3	0.8

Note: Figures are percent differences from baseline real values. Dashes indicate variable is exogenous in this simulation.

Table 4.23
U.S. Fiscal Expansion: Absolute Effects on Japanese Industry Output

	CHANGE FROM BASELINE SIMULATION	
	ABSOLUTE DIFFERENCES	PERCENT OF TOTAL OUTPUT
Natural Textiles	12.1	0.002
Chemical Textiles	5.8	0.001
Other Textiles	55.8	0.007
Wearing Apparel	26.5	0.003
Pulp, Paper	55.8	0.007
Basic, Int. Chems.	196.7	0.025
Final Chemicals	96.5	0.012
Petroleum Prods.	121.2	0.015
Coal Products	12.3	0.002
Rubber Products	61.4	0.008
Leather Products	2.0	0.000
Wood Products	49.0	0.006
Furniture	26.2	0.003
Cement	10.4	0.013
Other Ceramics	69.1	0.009
Iron Products	37.9	0.048
Roll., Cast., Forg.	113.2	0.014
Aluminum	——	——
Oth. Nonfer. Metal	292.3	0.037
Metal Products	165.6	0.021
Nonelect. Machinery	573.8	0.072
Electrical Machinery	987.8	0.124
Aircraft	——	——
Oth. Transp. Equip.	694.3	0.087
Automobiles	496.0	0.063
Instruments	92.9	0.012
Misc. Manufactures	109.5	0.014
Manuf. Total	4364.1	0.605

Notes: Figures give effects in the sixth year of the simulation. Dashes indicate the variable is exogenous in the simulation.

Table 4.24
U.S. Fiscal Expansion: Decomposition of
Japan Output Effects for Selected Industries

		F	E	M	IV	X^I	X
Basic, Int. Chems.	Year 1	0.0	9.1	7.3	3.2	58.3	63.2
	Year 2	0.0	-15.9	2.9	0.8	69.2	51.2
	Year 6	0.0	31.7	10.6	4.6	171.0	196.7
Final Chemicals	Year 1	1.2	8.2	4.0	2.9	15.4	23.7
	Year 6	7.5	36.2	5.9	3.0	55.7	96.5
Iron Products	Year 1	-0.3	0.5	0.4	13.2	91.1	104.0
	Year 6	-1.2	0.4	-0.1	-2.5	41.2	37.9
Roll., Cast., Forg.	Year 1	0.0	73.2	4.4	0.0	48.6	117.3
	Year 6	0.0	121.6	3.7	-2.4	-2.3	113.2
Nonel. Machinery	Year 1	23.4	70.0	3.2	32.7	97.5	220.4
	Year 6	84.6	149.2	-2.9	21.9	315.2	573.8
Electr. Machinery	Year 1	32.8	15.0	3.3	22.7	65.5	132.7
	Year 6	142.4	460.2	7.3	41.6	350.9	987.8
Automobiles	Year 1	12.7	91.8	1.8	6.0	42.7	151.4
	Year 6	54.4	279.3	0.7	8.9	154.0	496.0

Notes: Figures are differences from baseline simulation in billions of 1980 yen.
Symbols are defined in the text.

Table 4.25
U.S. Fiscal Expansion: Effects on "Nontraded" Japanese Industry Output

	PERCENT CHANGE		ABSOLUTE CHANGE
	YEAR 1	YEAR 6	YEAR 6
Housing Construction	0.3	0.7	154.9
Industrial Construction	0.2	0.6	141.0
Public Construction	0.0	0.0	5.8
Other Construction	0.1	0.4	70.2
Electric Power	0.3	0.6	80.6
Gas	0.1	0.5	7.4
Water and Sanitary Service	0.1	0.3	13.1
Wholesale and Retail Trade	0.1	0.5	365.2
Real Estate	0.1	0.5	197.7
Railways	0.1	0.4	12.4
Trucks and Buses	0.2	0.4	50.1
Other Transportation	0.3	0.5	36.7
Communications	0.2	0.8	53.4
Finance and Insurance	0.2	0.7	172.5
Government Services	——	——	——
Public Services	0.1	0.4	163.0
Other Services	0.1	0.3	162.8

Notes: Absolute figures are in billions of 1980 yen. Dashes indicates the industry is exogenous.

Table 4.26
Japan Fiscal Expansion: Industry-Level Effects in Japan and the U.S.

	JAPAN				U.S.	
	OUTPUT		IMP. FR. U.S.		OUTPUT	
	YR. 1	YR. 6	YR. 1	YR. 6	YR. 1	YR. 6
General Crops	0.2	0.2	0.1	0.5	0.0	0.1
Industrial Crops	0.9	1.2	1.0	1.3		
Livestock,Textiles	—	—	1.3	1.0		
Livestock	0.6	0.8	1.1	1.9		
Forestry	0.0	0.0	7.4	3.2		
Fisheries	0.3	0.2	0.0	1.9		
Coal Mining	0.7	1.0	2.1	2.0	0.0	0.4
Iron Ores	—	—	—	—	0.1	0.3
Nonfer. Metal Ore	—	—	1.1	1.0		
Crude Petroleum	—	—	—	—	—	—
Natural Gas	—	—	—	—	—	—
Other Mining	4.4	3.2	2.8	2.3	0.1	0.2
Meat, Dairy	0.6	1.0	0.5	0.7	0.0	0.1
Grain Products	-0.2	-0.2	-0.2	0.0		
Manuf. Sea Food	0.3	0.4	0.6	0.9		
Other Foods	0.3	0.6	0.2	0.6		
Beverages	0.8	0.8	—	—		
Tobacco	0.4	0.4	—	—	0.0	0.1
Natural Textiles	1.7	0.7	-0.3	1.6	0.0	0.1
Chemical Textiles	1.3	0.8	1.1	0.9		
Other Textiles	1.5	0.8	-0.2	2.4		
Wearing Apparel	0.4	0.8	0.5	1.4	0.0	0.1
Wood, Products	3.7	1.9	0.0	1.8	0.0	0.0
Furniture	1.9	1.3	2.2	3.1	0.0	0.1
Pulp, Paper	3.7	1.9	0.6	1.5	0.0	0.1
Leather Products	0.3	0.2	1.2	1.6	0.0	0.1
Rubber Products	1.8	0.4	—	—	0.0	0.1
Basic, Int. Chems.	0.9	0.4	1.1	0.9	0.1	0.6
Final Chemicals	0.6	0.4	1.0	0.5	0.0	0.0
Petroleum Prods.	0.9	1.2	1.1	1.9	0.0	0.1
Coal Products	2.4	1.6	4.0	7.2		
Cement	3.9	2.7	3.2	2.5	0.0	0.1
Other Ceramics	3.4	2.5	—	—	0.0	0.1
Iron Products	1.0	0.8	0.2	0.5	0.1	0.2
Roll., Cast., Forg.	0.8	0.7	3.7	2.1		
Aluminum	—	—	1.4	0.6	0.2	0.4
Oth. Nonfer. Met.	1.3	0.8	1.6	1.6	0.0	0.2
Metal Products	2.2	2.2	2.4	2.8	0.0	0.1
Nonel. Machinery	1.5	1.4	1.2	1.5	0.0	0.1
Electr. Machinery	2.5	1.7	1.4	2.0	0.0	0.1
Automobiles	0.8	0.5	1.2	0.9	0.1	0.3
Aircraft	—	—	0.5	0.8	0.0	0.1
Oth. Transp. Equip.	1.6	1.3	0.0	0.1	0.0	0.0
Instruments	1.6	1.5	2.1	2.1	0.0	0.1
Misc. Manufs.	1.1	0.9	0.6	1.3	0.1	0.2
Total	1.7	1.4	1.2	1.3	0.02	0.06

Note: Figures are percent differences from baseline real values. Dashes indicate variable is exogenous in this simulation.

Table 4.27

Fiscal Expansion in Other Big Seven Countries: U.S. Macro Summary

	1988	%CHG	1989	%CHG	1990	%CHG	1991	%CHG	1992	%CHG
Selected Economic Indicators										
GNP (72$ billion)	1.3	0.1	1.9	0.1	2.3	0.1	2.1	0.1	1.8	0.1
Nominal GNP ($b)	3.6	0.1	6.7	0.1	10.4	0.2	13.4	0.2	15.4	0.2
GNP Deflator	0.0	0.0	0.1	0.0	0.2	0.1	0.3	0.1	0.5	0.2
Consumer Prices	0.0	0.0	0.1	0.0	0.3	0.1	0.5	0.1	0.7	0.1
Employment (mil.)	0.0	0.0	0.1	0.1	0.1	0.1	0.1	0.1	0.1	0.1
Unemployment Rate (%)	0.0	-0.4	0.0	-0.8	-0.1	-0.9	-0.1	-1.0	-0.1	-0.9
3-Month CD Rate (%)	0.0	0.1	0.0	0.2	0.0	0.4	0.1	0.6	0.1	0.6
M2 ($b)	1.7	0.1	3.5	0.1	5.5	0.2	7.3	0.2	8.7	0.2
Federal Surplus ($b)	1.0	-0.7	1.8	-1.1	2.3	-1.1	2.5	-1.5	2.3	-1.4
Current Account ($b)	1.2	-0.8	1.9	-1.3	2.2	-1.5	2.0	-1.3	1.9	-1.2
W.A. $ Exchange Rate	0.0	0.0	0.0	0.0	0.0	0.0	0.0	0.0	0.0	0.0
Real Gross National Product by Category (72$ billion)										
Personal Consumption	0.4	0.0	0.8	0.1	1.1	0.1	1.1	0.1	1.1	0.1
Durable Goods	0.2	0.1	0.4	0.2	0.5	0.2	0.4	0.2	0.3	0.1
Nondurable Goods	0.1	0.0	0.2	0.1	0.3	0.1	0.3	0.1	0.3	0.1
Services	0.1	0.0	0.2	0.0	0.3	0.0	0.4	0.1	0.4	0.1
Gross Private Investment	0.4	0.1	0.5	0.1	0.5	0.2	0.3	0.1	0.1	0.0
Fixed Investment	0.3	0.1	0.3	0.1	0.3	0.1	0.2	0.1	0.1	0.0
Nonresidential	0.1	0.1	0.2	0.1	0.3	0.1	0.3	0.1	0.3	0.1
Residential	0.1	0.2	0.1	0.1	0.0	0.0	-0.1	-0.1	-0.2	-0.3
Change in Bus. Inventories	0.1	0.9	0.2	1.4	0.2	15.5	0.1	0.6	0.0	-0.1
Net Exports, Goods and Srvcs.	0.5	-2.3	0.7	-2.9	0.7	-3.7	0.7	-2.5	0.6	-2.0
Exports	0.6	0.4	0.9	0.5	1.0	0.6	1.0	0.5	0.9	0.5
Imports	0.1	0.1	0.2	0.1	0.3	0.1	0.3	0.1	0.3	0.2
Government Purchases	0.0	0.0	0.0	0.0	0.0	0.0	0.0	0.0	0.0	0.0

Note: Figures are differences and percent differences from the baseline solution in billions of 1972 dollars, unless otherwise noted. "Other Big Seven" includes Canada, United Kingdom, France, Italy, and the Federal Republic of Germany.

Table 4.28

Fiscal Expansion in Other Big Seven Countries: Japan Macro Summary

	1988	%CHG	1989	%CHG	1990	%CHG	1991	%CHG	1992	%CHG
Selected Economic Indicators										
GNE (80¥ billion)	138.9	0.0	292.8	0.1	369.3	0.1	385.7	0.1	405.6	0.1
Nominal GNE (¥b)	103.8	0.0	252.4	0.1	360.5	0.1	425.3	0.1	482.1	0.1
GNE Deflator	0.0	0.0	0.0	0.0	0.0	0.0	0.0	0.0	0.0	0.0
Pers. Cons. Deflator	0.0	0.0	0.0	0.0	0.0	0.0	0.0	0.0	0.0	0.0
Employment (thous.)	3.5	0.0	8.9	0.0	13.5	0.0	16.3	0.0	18.2	0.0
Unemployment Rate (%)	0.0	0.0	0.0	-0.1	0.0	-0.1	0.0	-0.1	0.0	-0.1
Bank Lending Rate (%)	0.0	0.0	0.0	0.0	0.0	0.0	0.0	0.0	0.0	0.0
Govt. Surplus (¥b)	11.6	-0.1	30.9	-0.1	47.8	-0.2	57.9	-0.2	64.2	-0.2
Current Account ($b)	0.3	0.4	0.7	0.9	0.9	1.2	1.0	1.3	1.1	1.5
¥/$ Exchange Rate	0.0	0.0	0.0	0.0	0.0	0.0	0.0	0.0	0.0	0.0
Real Gross National Expenditure by Category (80¥ billion)										
Private Consumption	18.1	0.0	46.8	0.0	69.4	0.0	81.6	0.0	90.2	0.0
Nonprofit Consumption	0.0	0.0	0.0	0.0	0.0	0.0	0.0	0.0	0.0	0.0
Government Consumption	0.0	0.0	0.0	0.0	0.0	0.0	0.0	0.0	0.0	0.0
Business Investment	28.5	0.1	69.8	0.1	92.9	0.2	93.6	0.2	89.0	0.1
Residential Investment	12.6	0.1	31.9	0.1	35.2	0.1	25.8	0.1	19.0	0.1
Government Investment	0.0	0.0	0.0	0.0	0.0	0.0	0.0	0.0	0.0	0.0
Priv. Inventory Invest.	25.1	0.8	38.7	1.3	31.6	1.1	19.1	0.6	13.8	0.3
Govt. Inventory Invest.	0.0	0.0	0.0	0.0	0.0	0.0	0.0	0.0	0.0	0.0
Net Exports	54.0	1.5	105.0	3.6	140.0	3.5	166.0	2.7	193.6	2.2
Exports	80.2	0.1	159.1	0.3	208.1	0.3	236.2	0.3	264.8	0.4
Imports	26.2	0.0	54.1	0.1	68.1	0.1	70.2	0.1	71.2	0.1

Note: Figures are differences and percent differences from the baseline solution in billions of 1980 yen, unless otherwise noted. "Other Big Seven" include Canada, United Kingdom, France, Italy, and the Federal Republic of Germany.

Table 4.29
Fiscal Expansion in Other Big Seven Countries: World Trade by Region (f.o.b.)

	1988	%DIF	1989	%DIF	1990	%DIF	1991	%DIF	1992	%DIF
United States										
Exports	1.5	0.5	2.4	0.7	3.0	0.8	2.9	0.7	2.9	0.7
Imports	0.4	0.1	0.8	0.2	1.2	0.2	1.6	0.3	2.0	0.3
Balance	1.1		1.6		1.8		1.4		1.0	
Japan										
Exports	0.5	0.2	1.1	0.4	1.5	0.5	1.6	0.5	1.8	0.5
Imports	0.1	0.1	0.2	0.1	0.3	0.2	0.4	0.2	0.4	0.2
Balance	0.4		0.9		1.2		1.3		1.4	
Other Industr. Countries										
Exports	7.7	0.5	13.6	0.9	16.6	1.0	17.6	1.0	19.2	1.0
Imports	10.8	0.8	18.7	1.2	22.4	1.4	23.2	1.3	24.5	1.2
Balance	-3.2		-5.1		-5.9		-5.6		-5.3	
Canada										
Exports	0.2	0.2	0.4	0.3	0.5	0.4	0.6	0.4	0.7	0.4
Imports	0.9	0.8	1.1	1.0	1.3	1.1	1.0	0.8	0.7	0.5
Balance	-0.7		-0.7		-0.8		-0.4		0.1	
EC										
Exports	6.2	0.6	10.8	1.0	13.1	1.1	13.9	1.0	15.2	1.0
Imports	9.6	0.9	16.7	1.5	19.7	1.6	20.6	1.5	22.0	1.5
Balance	-3.4		-5.8		-6.6		-6.7		-6.8	
Developing Countries										
Exports	1.6	0.3	2.8	0.5	3.6	0.5	4.1	0.5	4.5	0.5
Imports	0.3	0.1	0.9	0.2	1.5	0.2	2.0	0.3	2.4	0.3
Balance	1.2		1.9		2.1		2.1		2.1	
Asia Including China										
Exports	0.6	0.2	1.1	0.3	1.4	0.4	1.6	0.4	1.8	0.4
Imports	0.2	0.0	0.4	0.1	0.7	0.2	0.9	0.2	1.2	0.2
Balance	0.4		0.7		0.7		0.7		0.7	
CPEs Excluding China										
Exports	0.4	0.2	0.8	0.4	1.1	0.4	1.3	0.5	1.4	0.5
Imports	0.0	0.0	0.1	0.1	0.3	0.1	0.4	0.2	0.5	0.2
Balance	0.4		0.7		0.8		0.7		0.9	
World Exports	11.6	0.4	20.8	0.7	25.7	0.8	27.6	0.8	29.8	0.8
World Export Price	0.0	0.0	0.0	0.1	0.0	0.1	0.0	0.2	0.0	0.2
World Exports Real (70Sb.)	3.1	0.4	5.1	0.6	5.8	0.7	5.6	0.6	5.6	0.6

Notes: Figures are differences from the baseline simulation in billions of U.S. dollars and percent. CPE refers to the centrally-planned economies; "Other Big Seven" includes Canada, Kingdom, France, Italy, and the Federal Republic of Germany.

Table 4.30
Fiscal Expansion in Other Big Seven Countries: World GNP by Region

	1988	%CHG	1989	%CHG	1990	%CHG	1991	%CHG	1992	%CHG
U.S.	1.2	0.1	1.8	0.1	2.1	0.1	1.9	0.1	1.6	0.1
Japan	0.2	0.0	0.4	0.1	0.5	0.1	0.5	0.1	0.5	0.1
Other Industr. Countries	15.8	0.8	21.6	1.0	22.9	1.0	22.0	1.0	20.6	0.9
Canada	2.2	1.3	3.2	1.9	4.1	2.4	4.9	2.7	5.6	2.9
EC	13.3	0.8	17.7	1.1	17.9	1.0	16.1	0.9	14.0	0.8
Australia, N.Z.	0.0	0.1	0.1	0.1	0.1	0.1	0.1	0.1	0.1	0.1
Rest of Industrialized	0.2	0.1	0.6	0.2	0.8	0.3	1.0	0.4	1.0	0.4
Developing Countries	0.3	0.0	0.6	0.1	0.8	0.1	0.8	0.1	0.8	0.1
OPEC	0.1	0.1	0.1	0.1	0.1	0.1	0.1	0.1	0.1	0.1
Africa	0.1	0.1	0.1	0.2	0.1	0.2	0.1	0.2	0.1	0.2
Asia Including China	0.1	0.0	0.2	0.0	0.3	0.1	0.3	0.0	0.2	0.0
Asian NIEs	0.1	0.1	0.1	0.1	0.1	0.1	0.1	0.1	0.1	0.1
Middle East Nonoil	0.0	0.1	0.1	0.1	0.1	0.2	0.1	0.2	0.1	0.2
Western Hemisphere	0.1	0.0	0.1	0.1	0.2	0.1	0.2	0.1	0.2	0.1
C.P.E. Excluding China	0.0	0.0	0.0	0.0	0.1	0.0	0.1	0.0	0.2	0.0
World Total	17.5	0.3	24.4	0.4	26.3	0.4	25.4	0.4	23.6	0.3

Note: Figures are differences and percent differences from the baseline solution in billions of 1970 dollars. NIEs are newly industrializing economies; CPE refers to the centrally-planned economies. "Other Big Seven" includes Canada, United Kingdom, France, Italy, and the Federal Republic of Germany.

EXCHANGE RATE CHANGES IN THE
U.S.-JAPAN MODEL SYSTEM

The volatility of exchange rates in recent years and their potential for disrupting markets have shown the need for a more complete understanding of the role of exchange rates in the world economy. The research agenda in this area is very broad, including efforts to explain or predict exchange rate movements, evaluations of the macroeconomic effects of exchange rate fluctuations, and analyses of the microeconomic behavior of agents facing exchange rate change. The present analysis sidesteps the first (and most difficult) of these tasks in order to focus on elements of the latter two areas, analyzing the macroeconomic impact of "given" exchange rate shocks and the role of strategic pricing behavior in the adjustment to such shocks.

In the first section of this chapter, we evaluate the effects of substantial exchange rate changes on the U.S.-Japan-world economy. Through simulations of assumed changes in the value of the yen and dollar, we examine the mechanisms by which exchange rate movements influence prices, patterns of trade, and the distribution of economic activity internationally.

The ultimate impact of exchange rate adjustment depends on the actions of economic agents in response to exchange rate movements. An important characteristic of recent exchange rate fluctuation episodes has been the apparent willingness of Japanese exporting firms to limit the extent to which they "pass through" yen appreciation into higher dollar export prices. The export price equations of the Japan model exhibit such limited pass-through and so provide a means for estimating the effect of strategic export pricing behavior. In the second section of this chapter, we compare the effect of yen appreciation under partial and full price pass-through.

MACROECONOMIC AND INDUSTRY EFFECTS OF EXCHANGE RATE CHANGE

In this section, we evaluate the effect on trade, prices, and domestic economies of assumed changes in currency values. The simulations presented involve an exogenous 8% appreciation of the yen against all currencies and a 10% appreciation of the dollar against major currencies.[1] The influence of the exchange rate change is traced from the effect of the initial shock on international prices, through impacts on industry trade volumes and prices, to ultimate effects on economic activity, inflation, and the industrial composition of output and price effects.

Yen Appreciation

Table 5.1 summarizes the effect of a yen appreciation on the U.S., Japan, and world economies. The assumed appreciation has a strong contractionary effect on the Japanese economy. The 8% once-and-for-all appreciation of the yen reduces yen import prices 7.2%, slightly less than one-for-one because of some induced inflation abroad.[2] Real imports rise about 1% above base. Including some offsetting decline in yen prices (discussed further below), Japanese export prices rise about 4% in dollar terms. As a result, real exports fall 2.5% by 1992. The trade surplus in yen is about 0.5% of GNE smaller than in the base simulation, and GNE falls 0.8% below base levels.

Since Japanese goods are 19% of U.S. imports in the baseline, the 8% yen appreciation represents a 1.5% increase in the U.S. effective exchange rate. Overall import prices rise slightly more than 1% as a result, causing a fairly substantial drop in U.S. real imports—1.3% by 1992—which raises activity 0.4% above base. Although nominal exports are up nearly $3 billion by 1992, higher export prices mean that real exports are virtually unchanged from baseline levels.

In Japan, the effect of plunging import prices creates a pronounced deflation, with consumer prices almost 2% lower than base by 1992. The price effects on the United States are also significant. Higher import prices and the expansionary effect of an improved trade balance contribute to a 0.6% increase in U.S. consumer prices over the forecast period.

The strong decline in U.S. imports under the yen appreciation is not matched by other countries. As Table 5.2 shows, all other regions experience some increase in nominal imports (although these represent small declines in real terms). As a consequence, the United States contributes a disproportionately large share of the negative trade effect experienced by Japan. Nominal Japanese exports to the U.S. fall 9.6% by 1992 (not shown), compared with a roughly 6% overall decline in Japanese nominal exports.

In addition to the large overall decline in U.S. imports, the decline in Japanese competitiveness leads to a reduction in the Japanese share in U.S. imports (the Japanese share of manufacturing imports declines by half a percentage point), compounding the adverse trade effects on Japan. In the world economy (Table 5.2), the increased export shares of the industrial countries as a group, and the Asian newly industrializing economics (NIEs)—Korea, Taiwan, Hong Kong, and Singapore—lead to initial increases in their exports of about 0.6%. By 1992, rising world trade prices reduce overall import demand in the United States and other countries, so that much of the nominal export gains are erased. The 0.7% rise in world trade prices reduces real world exports by 0.5% by 1992. World economic activity (Table 5.3) is slightly above base because of lower real imports, but there are notable declines in activity in the Asian NIEs, who depend heavily on U.S. import demand.

Overall, the yen appreciation creates a measurable transfer of economic activity from Japan to the United States, as the trade balance moves in favor of the United States. By increasing U.S. market shares at the expense of the Japanese, other industrialized economies also gain, although to a lesser extent. Again, the U.S. economy is seen to exert a strong influence on economic activity in Japan and other countries.

The distribution of trade and output effects across industries in the Japanese and U.S. economies depends on the direct effects of relative trade price changes on the bilateral import equations of the two models, and on induced changes in prices and activity as the trade effects filter through the interindustry structure. The yen appreciation is reflected in uniformly lower Japanese import prices at the industry level, as shown in the first column of Table 5.4. The roughly 7.2% lower import prices stimulate strong increases in most categories of real imports, although there is considerable variety in the extent of the increases. Imports of natural textiles and refined coal products jump more than 10% in the first year. Mining, other textiles, pulp and paper, leather, machinery, aircraft, and instruments are also up significantly. Since the import price decline is fairly uniform across industries, differences in import volume changes are due primarily to differing import price elasticities and changes in overall industry demand. Some industries (even ones with substantial price elasticities) actually experience decreased imports because of falling industry demand or high demand elasticities.

The distribution of export losses across Japanese industries is largely determined by the pattern of response of U.S. imports to increased Japanese export prices. This is partly the result of the relatively large reduction in U.S. imports that occurs, but it is also due to model characteristics; industry-level Japanese exports to ROW countries are fixed shares of total exports in the four broad SITC categories; changes in ROW demand change the composition of exports only at the four-category level, not at the level of individual industries.

As illustrated in Table 5.5, the yen appreciation is reflected unevenly in

Japanese export prices. Yen prices in general decline, partially offsetting the effect of the exchange rate change on dollar export prices. Prices falling less than 8% represent price increases in dollar terms, whereas those falling by more than 8% (there are a few: nonferrous metals, other mining, and the chemical categories) represent dollar price declines.

Although some of the price declines reflect general deflationary pressure in the economy, most are due to an inverse dependence between exchange rates and prices built into the behavioral export price equations. Negative elasticities with respect to the exchange rate reflect the tendency of Japanese exporters to limit price increases during an appreciation to maintain their competitive position in foreign markets. The assumption of less than complete pass-through is very different from the U.S. model, where complete pass-through has been assumed. In the Japan model, the extent of restricted "pass-through" varies across industries; the weighted average elasticity is -0.42, indicating that on average only about 60% of a yen appreciation is reflected in higher dollar export prices. The consequences of partial pass-through of yen movements to dollar export price are analyzed more fully below.[3] Limiting of pass-through is strongest in nonferrous metals, grains, chemicals, and some metal and machinery categories. The overall price declines in Table 5.5 reflect this behavior, as well as the general deflation in output prices experienced in most industries under the yen appreciation.

The net result of the exchange rate change and the partially offsetting movements in Japanese yen export prices is the pattern of changes in U.S. dollar import prices for Japanese goods shown as the first column in Table 5.6. Instruments show the largest price increase (7.9%), and chemicals the only significant decline.[4] Since prices of manufacturing imports from other countries rise just over 0.1% in dollar terms, overall U.S. manufacturing import prices rise less than prices of imports from Japan, as shown in this second column of the table. The result is that, in addition to a general decline in U.S. manufacturing imports, there is a significant shift of U.S. imports away from Japan in favor of other country exports. In nominal terms, total U.S. manufacturing imports fall 1.2% by 1992, and 1.5% for imports from Japan. In real terms, U.S. manufacturing imports are off 2.3%; imports from Japan are 4% lower.

The right-hand columns of Table 5.6 give the resulting changes, after six years, in overall U.S. real imports and real imports from Japan. For particular industries, the competitive deterioration of Japanese exports is dramatic. Japanese exports to the United States fall more than five times faster than overall U.S. imports in seven industries (textiles, apparel, nonindustrial chemicals, rubber, leather, lumber, and nonelectrical machinery), with 20%+ reductions in industrial chemicals, leather, other nonferrous metals, aircraft, and other transportation equipment.[5] Imports from Japan in two industries (autos and nonelectrical machinery) fall in absolute terms by more than overall imports, implying an increase in U.S. demand for exports of ROW countries in these categories. The only Japanese sectors to increase their real dollar exports to the United States are paper and pulp, iron and steel, and miscellaneous manufactures.

The pattern of change that emerges for U.S. imports from Japan depends on the extent of Japanese export price change, the extent of overall U.S. import price change, overall and bilateral U.S. import price elasticities, and changes in the sectoral composition of U.S. output. In particular, note that the industries for which Japan suffers the greatest export losses are not necessarily those with highest trade share price elasticities.

Overall changes in Japanese industry exports, imports, and output are shown in Table 5.7. For Japanese manufacturing exports, the pattern of change closely follows that of U.S. imports, except for the large decline by 1992 in iron products (which show a slight gain in the United States). This Japanese decline is a value effect of rising export prices for this category. Among nonmanufacturing exports, the sharp rise in exports of nonferrous metal ores is interesting, although it is on a small volume. It results from a very large drop in Japanese export prices of these materials. In absolute terms, the biggest decline is in automobiles, down 1980¥ 622 billion by the sixth year.

The net results for Japanese output are shown in the third and sixth column pairs of Table 5.7. In percent terms, the biggest losers are other transportation equipment, textiles, autos, the machinery categories, other nonferrous metals, instruments, and rubber products. Small gains are made by iron and steel, food and beverages, and energy industries. In absolute terms, autos and machinery swamp all other changes, accounting for over half the total declines. The large declines in these industries are due to reductions in exports to the United States via the direct bilateral linkage equations and also reductions in exports to third countries in the LINK system.

In the U.S. economy (Table 5.8), the most affected industries are generally those for which there are the largest declines in overall U.S. imports in response to the rise in import prices from Japan as discussed above. Output in aluminum and other nonferrous metals industry is up over 4% from base levels by 1992, with strong growth also in chemicals, autos, aircraft, and transportation equipment. Other industries, notably the mining industries, benefit from increased exports to Japan. However, by 1992, much of the net gain in U.S. exports is canceled out by rising U.S. export prices. The metals industries also expand, apparently because of increased indirect demand in the expanding auto and transportation industries.

Just as the multiplier simulations of the previous chapter provided an opportunity to evaluate the interindustry transmission of economic activity, so the exchange rate simulation under consideration here permits an evaluation of the manner in which relative price shocks are channeled through the industrial structure of the economy.

The extent of pass-through of the yen appreciation into Japanese domestic prices depends on the pass-through to import prices (which we have seen to be nearly complete and uniform across industries) and on the input-output structure by which industry output prices become input costs to other industries. Table 5.9 illustrates these relationships by giving for each Japanese industry the percentage change from base levels of value-added price *(PV)*, price of intermediate inputs *(PI)*, gross output price *(PX)*, and composite gross output price *(P)*.

Value-added prices, the returns to primary factors of production, fall by up to 2% (except for the peculiar rise in other transportation equipment) because of the general deflation in the Japan economy. Intermediate prices show much more variation, with some declining more than 4% and others showing little decline or even small increases. The differences primarily reflect differing dependence on direct and indirect imported inputs. Considerations of industrial structure also play a role. Pricing in primary materials industries is likely to be more closely related to competitive world prices than in manufactures where producers have substantial leeway for strategic price decisions. Intermediate input prices are a weighted average of supplying industry composite output prices:

$$PI_j - \sum_i a_{ij} P_i \qquad\qquad (5.1)$$

where α_{ij} (elements of the technical coefficients matrix) gives requirements of industry i output per unit of industry j output, and P_i is the composite gross output price, reflecting prices of both domestic and imported inputs:

$$F_i - (1 - \mu_i)PX_i + \mu_i PM_i \qquad\qquad (5.2)$$

Here μ_i is the import share of industry i sales. The large shifts in import prices are passed through to intermediate input costs through this input-output structure. In Table 5.9, we see indeed that the industries experiencing the sharpest declines in intermediate input costs are those most heavily dependent directly or indirectly on imported inputs. The agricultural categories of general crops and grain products are heavy importers and show 4.2% and 3.7% input price declines, respectively. The other largest intermediate price declines, in basic chemicals, cement, and coal mining, are in industries that are heavy consumers of imported oil and electricity (which uses imported oil). Compare these changes to the small declines in the input price of the auto industry, down just 0.7%. The auto industry's principal suppliers are rubber and steel, with much smaller dependence on energy inputs.

The gross output price, *PX*, is a behavioral function of total unit input costs (the weighted sum of value-added and intermediate input prices), with capacity utilization entering the specification to account for supply constraints. In addition, import prices enter some equations directly, reflecting competitive trade effects. In instances where gross output prices decline substantially more than intermediate input prices (for example, iron ores, crude petroleum, and pulp and paper), it is due to a substantial positive coefficient on import prices.[6]

Finally, the composite output prices *(P)*, which form the basis for macro-expenditure deflators, average in the prices of the imported share of industry demand. The additional decline in *P*, over *PX*, is greatest of course where imports are a substantial share of total industry demand: agricultural goods, forestry, oil, and the mining industries.

Dollar Depreciation Against "Big Seven" Countries

The scenario discussed in the previous section simulates an appreciation of the yen against the dollar and all other foreign currencies. From a U.S. perspective, the exercise represents a dollar depreciation against the yen, with other exchange rates unchanged. In this section, we describe a simulation of dollar depreciation against the six other Big Seven countries. The effects on the U.S., Japan, and the world of this general dollar depreciation are compared to the dollar/yen depreciation of the previous section.

The exchange rate shock considered is a 10% appreciation against the dollar of the pound sterling, the Deutsche mark, the French franc, the Italian lira, and the Japanese yen, with a 5% appreciation of the Canadian dollar. The close interdependence of the Canadian and U.S. economies makes a 10% appreciation of the Canadian dollar a disproportionately large shock both in terms of realism and the behavior of the models.

The effect of the simulation on the U.S., Japan, and world economies is summarized in Table 5.10. The schedule of currency appreciations represents a 4.4% decrease in the effective value of the dollar, using 1988 nominal import trade weights.[7] U.S. import prices rise by precisely this amount in 1988. As a result, real imports decline 1.4% in 1988 and 2.3% by 1993. Real exports rise in similar proportion: 2% in 1988 and 1% by 1993. The J-curve effect generates a nominal trade balance deterioration initially, which is reversed by 1990. U.S. output expands to 0.8% above the baseline level over the simulation horizon, with prices up nearly 2%.

Comparing these results for the United States with those of the yen appreciation scenario, three points stand out. First, although the increase in U.S. import prices is about four times as large in the current simulation, the effects on U.S. trade and output are only about twice as great. Second, where before most U.S. output gains came from U.S. real import reductions, here export increases are equally important, at least in early years. These observations are related: the stronger export performance under the current scenario stimulates activity and keeps import volumes from falling as far as they otherwise would. The stronger export growth reflects stronger import growth in the other Big

Seven countries than in Japan, as illustrated in Table 5.11. While Japan nominal dollar imports rise 2.8% in the first year, the non-Japan weighted average increase is 3.8%. Canada, which experiences only a 5% currency appreciation, increases nominal dollar imports by 4.6%.

The third point to make is that the effect on U.S. prices is relatively stronger in the current simulation than in the yen appreciation scenario. In that simulation, both U.S. real output and prices were up about 0.5% by 1993; here, prices are up nearly 2% by 1993, whereas real GNP is just 0.7% to 0.8% above base. The large price increase contributes to higher nominal interest rates (up forty basis points by 1993), which pull down investment activity after the first several years.

The results for the Japan economy are similar to those of the yen-against-all-currencies simulation, with price and import effects a bit larger because of the larger assumed exchange rate change. Real exports are somewhat less adversely affected here, since Japan does not suffer a competitive disadvantage relative to the other non-U.S. Big Seven countries.

In the world economy (Tables 5.12, 5.13), trade is up about 3% in current dollars, but down slightly in real terms. World GDP rises 0.25% in the fourth year, but is only 0.08% above base by 1993, because of a decline in activity in the EC countries. These overall output effects are negligible compared to changes in the distribution of world trade and product. The EC experiences a nominal dollar trade balance deterioration, as do Korea and Taiwan. The dollar depreciation transfers activity from the appreciating economies to the United States and to economies that export to the United States, such as the "other industrialized countries." Exporters to the appreciating currency countries, for example Taiwan, suffer from declining activity in those markets.

CURRENCY APPRECIATION UNDER PARTIAL AND FULL PASS-THROUGH

As discussed in the previous section, export prices in the Japan model do not fully reflect exchange rate fluctuations. In response to a yen appreciation, local currency prices fall to offset partially the potential rise of dollar-denominated prices. This phenomenon of foreign firms limiting the "pass-through" of exchange appreciation has been frequently noted and much studied during the past decade. A number of writers (Mann, 1986; Baldwin, 1988; Foster, 1986) have observed that measures of aggregate pass-through appear to be lower than for earlier periods. Others (Krugman, 1986; Dornbusch, 1987) have noted that the extent of pass-through, as measured by exchange rate elasticities similar to those of the Japan model, varies considerably across industries and destination markets.

The degree to which pass-through is restricted, and the distribution of such behavior across industries, may have important effects on the magnitude and composition of gains and losses under an exchange rate change. In this section, we examine the macroeconomic and industry implications of limited exchange rate pass-through by comparing the partial pass-through scenario of the previous section with an alternative full pass-through simulation. We find that restricting their dollar export price increases permits firms in some Japanese industries to reduce by half the competitive losses resulting from yen appreciation, with competing U.S. industries capturing correspondingly smaller output gains. The macroeconomic effects of the 8% yen appreciation are reduced to 60% to 80% of the full pass-through case.

Partial pass-through is incorporated in the Japan model through a (generally) inverse dependence of local-currency export prices on the exchange value of the yen. Export price equations are of the form:

$$\ln(PE_i) - \alpha_i + \beta_{i1} \cdot \ln(PX_i) + \beta_{i2} \cdot \ln(REX) + \beta_{i3} \cdot \ln(ROX_i) + e_i \qquad (5.3)$$

where PX is the gross output price, ROX is rate of capacity utilization, and REX is the dollar/yen exchange rate index. Some equations include once-lagged values of REX. The coefficient β_{12} indicates the extent to which the effect of yen appreciation on dollar export prices is limited by a reduction in Japanese yen export prices. Coefficients near zero represent nearly complete pass-through, whereas large negative coefficients indicate very limited pass-through.

Table 5.14 gives the pass-through elasticities for each industry. Both first-year and long-run effects are reported, which differ if a lagged response of yen prices to exchange rate shocks is permitted. The long-run weighted average elasticity is -0.42, indicating that on average 58% of an exchange rate change is passed through to dollar export prices. Most elasticities lie between zero and one, as expected. Nearly complete pass-through occurs in the autos, pulp and paper, and furniture industries, among others, whereas pass-through is very limited in nonferrous metals, grains, chemicals, and some metal and machinery categories. The several positive elasticities make little sense as pricing behaviors in response to exchange rate changes, and probably reflect ideosyncratic movements in industry prices during the estimation period.

To assess the influence of limited pass-through in the model, we perform an alternative yen appreciation simulation with all of the pass-through elasticities in Table 5.14 constrained to equal zero. Effects of the 8% yen appreciation on trade prices, flows, and economic activity can then be compared with the partial pass-through simulation results above.

Differences between the two simulations in aggregate terms are summarized in Table 5.15. The table compares partial and full pass-through effects in the second and sixth years of the simulation period.[8] Under full pass-through, Japan yen-denominated export prices fall just 2% in the second year, rather than the 3.6% of the partial pass-through scenario, resulting in a 1.5% greater increase in the dollar price of United States imports from Japan. Japanese real exports decline an additional two percentage points by year six, driven by a 2% larger decline in U.S. imports from Japan. Both the Japanese and American dollar current account balances move more strongly into surplus. Overall effects on output are small: about 0.2% to 0.3% greater declines in Japan and expansion in the United States by year six. World GNP is only slightly greater under the full pass-through scenario. Overall, the effect of complete pass-through is to increase the trade and activity effects by about 30% to 50%.

Although the macro effects of greater pass-through may be considered modest, cross-industry differences in pass-through coefficients imply more varied responses at the industry level. Tables 5.16 and 5.17 show the effect of the 8% yen appreciation on Japanese industry export prices, real exports, and output under the partial and full pass-through simulations. Yen export price declines are half as large under the full pass-through simulation for furniture, other ceramics, the steel category, metal products, electrical machinery, and the unallocated category, corresponding to larger-than-average pass-through coefficients for these industries in Table 5.14. The resulting declines in exports in these industries lead to appreciably greater declines in output for the sectors. As a particular example, electrical machinery output declines 3% in year two under the full pass-through simulation, compared with 1.6% in the partial pass-through case. Yen export prices also fall considerably less in a number of agricultural categories, but although the resulting sharp declines in exports are significant, the small shares of trade in agricultural production mean that output in these sectors is little affected.[9]

In the United States (Tables 5.18 and 5.19), the effects of more complete pass-through are concentrated in the same set of industries: other ceramics, iron, metal products, electrical machinery and miscellaneous manufactures. Again, output effects, in percentage terms, are quite small compared with differences in imports from Japan.

In summary, the impacts of restricting exchange rate pass-through are concentrated in those industries exercising such behavior. Although they are of limited macroeconomic importance, for certain Japanese industries, restricting dollar price increases can reduce by half the adverse effects of a yen appreciation, permitting them to hold on to a significant portion of the U.S. market share they would otherwise lose to U.S. or third-country competitors.

Table 5.1

Yen Appreciates 8%: U.S., Japan, World Macro Summary

	1987	%DIF	1988	%DIF	1989	%DIF	1990	%DIF	1991	%DIF	1992	%DIF
JAPAN:												
GNE (80¥ billion)	-2185.00	-0.7	-2576.00	-0.8	-2799.00	-0.8	-2507.00	-0.7	-2565.00	-0.7	-2741.00	-0.7
Nominal GNE (¥b.)	-3152.00	-1.0	-5702.00	-1.6	-6373.00	-1.7	-6293.00	-1.6	-6518.00	-1.6	-7071.00	-1.6
GNE Deflator	-0.31	-0.3	-0.68	-0.6	-0.78	-0.7	-0.84	-0.7	-0.84	-0.7	-0.88	-0.7
Net Exports (80¥b.)	-1519.00	-70.5	-1537.00	-42.3	-1756.00	-59.8	-1962.00	-49.4	-2201.00	-35.9	-2388.00	-27.2
Exports	-1224.00	-2.3	-929.00	-1.6	-1151.00	-1.9	-1340.00	-2.1	-1580.00	-2.3	-1818.00	-2.5
Imports	295.14	0.6	607.25	1.1	605.52	1.1	621.93	1.0	620.97	1.0	570.19	0.9
Current Account ($b.)	5.07	9.7	4.20	5.2	3.65	4.7	3.14	4.1	2.63	3.6	2.31	3.2
¥/$ Exchange Rate	-10.71	-7.4	-9.54	-7.4	-9.17	-7.4	-8.99	-7.4	-9.00	-7.4	-9.02	-7.4
Pers. Cons. Deflator	-1.16	-1.1	-1.62	-1.5	-1.72	-1.6	-1.79	-1.6	-1.85	-1.6	-1.97	-1.7
Employment (thous.)	-87.20	-0.2	-129.00	-0.2	-147.90	-0.3	-150.20	-0.3	-153.20	-0.3	-162.90	-0.3
Unemployment Rate (%)	0.01	0.5	0.02	0.7	0.02	0.8	0.02	0.7	0.01	0.5	0.01	0.4
Bank Lending Rate (%)	-0.01	-0.1	-0.02	-0.3	-0.01	-0.2	0.00	-0.1	0.00	0.0	0.00	0.0
UNITED STATES:												
GNP (72$ billion)	0.84	0.0	3.01	0.2	4.12	0.2	5.18	0.3	6.25	0.3	7.48	0.4
Nominal GNP ($b.)	2.74	0.1	10.75	0.2	19.22	0.4	29.74	0.5	42.13	0.7	56.05	0.9
GNP Deflator	0.04	0.0	0.15	0.1	0.41	0.1	0.76	0.3	1.17	0.4	1.59	0.5
Net Export G&S (72$b.)	1.32	-5.1	1.47	-7.1	1.82	-7.8	2.12	-10.4	2.44	-9.2	2.84	-9.7
Exports	0.27	0.2	0.18	0.1	0.12	0.1	0.07	0.0	-0.01	0.0	-0.13	-0.1
Imports	-1.05	-0.6	-1.29	-0.7	-1.70	-0.9	-2.05	-1.0	-2.46	-1.2	-2.97	-1.3
Current Account ($b.)	-2.37	1.6	-0.32	0.2	0.56	-0.4	1.63	-1.1	2.75	-1.8	4.29	-2.8
W. Ave. $ Exch. Rate	1.35	1.5	1.43	1.5	1.46	1.5	1.48	1.5	1.47	1.5	1.46	1.5
Consumer Prices	0.42	0.1	0.54	0.1	0.92	0.2	1.39	0.3	1.95	0.5	2.53	0.6
Employment (thous.)	13.70	0.0	73.00	0.1	135.40	0.1	196.50	0.2	256.90	0.2	232.30	0.3
Unemployment Rate (%)	-0.01	-0.1	-0.07	-1.0	-0.11	-1.7	-0.15	-2.0	-0.18	-2.7	-0.22	-3.2
3-Month CD Rate (%)	0.02	0.2	0.05	0.6	0.09	0.8	0.13	1.3	0.15	1.7	0.17	2.0
Fed. Budget Surplus ($b.)	-1.14	0.8	1.34	-0.9	2.61	-1.5	3.80	-1.9	5.46	-3.2	7.17	-4.3
WORLD:												
Nominal Exports ($b.)	10.89	0.4	7.35	0.3	7.51	0.2	8.30	0.3	9.18	0.3	9.65	0.2
Export Price	0.02	0.6	0.02	0.5	0.02	0.6	0.02	0.6	0.03	0.7	0.03	0.7
Real Exports (70$b.)	-1.25	-0.2	-1.78	-0.2	-2.68	-0.3	-3.19	-0.4	-3.83	-0.4	-4.53	-0.5
Gross Dom. Prod. (70$b.)	0.16	0.0	2.35	0.0	2.56	0.0	4.00	0.1	4.99	0.1	5.75	0.1

Note: Figures are differences and percent differences from the baseline solution.

Table 5.2
Yen Appreciates 8%: World Trade by Region (f.o.b.)

	1987	%DIF	1988	%DIF	1989	%DIF	1990	%DIF	1991	%DIF	1992	%DIF
United States												
Exports	1.40	0.6	1.13	0.4	1.25	0.4	1.51	0.4	1.70	0.4	1.89	0.4
Imports	1.66	0.4	-0.65	-0.1	-1.67	-0.4	-2.78	-0.6	-3.89	-0.7	-5.51	-0.9
Balance	-0.26		1.78		2.92		4.28		5.58		7.40	
Japan												
Exports	1.97	0.9	0.51	0.2	0.40	0.1	0.25	0.1	0.20	0.1	0.16	0.0
Imports	1.10	0.9	2.00	1.4	2.22	1.4	2.54	1.5	2.78	1.5	2.84	1.4
Balance	0.87		-1.49		-1.81		-2.29		-2.58		-2.68	
Other Industr. Countries												
Exports	5.21	0.4	3.36	0.2	3.49	0.2	3.96	0.2	4.49	0.2	4.74	0.2
Imports	4.38	0.4	2.93	0.2	3.36	0.2	4.33	0.3	5.44	0.3	6.65	0.3
Balance	0.83		0.43		0.13		-0.38		-0.96		-1.91	
EC												
Exports	3.81	0.4	2.47	0.2	2.70	0.2	3.25	0.3	3.88	0.3	4.39	0.3
Imports	3.14	0.3	1.96	0.2	2.25	0.2	3.07	0.2	4.09	0.3	5.21	0.3
Balance	0.67		0.51		0.45		0.17		-0.21		-0.82	
Developing Countries												
Exports	1.92	0.4	1.98	0.3	1.92	0.3	2.06	0.3	2.18	0.3	2.16	0.3
Imports	3.60	0.8	2.85	0.5	3.33	0.6	3.83	0.6	4.36	0.6	5.15	0.6
Balance	-1.68		-0.87		-1.41		-1.77		-2.17		-2.98	
Asia Including China												
Exports	1.55	0.6	1.21	0.4	1.22	0.3	1.25	0.3	1.23	0.3	1.11	0.2
Imports	2.42	1.0	1.72	0.5	2.14	0.6	2.23	0.6	2.56	0.6	3.06	0.6
Balance	-0.87		-0.51		-0.91		-0.99		-1.33		-1.96	
Asian NIEs												
Exports	0.99	0.6	0.58	0.3	0.53	0.2	0.47	0.2	0.37	0.1	0.21	0.1
Imports	1.65	1.1	1.29	0.7	1.57	0.7	1.73	0.7	1.90	0.7	2.04	0.7
Balance	-0.66		-0.71		-1.04		-1.26		-1.53		-1.83	
CPEs Excluding China												
Exports	0.39	0.2	0.37	0.2	0.44	0.2	0.52	0.2	0.61	0.2	0.70	0.2
Imports	0.14	0.1	0.19	0.1	0.24	0.1	0.29	0.1	0.34	0.1	0.40	0.1
Balance	0.25		0.18		0.20		0.23		0.27		0.30	
World Exports	10.89	0.4	7.35	0.3	7.51	0.2	8.30	0.3	9.18	0.3	9.65	0.2
World Export Price	0.02	0.6	0.02	0.5	0.02	0.6	0.02	0.6	0.03	0.7	0.03	0.7
World Exports Real (70$b.)	-1.25	-0.2	-1.78	-0.2	-2.68	-0.3	-3.19	-0.4	-3.83	-0.4	-4.53	-0.5

Notes: Figures are differences from the baseline simulation in billions of U.S. dollars and percent. NIEs are newly industrializing economies; CPE refers to the centrally-planned economies.

Table 5.3
Yen Appreciates 8%: World GNP by Region

	1987	%DIF	1988	%DIF	1989	%DIF	1990	%DIF	1991	%DIF	1992	%DIF
U.S.	0.76	0.1	2.72	0.2	3.72	0.2	4.67	0.3	5.65	0.3	6.76	0.4
Japan	-2.92	-0.7	-3.44	-0.8	-3.74	-0.8	-3.35	-0.7	-3.43	-0.7	-3.66	-0.7
Other Industr. Countries	2.14	0.1	2.51	0.1	2.24	0.1	2.09	0.1	2.22	0.1	2.13	0.1
Canada	0.23	0.2	0.13	0.1	0.13	0.1	0.08	0.1	0.01	0.0	-0.17	-0.1
Australia, N.Z.	0.03	0.1	0.04	0.1	0.05	0.1	0.05	0.1	0.04	0.1	0.04	0.1
EC	1.76	0.1	2.25	0.1	1.95	0.1	1.82	0.1	1.97	0.1	2.05	0.1
Rest of Industrialized	0.11	0.1	0.10	0.0	0.10	0.0	0.14	0.1	0.20	0.1	0.20	0.1
Developing Countries	0.19	0.0	0.54	0.1	0.33	0.0	0.58	0.1	0.53	0.0	0.48	0.0
OPEC	-0.10	-0.1	0.18	0.2	0.05	0.1	0.13	0.1	0.09	0.1	0.14	0.1
Africa	0.03	0.1	0.02	0.0	0.03	0.1	0.03	0.1	0.04	0.1	0.05	0.1
Asia Including China	0.23	0.1	0.30	0.1	0.33	0.1	0.53	0.1	0.57	0.1	0.53	0.1
Asian NIEs	-0.08	-0.1	-0.12	-0.1	-0.17	-0.2	-0.24	-0.3	-0.30	-0.3	-0.38	-0.3
Middle East Nonoil	-0.02	0.0	0.02	0.0	0.00	0.0	0.00	0.0	-0.01	0.0	-0.01	0.0
Western Hemisphere	0.05	0.0	0.01	0.0	-0.07	0.0	-0.12	0.0	-0.17	-0.1	-0.22	-0.1
C.P.E. Excluding China	-0.01	0.0	0.01	0.0	0.01	0.0	0.01	0.0	0.03	0.0	0.04	0.0
World Total	0.16	0.0	2.35	0.0	2.56	0.0	4.00	0.1	4.99	0.1	5.75	0.1

Note: Figures are differences and percent differences from the baseline solution in billions of 1970 dollars. NIEs are newly industrializing economies; CPE refers to the centrally-planned economies.

Table 5.4
Yen Appreciates 8%: Japan Import Prices and Real Imports

	IMPORT PRICE	IMPORTS	
	%DIF	DIF	%DIF
General Crops	-7.5	16.1	1.0
Industrial Crops	-7.6	-2.2	-0.2
Livestock, Textiles	-7.7	1.6	0.9
Livestock	-7.7	1.5	1.6
Forestry	-7.6	-39.4	-2.9
Fisheries	-7.6	0.0	0.0
Iron Ores	-7.7	22.3	2.9
Nonfer. Metal Ore	-7.7	1.6	0.1
Coal Mining	-7.1	96.1	4.9
Crude Petroleum	-6.9	-113.6	-0.9
Natural Gas	-6.9	4.3	0.4
Other Mining	-7.7	19.3	4.4
Meat, Dairy	-7.6	13.4	1.2
Grain Products	-7.6	0.0	0.2
Manuf. Sea Food	-7.7	-0.4	0.0
Other Foods	-7.7	2.7	0.2
Beverages	-7.8	7.9	1.7
Tobacco	-7.8	5.3	4.0
Natural Textiles	-8.2	16.7	10.1
Chemical Textiles	-7.6	-0.1	-1.0
Other Textiles	-8.2	23.0	3.5
Wearing Apparel	-8.1	7.2	1.3
Paper, Pulp	-7.9	10.3	3.2
Print., Publish.	-8.2	1.0	2.0
Basic, Int. Chems.	-7.8	20.8	1.8
Final Chemicals	-8.0	16.6	1.7
Petroleum Prods.	-7.0	-42.0	-1.1
Coal Products	-7.2	0.3	10.9
Rubber Products	-8.2	1.5	1.1
Leather Products	-8.1	4.0	5.2
Wood Products	-7.9	0.0	0.0
Furniture	-8.2	-0.6	-0.6
Cement	-7.9	0.0	-0.8
Other Ceramics	-8.2	-1.3	-0.9
Iron Products	-8.0	0.1	0.0
Roll., Cast., Forg.	-8.1	0.3	0.2
Aluminum	-8.0	4.7	0.6
Oth. Nonfer. Metal	-8.1	-30.7	-1.7
Metal Products	-7.9	0.4	0.3
Nonelect. Machinery	-7.4	15.5	3.0
Electrical Machinery	-7.7	24.0	2.0
Aircraft	-7.6	12.5	4.5
Oth. Transp. Equip.	-8.1	0.0	0.0
Automobiles	-7.9	-3.5	-1.8
Instruments	-7.6	21.6	5.1
Misc. Manufactures	-7.9	47.0	6.8
Unallocated	-8.2	28.8	2.4
Total	-7.2	256.3	0.5

NOTES: Price column gives percent differences from 1987 baseline yen price
indices (1980=100); import columns give 1987 differences and percent
differences from baseline in billions of 1980 yen.

Table 5.5
Yen Appreciates 8%: Japan Export Prices

	1987	1988	1989	1990	1991	1992
General Crops	-2.3	-7.4	-6.7	-7.0	-6.9	-7.4
Industrial Crops	-1.7	-1.7	-1.7	-1.7	-1.7	-1.7
Livestock, Textiles	0.0	0.0	0.0	0.0	0.0	0.0
Livestock	-0.3	-0.6	-0.6	-0.6	-0.5	-0.6
Forestry	4.7	0.1	0.1	0.1	0.1	0.1
Fisheries	-2.5	-3.5	-3.3	-3.5	-3.4	-3.4
Coal Mining	-4.6	-4.6	-4.6	-4.6	-4.6	-4.6
Iron Ores	0.0	0.0	0.0	0.0	0.0	0.0
Nonfer. Metal Ore	0.2	-14.9	-15.1	-14.8	-14.8	-15.0
Crude Petroleum	0.0	0.0	0.0	0.0	0.0	0.0
Natural Gas	0.0	0.0	0.0	0.0	0.0	0.0
Other Mining	-6.0	-8.3	-8.5	-8.5	-8.6	-8.7
Meat, Dairy	-3.4	-3.8	-3.8	-3.8	-3.8	-3.9
Grain Products	0.0	0.0	0.0	0.0	0.0	0.0
Manuf. Sea Food	-4.7	-5.0	-5.0	-5.0	-5.0	-5.1
Other Foods	-3.3	-3.6	-3.8	-3.5	-3.5	-3.5
Beverages	-4.5	-4.1	-4.2	-4.2	-4.3	-4.2
Tobacco	-1.8	-0.6	-0.7	-0.6	-0.7	-0.7
Natural Textiles	-2.8	-0.1	-0.3	-0.4	-0.5	-0.6
Chemical Textiles	-6.8	-1.0	-1.1	-1.1	-1.1	-1.1
Other Textiles	-1.4	-2.2	-2.3	-2.4	-2.4	-2.4
Wearing Apparel	-2.1	-3.0	-3.5	-3.5	-3.5	-3.5
Wood Products	-0.4	1.7	1.6	1.6	1.5	1.4
Furniture	-1.9	-2.2	-2.3	-2.4	-2.3	-2.3
Pulp, Paper	-5.6	-6.3	-6.3	-6.3	-6.3	-6.3
Print., Publish.	0.4	-1.5	-1.6	-1.6	-1.6	-1.6
Leather Products	-0.1	-4.4	-3.6	-2.9	-2.8	-3.1
Rubber Products	-3.0	-5.7	-5.7	-5.5	-5.5	-5.6
Basic, Int. Chems.	-9.6	-10.2	-9.9	-9.5	-9.2	-9.0
Final Chemicals	-8.6	-9.0	-9.1	-9.1	-9.1	-9.1
Petroleum Prods.	-4.5	-7.3	-7.2	-7.2	-7.2	-7.2
Coal Products	0.0	0.0	0.0	0.0	0.0	0.0
Cement	-2.8	-3.6	-3.5	-3.5	-3.4	-3.3
Other Ceramics	-3.9	-4.2	-4.3	-4.2	-4.2	-4.2
Iron Products	-6.0	6.4	6.3	6.6	6.6	6.6
Roll., Cast., Forg.	-6.0	-6.3	-6.1	-6.1	-6.1	-6.2
Aluminum	-5.5	-2.4	-2.4	-2.3	-2.2	-2.3
Oth. Nonfer. Metal	-2.9	0.7	0.8	0.9	0.9	0.9
Metal Products	-4.2	-4.5	-4.4	-4.5	-4.6	-4.7
Nonelect. Machinery	-4.3	-5.7	-5.1	-5.0	-4.6	-4.6
Electrical Machinery	0.0	-4.4	-4.4	-4.5	-4.5	-4.5
Automobiles	-3.3	-4.7	-4.3	-4.1	-3.9	-3.8
Aircraft	0.0	0.0	0.0	0.0	0.0	0.0
Oth. Transp. Equip.	0.0	0.0	0.0	0.0	0.0	0.0
Instruments	-2.1	3.3	3.3	3.3	3.3	3.3
Misc. Manufactures	-6.1	-6.4	-6.3	-6.2	-6.2	-6.3
Unallocated	-7.6	-7.7	-7.7	-7.7	-7.7	-7.8
Total	-2.8	-4.1	-4.0	-4.0	-3.9	-4.0

Notes: Figures are percent differences from the baseline solution, yen price indexes, 1980 = 100.

Table 5.6
Yen Appreciates 8%: U.S. Import Prices and Quantities

	U.S. IMPORT PRICE		U.S. REAL IMPORTS			
	FROM JA.	TOTAL	FROM JAPAN		TOTAL	
	%DIF	%DIF	DIF	%DIF	DIF	%DIF
Textiles	3.7	1.6	-0.01	-1.5	-0.01	-0.3
Apparel	2.6	1.2	-0.02	-5.6	0.01	0.1
Paper, Pulp	-0.1	1.1	0.00	2.7	0.00	0.0
Industrial Chemicals	-1.7	0.9	-0.06	-23.1	-0.49	-14.5
Nonind. Chemicals	-1.1	0.5	-0.04	-4.5	0.00	0.0
Rubber, Plastics	1.9	1.3	-0.02	-4.9	-0.01	-0.7
Leather	2.9	1.1	0.00	-20.5	-0.01	-0.8
Lumber, Wood Prod.	6.5	1.3	0.00	-6.2	-0.01	-0.5
Furniture	3.6	1.2	0.00	-4.5	-0.04	-1.7
Cement	3.0	1.1	—	—	—	—
Oth. Stone, Clay, Gl.	2.2	1.3	-0.02	-2.7	-0.05	-1.6
Iron, Steel	0.9	1.1	0.01	1.2	0.07	1.2
Aluminum	3.6	1.6	-0.02	-7.8	-0.05	-4.7
Oth. Nonfer. Metal	6.1	1.3	-0.05	-27.8	-1.41	-21.4
Fabr. Metal Products	2.0	1.3	-0.02	-6.5	-0.13	-2.3
Nonelect. Machinery	2.4	1.5	-0.27	-2.8	-0.07	-0.3
Electrical Machinery	2.5	1.5	-0.42	-2.6	-0.65	-1.6
Aircraft	5.6	1.3	-0.02	-25.4	-0.22	-8.4
Oth. Transp. Equip.	5.6	3.2	-0.19	-25.0	-0.31	-19.2
Motor Vehicles	3.3	1.8	-0.80	-7.5	-0.61	-2.4
Instruments	7.9	5.0	-0.02	-0.8	0.03	0.6
Misc. Manufactures	0.7	1.0	0.03	1.0	0.01	0.1
Total	2.8	1.3	-1.93	-4.0	-3.96	-2.3

Notes: Figures are 1992 differences and percent differences from the baseline simulation.
Dashes indicate the variable is exogenous in the simulation.

Table 5.7

Yen Appreciates 8%: Japan Exports, Imports and Output by Industry

	1987 EXPORTS		1987 IMPORTS		1987 OUTPUT		1992 EXPORTS		1992 IMPORTS		1992 OUTPUT	
	DIF	%DIF	DIF	%DIF	DIF	%DIF	DIF	%DIF	DIF	%DIF	DIF	%DIF
General Crops	-0.4	-3.0	16.1	1.0	-3.3	0.0	0.4	1.8	14.4	0.6	-10.9	-0.1
Industrial Crops	-0.3	-3.6	-2.2	-0.2	-6.5	-1.2	-0.5	-4.6	24.3	1.7	4.6	0.7
Livestock, Textiles	—	—	1.6	0.9	—	—	—	—	3.1	1.6	—	—
Livestock	-0.1	-6.0	1.5	1.6	-3.7	-0.1	-0.2	-6.2	1.2	1.3	-9.3	-0.2
Forestry	-1.6	-9.9	-39.4	-2.9	-19.0	-1.3	-1.7	-6.6	-12.4	-0.6	-18.3	-1.4
Fisheries	-0.5	-3.3	0.0	0.0	8.7	0.3	-1.0	-3.3	1.8	0.4	-3.3	-0.1
Coal Mining	0.0	-2.4	96.1	4.9	4.2	1.7	0.0	-2.6	115.1	4.5	5.8	2.2
Iron Ores	0.0	-5.9	22.3	2.9	—	—	0.0	-6.6	42.5	4.5	—	—
Nonfer. Metal Ore	-0.1	-5.3	1.6	0.1	—	—	0.4	11.1	67.5	3.6	—	—
Crude Petroleum	0.0	-6.6	-113.6	-0.9	—	—	0.0	-6.7	94.8	0.6	—	—
Natural Gas	—	—	4.3	0.4	—	—	—	—	2.3	0.2	—	—
Other Mining	-0.1	-0.8	19.3	4.4	-26.7	-1.3	0.4	1.5	15.8	3.3	-21.8	-0.9
Meat, Dairy	-0.4	-2.8	13.4	1.2	10.4	0.2	-0.6	-2.7	10.8	0.5	-0.5	0.0
Grain Products	-1.1	-5.4	0.0	0.2	8.6	0.2	-1.7	-5.9	0.3	1.2	3.5	0.1
Manuf. Sea Food	-1.7	-1.0	-0.4	0.0	-0.6	0.0	-2.9	-1.1	3.6	0.3	-15.3	-0.5
Other Foods	-1.2	-3.1	2.7	0.2	28.1	0.2	-1.9	-3.3	14.6	1.0	40.0	0.3
Beverages	-0.3	-1.1	7.9	1.7	50.0	1.0	-0.6	-1.8	8.7	1.3	29.1	0.5
Tobacco	-0.1	-2.2	5.3	4.0	16.6	0.6	-0.1	-4.0	3.9	2.4	11.3	0.4
Natural Textiles	-2.3	-3.8	16.7	10.1	-35.4	-4.0	-4.5	-6.1	11.4	5.6	-28.8	-3.0
Chemical Textiles	0.2	0.4	-0.1	-1.0	-4.7	-1.2	-4.4	-5.5	-0.2	-2.1	-9.4	-2.2
Other Textiles	-48.7	-5.1	23.0	3.5	-119.0	-1.9	-55.5	-4.3	-5.0	-0.5	-93.7	-1.4
Wearing Apparel	-6.0	-6.0	7.2	1.3	-60.3	-1.0	-7.1	-5.6	1.3	0.2	-69.9	-1.0
Wood Products	-1.7	-6.3	0.0	0.0	-57.0	-1.1	-2.8	-8.5	-0.1	0.0	-8.5	-0.1
Furniture	-1.9	-4.7	-0.6	-0.6	-20.5	-0.6	-2.9	-5.1	0.0	0.0	-15.9	-0.4
Pulp, Paper	-2.1	-0.9	10.3	3.2	-53.3	-0.7	-1.0	-0.3	6.6	1.9	-40.1	-0.5
Print., Publish.	0.0	-0.4	1.0	2.0	-34.3	-0.4	0.0	1.6	0.8	1.5	-38.4	-0.5
Leather Products	-3.3	-6.7	4.0	5.2	-12.0	-2.3	-3.4	-4.3	5.6	4.6	-6.9	-1.2
Rubber Products	-21.5	-4.0	1.5	1.1	-74.5	-2.9	-16.2	-2.0	-0.6	-0.3	-81.9	-2.6
Basic, Int. Chems.	38.8	2.2	20.8	1.8	-117.4	-0.8	15.9	0.6	16.4	1.1	-121.0	-0.7
Final Chemicals	22.2	1.4	16.6	1.7	-37.2	-0.4	59.3	1.8	19.5	1.5	-23.4	-0.2
Petroleum Prods.	-14.0	-2.6	-42.0	-1.1	-150.5	-0.9	0.8	0.1	69.3	1.2	121.1	0.6
Coal Products	-3.2	-7.0	0.3	10.9	2.6	0.1	-3.3	-7.1	0.6	5.2	18.2	0.7

Table 5.7—Continued

	1987 EXPORTS DIF	%DIF	IMPORTS DIF	%DIF	OUTPUT DIF	%DIF	1992 EXPORTS DIF	%DIF	IMPORTS DIF	%DIF	OUTPUT DIF	%DIF
Cement	-4.6	-3.9	0.0	-0.8	-9.4	-1.0	-5.9	-3.5	0.0	0.1	1.4	0.1
Other Ceramics	-14.6	-3.1	-1.3	-0.9	-35.4	-0.5	-18.4	-3.2	-1.4	-0.7	-36.3	-0.4
Iron Products	-0.2	-0.7	0.1	0.0	41.7	0.5	-2.4	-12.4	4.6	1.8	154.1	1.5
Roll, Cast, Forg.	-29.3	-0.7	0.3	0.2	8.3	0.0	-22.2	-0.4	6.6	2.8	196.5	1.0
Aluminum	-0.6	-2.0	4.7	0.6	—	—	-2.6	-7.7	-0.7	-0.1	—	—
Oth. Nonfer. Met.	-19.7	-3.4	-30.7	-1.7	-96.0	-1.4	-115.7	-14.0	-70.0	-3.1	-175.3	-2.1
Metal Products	-23.5	-2.4	0.4	0.3	-119.5	-0.9	-31.4	-2.6	2.6	1.4	76.9	0.4
Nonel. Machinery	-150.0	-2.8	15.5	3.0	-646.6	-2.2	-197.8	-2.5	10.1	2.2	-918.4	-2.4
Electr. Machinery	-533.8	-5.7	24.0	2.0	-1059.0	-2.5	-394.9	-2.7	28.0	1.6	-798.0	-1.2
Automobiles	-271.3	-3.4	-3.5	-1.8	-302.4	-1.2	-622.3	-4.8	12.5	4.1	-925.6	-2.6
Aircraft	-11.7	-16.7	12.5	4.5	—	—	-26.3	-21.6	7.6	2.4	—	—
Oth. Transp. Equip.	-168.4	-7.9	0.0	0.0	-246.1	-7.0	-318.4	-9.8	0.0	0.0	-402.8	-7.8
Instruments	-45.1	-3.8	21.6	5.1	-95.2	-2.2	-104.8	-7.2	15.1	2.9	-167.8	-3.2
Misc. Manufs.	-5.6	-0.6	47.0	6.8	-91.2	-0.8	-5.3	-0.3	43.6	5.0	-68.2	-0.5
Housing	—	—	—	—	36.1	0.2	—	—	—	—	87.7	0.4
Indus. Construction	—	—	—	—	-73.5	-0.4	—	—	—	—	-98.5	-0.4
Public Construction	—	—	—	—	-3.2	0.0	—	—	—	—	-4.1	0.0
Oth. Construction	—	—	—	—	-38.7	-0.3	—	—	—	—	-50.1	-0.3
Electric Power	—	—	—	—	76.2	0.7	—	—	—	—	45.1	0.4
Gas	—	—	—	—	-17.2	-1.2	—	—	—	—	-27.4	-1.7
Water, Sanitary	—	—	—	—	-7.1	-0.2	—	—	—	—	-18.9	-0.5
Wholesale, Retail	—	—	24.8	2.9	201.0	0.3	—	—	18.8	1.8	-63.3	-0.1
Real Estate	—	—	—	—	-78.8	-0.2	—	—	—	—	-143.1	-0.4
Railways	—	—	-0.1	-0.3	-11.9	-0.3	—	—	-0.2	-0.4	-17.0	-0.5
Trucks, Buses	—	—	7.8	4.8	-39.1	-0.4	—	—	5.3	2.7	-44.8	-0.4
Oth. Transport.	—	—	-0.6	0.0	-8.0	-0.1	—	—	-1.6	-0.1	-9.6	-0.1
Communications	—	—	-0.2	-0.7	-30.3	-0.5	—	—	-0.2	-0.7	-74.3	-1.1
Finance, Insurance	—	—	-2.5	-0.7	-61.3	-0.3	—	—	-2.0	-0.4	-48.9	-0.2
Public Services	—	—	—	—	-106.4	-0.3	—	—	—	—	-299.5	-0.7
Other Services	—	—	12.7	1.4	-84.1	-0.2	—	—	9.1	0.8	-114.8	-0.2
Unallocated	38.3	2.2	28.8	2.4	-65.0	-0.7	50.5	1.9	29.2	1.5	-48.3	-0.4
Total	-1292.0	-2.7	256.3	0.5	-3668.0	-0.6	-1853.0	-2.7	654.8	1.0	-4376.0	-0.6

Notes: Figures are differences and percent differences from the baseline solution in billions of 1980 yen. Dashes indicate the value is exogenous in the simulation.

Table 5.8
Yen Appreciates 8%: U.S. Exports, Imports and Output by Industry

	1987						1992					
	EXPORTS		IMPORTS		OUTPUT		EXPORTS		IMPORTS		OUTPUT	
	DIF	%DIF	DIF	%DIF	DIF	%DIF	DIF	%DIF	DIF	%DIF	DIF	%DIF
Agric., For., Fish.	0.01	0.1	—	—	0.08	0.1	0.01	0.1	—	—	0.49	0.4
Metal Mining	0.00	0.4	—	—	0.03	0.6	0.01	0.9	—	—	0.19	4.0
Coal Mining	0.03	1.9	—	—	0.01	0.1	0.03	2.0	—	—	0.11	1.3
Nonmetal Mining	0.00	0.8	—	—	0.01	0.2	0.00	-0.2	—	—	0.04	0.8
Resid. Construction	—	—	—	—	-0.14	-0.3	—	—	—	—	-0.08	-0.2
Nonres. Construction	—	—	—	—	0.02	0.0	—	—	—	—	0.09	0.2
Other Construction	—	—	—	—	0.02	0.1	—	—	—	—	0.13	0.3
Food and Beverages	0.00	0.1	—	—	0.07	0.1	-0.01	-0.2	—	—	0.52	0.3
Tobacco	0.00	0.0	—	—	0.00	0.0	0.00	-0.1	—	—	0.04	0.5
Textiles	0.00	0.1	-0.01	-0.5	-0.02	0.0	-0.04	-0.9	-0.01	-0.3	0.18	0.4
Apparel	0.00	-0.2	-0.04	-0.3	-0.05	-0.2	0.00	-0.4	0.01	0.1	0.11	0.4
Paper, Pulp	0.00	0.3	—	—	0.03	0.1	-0.01	-0.3	—	—	0.19	0.4
Printing, Publish.	—	—	—	—	0.00	0.0	—	—	—	—	0.17	0.3
Industrial Chemicals	0.02	0.5	-0.05	-1.5	0.07	0.3	0.00	-0.1	-0.49	-14.5	0.49	2.1
Nonind. Chemicals	0.03	0.6	-0.01	-0.4	0.07	0.1	0.01	0.2	0.00	0.0	0.35	0.4
Petr., Coal Refining	0.00	-0.1	—	—	0.02	0.0	0.00	0.6	—	—	0.20	0.6
Rubber, Plastics	0.00	0.5	-0.03	-2.0	0.06	0.2	0.00	0.1	-0.01	-0.7	0.22	0.6
Leather	0.00	0.4	-0.01	-1.1	0.00	0.0	0.00	0.1	-0.01	-0.8	0.03	0.6
Lumber, Wood Prod.	0.00	0.1	-0.02	-1.5	0.00	0.0	0.00	-0.5	-0.01	-0.5	0.10	0.3
Furniture	0.00	0.2	-0.02	-1.3	0.01	0.1	0.00	-0.3	-0.04	-1.7	0.09	0.6
Cement	0.00	0.9	—	—	0.00	0.1	0.00	-0.1	—	—	0.01	0.4
Oth. Stone, Clay, Gl.	0.00	0.4	-0.03	-1.1	0.03	0.2	0.00	0.0	-0.05	-1.6	0.14	0.6
Iron, Steel	0.00	0.4	-0.04	-0.8	0.11	0.4	0.00	0.1	0.07	1.2	0.41	1.6
Aluminum	0.00	-1.0	-0.01	-1.0	0.01	0.3	-0.01	-2.4	-0.05	-4.7	0.10	4.7
Oth. Nonfer. Metal	0.00	-0.1	-0.03	-0.8	0.08	0.2	0.00	0.1	-1.41	-21.4	1.83	4.2
Fabr. Metal Products	0.01	0.5	-0.05	-1.1	0.09	0.1	0.00	0.1	-0.13	-2.3	0.53	0.7
Nonelect. Machinery	0.06	0.3	-0.15	-0.7	0.22	0.2	-0.01	0.0	-0.07	-0.3	0.71	0.5
Electrical Machinery	0.02	0.2	-0.32	-1.0	0.29	0.3	0.01	0.1	-0.65	-1.6	0.98	0.8
Aircraft	0.04	0.7	-0.02	-1.3	0.07	0.3	0.00	0.0	-0.22	-8.4	0.30	1.3
Oth. Transp. Equip.	-0.01	-0.7	-0.04	-4.6	0.02	0.1	-0.02	-1.3	-0.31	-19.2	0.31	1.2
Motor Vehicles	0.00	0.0	-0.20	-1.0	0.08	0.1	0.01	0.1	-0.61	-2.4	1.55	1.5

Table 5.8—Continued

	1987						1992					
	EXPORTS		IMPORTS		OUTPUT		EXPORTS		IMPORTS		OUTPUT	
	DIF	%DIF	DIF	%DIF	DIF	%DIF	DIF	%DIF	DIF	%DIF	DIF	%DIF
Instruments	0.01	0.5	0.00	0.0	0.01	0.0	0.00	0.0	0.03	0.6	0.10	0.3
Misc. Manufactures	0.02	0.7	-0.09	-0.9	0.06	0.4	0.01	0.3	0.01	0.1	0.09	0.5
Rail Transportation	—	—	—	—	0.02	0.2	—	—	—	—	0.12	0.7
Passenger Transport.	—	—	—	—	0.00	0.0	—	—	—	—	0.02	0.5
Truck Transport.	—	—	—	—	0.02	0.1	—	—	—	—	0.21	0.5
Water Transport.	—	—	—	—	0.01	0.1	—	—	—	—	0.02	0.2
Air Transport.	—	—	—	—	0.01	0.0	—	—	—	—	0.10	0.4
Pipeline Transport.	—	—	—	—	0.00	0.0	—	—	—	—	0.01	0.3
Transport. Services	—	—	—	—	0.00	0.0	—	—	—	—	0.01	0.2
Communications	—	—	—	—	0.02	0.0	—	—	—	—	0.32	0.3
Electrical Utilities	—	—	—	—	0.01	0.0	—	—	—	—	0.23	0.4
Water, Sewer	—	—	—	—	0.00	0.0	—	—	—	—	0.04	0.2
Wholesale, Retail	—	—	—	—	-0.10	0.0	—	—	—	—	1.39	0.3
Fin., Ins., Real Estate	—	—	—	—	0.02	0.0	—	—	—	—	0.65	0.1
Oth. Nonmed. Servs.	—	—	—	—	0.05	0.0	—	—	—	—	0.93	0.3
Medical Services	—	—	—	—	0.00	0.0	—	—	—	—	0.24	0.2
Federal Enterprise	—	—	—	—	0.00	0.0	—	—	—	—	0.04	0.3
St., Local Enterprise	—	—	—	—	0.00	0.0	—	—	—	—	0.05	0.3
Total Manuf.	0.23 *	0.3 *	-1.16	-0.8	1.34	0.1	-0.04 *	0.0 *	-3.96	-2.3	9.73	0.8

NOTES: Figures are differences and percent differences from the baseline simulation in billions of 1972 dollars; output includes indirect business taxes. Dashes indicate the variable is not modeled at the industry level or is exogenous in this simulation.

*Total is for all export industries.

Table 5.9
Yen Appreciates 8%: Decomposition of Japan Price Effects

	PV	PI	PX	P
General Crops	-1.2	-4.2	-3.8	-4.4
Industrial Crops	-1.1	1.9	0.0	-4.4
Livestock, Textiles	0.0	0.0	0.2	-7.8
Livestock	-0.2	-1.5	-0.7	-0.9
Forestry	0.9	-1.4	0.0	-4.1
Fisheries	-0.9	-2.6	-1.0	-1.4
Coal Mining	0.0	-4.3	0.0	-5.9
Iron Ores	-1.1	0.1	-9.0	-7.8
Nonfer. Metal Ore	-0.6	0.0	1.7	-7.0
Crude Petroleum	-0.3	-2.5	-6.8	-6.7
Natural Gas	0.0	-2.8	0.0	-5.9
Other Mining	-1.8	-1.9	-4.5	-5.1
Meat, Dairy	-0.9	-1.3	-1.2	-2.4
Grain Products	0.0	-3.7	-3.5	-3.5
Manuf. Sea Food	-0.8	-1.5	-1.8	-3.3
Other Foods	-0.6	-2.0	-1.9	-2.3
Beverages	-0.4	-2.3	-0.1	-0.6
Tobacco	-0.2	-1.1	-2.9	-3.1
Natural Textiles	-2.4	-1.6	-2.2	-3.3
Chemical Textiles	-0.3	-0.7	-1.6	-1.7
Other Textiles	-0.6	-1.5	-1.4	-2.1
Wearing Apparel	-0.9	-1.7	-1.3	-1.8
Wood Products	-0.6	-3.2	-2.2	-2.6
Furniture	-0.7	-1.9	-1.0	-1.2
Pulp, Paper	-0.5	-3.6	-5.2	-5.3
Print., Publishing	-0.6	-3.4	-1.6	-1.7
Leather Products	-1.7	-1.9	-1.4	-2.7
Rubber Products	0.3	-2.8	-0.9	-1.4
Basic, Int. Chems.	-1.6	-4.3	-4.3	-4.5
Final Chemicals	-0.7	-2.5	-1.0	-1.6
Petroleum Prods.	-0.4	-4.9	-4.9	-5.2
Coal Products	-1.2	-1.8	-2.7	-2.7
Cement	-0.8	-7.4	-2.6	-2.6
Other Ceramics	0.0	-2.1	-1.0	-1.2
Iron Products	-1.4	-2.3	-1.6	-1.7
Roll., Cast., Forg.	-1.7	-1.3	-0.9	-1.0
Aluminum	-1.5	-2.7	-3.7	-4.7
Oth. Nonfer. Metal	0.0	-2.5	-2.3	-3.5
Metal Products	-1.3	-1.0	-0.9	-0.9
Nonelect. Machinery	0.1	0.0	-0.1	-0.1
Electrical Machinery	-0.4	-3.3	-1.3	-1.5
Automobiles	0.4	-0.7	-0.4	-0.5
Aircraft	-0.9	-0.7	-0.8	-2.9
Oth. Transp. Equip.	5.7	0.4	0.0	-0.8
Instruments	0.7	-1.3	-0.5	-1.1
Misc. Manufactures	-0.4	-3.1	-1.7	-2.1

Note: Figures are percent differences from 1992 baseline values, yen price indices, 1980 = 100.

Table 5.10
Dollar Depreciation Against Other Big Seven: U.S., Japan, World Macro Summary

	1988	%DIF	1989	%DIF	1990	%DIF	1991	%DIF	1992	%DIF	1993	%DIF
UNITED STATES:												
GNP (72$ billion)	5.2	0.3	12.1	0.6	14.8	0.8	15.6	0.8	15.4	0.8	15.2	0.7
Nominal GNP ($b.)	16.2	0.3	46.3	0.9	77.0	1.4	108.4	1.8	136.6	2.2	160.8	2.4
GNP Deflator	0.1	0.1	0.7	0.2	1.8	0.6	3.1	1.0	4.4	1.4	5.4	1.7
Net Exports (72$b.)	5.8	-25.4	6.2	-29.7	6.5	-40.1	6.6	-30.6	6.7	-27.0	7.1	-27.1
Exports	3.2	2.0	3.3	1.9	3.2	1.8	2.8	1.5	2.4	1.2	1.9	1.0
Imports	-2.6	-1.4	-2.9	-1.5	-3.3	-1.7	-3.8	-1.8	-4.3	-2.0	-5.2	-2.3
Current Account ($b.)	-5.9	3.8	-1.2	0.8	1.2	-0.8	3.1	-2.1	4.5	-2.8	6.0	-3.7
W. Ave. $ Exch. Rate	8.0	8.3	8.3	8.3	8.5	8.3	8.4	8.3	8.4	8.3	8.3	8.3
Consumer Prices	1.7	0.5	2.4	0.6	3.9	0.9	5.5	1.3	7.1	1.6	8.5	1.9
Employment (thous.)	93.7	0.1	318.4	0.3	520.4	0.5	661.0	0.6	747.1	0.6	799.8	0.7
Unemployment Rate (%)	-0.1	-0.9	-0.3	-4.2	-0.4	-5.3	-0.5	-6.7	-0.5	-6.7	-0.5	-6.4
3-Month CD Rate (%)	0.1	0.9	0.2	2.1	0.4	4.1	0.5	6.9	0.5	8.2	0.4	7.6
JAPAN:												
GNE (80¥ billion)	-1802.0	-0.6	-2169.0	-0.6	-2254.0	-0.6	-1841.0	-0.5	-1842.0	-0.5	-2124.0	-0.5
Nominal GNE (¥b.)	-3446.0	-1.0	-6359.0	-1.7	-7049.0	-1.8	-6825.0	-1.7	-6996.0	-1.6	-7644.0	-1.7
GNE Deflator	-0.5	-0.1	-0.1	-0.8	-1.1	-0.9	-1.1	-0.9	-1.1	-0.9	-1.1	-0.9
Net Exports (80¥b.)	-1470.0	-47.4	-1637.0	-58.9	-1729.0	-54.3	-1948.0	-44.7	-2200.0	-35.6	-2434.0	-28.5
Exports	-985.0	-1.7	-586.0	-1.0	-710.0	-1.1	-894.0	-1.4	-1147.0	-1.6	-1463.0	-2.0
Imports	485.3	0.9	1050.8	1.8	1018.9	1.7	1054.8	1.7	1053.0	1.7	970.9	1.5
Current Account ($b.)	11.1	14.4	8.0	10.5	8.0	11.4	7.4	11.8	6.5	11.5	4.7	11.1
¥/$ Exch. Rate	-12.9	-10.0	-12.4	-10.0	-12.1	-10.0	-12.2	-10.0	-12.2	-10.0	-12.2	-10.0
Consumer Prices	-1.4	-1.4	-2.1	-1.9	-2.2	-2.0	-2.3	-2.0	-2.3	-2.0	-2.5	-2.1
Employment (thous.)	-80.6	-0.1	-114.6	-0.2	-127.6	-0.2	-125.5	-0.2	-126.2	-0.2	-137.8	-0.2
Unemployment Rate (%)	0.0	0.4	0.0	0.6	0.0	0.6	0.0	0.5	0.0	0.3	0.0	0.3
Bank Lending Rate (%)	0.0	-0.2	0.0	-0.4	0.0	-0.2	0.0	-0.1	0.0	0.0	0.0	0.0
WORLD:												
Nominal Exports ($b.)	84.1	3.0	91.5	3.0	99.4	3.0	104.3	2.9	104.7	2.6	99.6	2.3
Export Price	0.1	3.6	0.1	3.1	0.1	2.9	0.1	2.9	0.1	2.9	0.1	2.9
Real Exports (70$b.)	-4.7	-0.6	-0.7	-0.1	0.4	0.0	0.3	0.0	-2.2	-0.2	-6.2	-0.6
Gross Natl. Prod. (70$b.)	-7.2	-0.1	5.7	0.1	14.2	0.2	17.3	0.3	12.6	0.2	5.8	0.1

Note: Figures are differences and percent differences from the baseline solution.

Table 5.11
Dollar Depreciation Against Other Big Seven: Growth in Nominal
Dollar Imports in Other Big Seven Countries

	1988	1989	1990	1993	WEIGHT
Japan	2.8	2.8	2.9	2.7	0.187
Canada	4.6	4.3	4.1	4.5	0.175
France	2.8	2.4	2.4	2.5	0.025
West Germany	2.8	4.7	5.5	4.2	0.065
Italy	2.6	2.0	1.7	2.9	0.027
United Kingdom	3.4	7.1	7.8	2.7	0.047
Non-Japan Weighted Average	3.8	4.4	4.6	3.9	

Note: Figures are percent differences from the baseline solution.

Table 5.12
Dollar Depreciation Against Other Big Seven: World Trade by Region (f.o.b.)

	1988	%DIF	1989	%DIF	1990	%DIF	1991	%DIF	1992	%DIF	1993	%DIF
Industrialized Countries												
Exports	67.18	3.4	72.37	3.3	79.11	3.3	82.32	3.2	81.85	2.9	77.38	2.5
Imports	67.00	3.4	76.10	3.5	82.82	3.5	86.56	3.3	85.04	3.0	77.90	2.5
Balance	0.17		-3.73		-3.71		-4.24		-3.19		-0.52	
North America												
Exports	14.55	3.5	14.88	3.2	15.77	3.1	16.35	2.9	16.80	2.8	16.45	2.5
Imports	16.20	3.0	12.40	2.1	10.72	1.7	10.06	1.5	10.12	1.3	8.93	1.1
Balance	-1.64		2.48		5.05		6.29		6.68		7.52	
Developed East												
Exports	9.34	3.2	8.72	2.7	9.53	2.8	10.03	2.7	10.39	2.6	10.20	2.4
Imports	5.46	3.0	6.61	3.2	7.04	3.2	7.65	3.2	8.31	3.2	8.71	3.1
Balance	3.88		2.11		2.49		2.39		2.07		1.50	
EC												
Exports	36.61	3.5	40.51	3.6	44.28	3.6	45.72	3.4	44.73	3.0	41.68	2.6
Imports	35.11	3.4	48.56	4.3	56.96	4.5	61.28	4.5	59.22	3.9	52.90	3.2
Balance	1.50		-8.05		-12.68		-15.56		-14.48		-11.23	
Rest of Industrialized												
Exports	6.67	2.9	8.26	3.3	9.53	3.5	10.22	3.5	9.93	3.1	9.05	2.6
Imports	10.23	4.3	8.52	3.3	8.10	2.9	7.58	2.6	7.39	2.3	7.36	2.2
Balance	-3.56		-0.27		1.43		2.64		2.53		1.69	
Developing Countries												
Exports	13.32	2.3	14.72	2.3	15.23	2.1	16.34	2.1	16.95	1.9	16.31	1.7
Imports	15.08	2.7	12.96	2.1	13.96	2.1	14.76	2.0	16.38	2.0	18.20	2.1
Balance	-1.76		1.77		1.26		1.57		0.56		-1.89	
Asia Including China												
Exports	7.29	2.2	7.29	2.0	7.41	1.8	7.41	1.6	7.38	1.4	6.79	1.2
Imports	7.68	2.4	6.25	1.7	6.66	1.7	6.91	1.5	7.71	1.5	8.63	1.6
Balance	-0.39		1.03		0.74		0.50		-0.34		-1.84	
Korea												
Exports	1.37	2.1	1.28	1.8	1.27	1.7	1.22	1.5	1.17	1.3	1.01	1.0
Imports	1.80	3.5	1.63	2.8	1.83	2.8	1.86	2.6	2.02	2.5	2.05	2.4
Balance	-0.42		-0.35		-0.57		-0.64		-0.85		-1.04	

Taiwan												
Exports	1.47	2.4	1.28	1.9	1.22	1.7	1.13	1.4	1.07	1.2	0.91	0.9
Imports	1.65	3.5	1.43	2.6	1.60	2.5	1.77	2.5	1.97	2.6	2.17	2.6
Balance	-0.18		-0.14		-0.38		-0.64		-0.90		1.26	
CPEs Excluding China												
Exports	3.64	1.7	4.36	1.9	5.06	2.1	5.61	2.1	5.95	2.1	5.93	1.9
Imports	2.27	1.1	2.59	1.1	2.86	1.2	3.17	1.2	3.56	1.2	3.78	1.2
Balance	1.37		1.77		2.20		2.44		2.39		2.16	
World Exports	84.14	3.0	91.45	3.0	99.40	3.0	104.27	2.9	104.74	2.6	99.62	2.3
World Export Price	0.13	3.6	0.11	3.1	0.11	2.9	0.11	2.9	0.12	2.9	0.12	2.9
World Exports Real (70$b.)	-4.66	-0.6	-0.65	-0.1	0.40	0.0	0.28	0.0	-2.21	-0.2	-6.20	-0.6

Notes: Figures are differences from the baseline simulation in billions of U.S. dollars and percent. CPEs are the centrally-planned economies.

Table 5.13
Dollar Depreciation Against Other Big Seven: World GNP by Region

	1988	%DIF	1989	%DIF	1990	%DIF	1991	%DIF	1992	%DIF	1993	%DIF
Industrialized Countries	-8.97	-0.2	2.89	0.1	10.94	0.3	13.47	0.3	8.28	0.2	1.36	0.0
North America	3.25	0.2	8.88	0.5	10.46	0.5	10.27	0.5	9.03	0.5	7.74	0.4
U.S.	4.73	0.3	10.90	0.6	13.34	0.8	14.10	0.8	13.90	0.8	13.76	0.7
Developed East	-2.12	-0.4	-2.57	-0.5	-2.69	-0.5	-2.15	-0.4	-2.17	-0.4	-2.56	-0.4
Japan	-2.41	-0.6	-2.90	-0.7	-3.01	-0.7	-2.46	-0.5	-2.46	-0.5	-2.84	-0.5
EC	-11.15	-0.7	-4.64	-0.3	1.76	0.1	3.86	0.2	-0.03	0.0	-5.20	-0.3
Rest of Industrialized	1.05	0.5	1.24	0.5	1.40	0.6	1.49	0.6	1.45	0.6	1.38	0.5
Developing Countries	1.80	0.2	2.72	0.3	3.04	0.3	3.52	0.3	3.81	0.3	3.52	0.3
OPEC	0.39	0.4	0.50	0.5	0.53	0.5	0.55	0.5	0.60	0.5	0.49	0.4
Africa	0.30	0.6	0.32	0.6	0.31	0.6	0.34	0.6	0.34	0.6	0.35	0.6
Asia Including China	0.60	0.1	1.10	0.2	1.44	0.2	1.74	0.3	1.94	0.3	1.70	0.2
Korea	0.26	0.7	0.23	0.6	0.24	0.5	0.20	0.4	0.16	0.3	0.14	0.3
Taiwan	-0.13	-0.5	-0.18	-0.7	-0.31	-1.0	-0.49	-1.5	-0.69	-1.9	-0.89	-2.3
Middle East Nonoil	-0.06	-0.1	0.18	0.3	0.16	0.3	0.27	0.5	0.27	0.5	0.22	0.4
Western Hemisphere	0.57	0.2	0.62	0.2	0.59	0.2	0.63	0.2	0.66	0.2	0.76	0.2
CPEs Excluding China	-0.06	0.0	0.08	0.0	0.20	0.0	0.28	0.0	0.50	0.0	0.89	0.1
World Total	-7.24	-0.1	5.69	0.1	14.17	0.2	17.27	0.3	12.60	0.2	5.77	0.1

Notes: Figures are difference from the baseline simulation in billions of 1970 U.S. dollars and percent. CPEs are the centrally-planned economies.

Table 5.14
Elasticity of Japanese Yen Export Prices
With Respect to the Dollar/Yen Exchange Rate

	SHORT-RUN	LONG-RUN
General Crops	0.00	-0.53
Industrial Crops	-0.22	-0.22
Livestock, Textiles	—	—
Livestock	—	—
Forestry	0.60	-0.01
Fisheries	-0.39	-0.39
Iron Ores	—	—
Nonfer. Metal Ore	0.00	-2.45
Coal Mining	-0.61	-0.61
Crude Petroleum	—	—
Natural Gas	—	—
Other Mining	0.00	-0.25
Meat, Dairy	-0.37	-0.37
Grain Products	-1.01	-1.01
Manuf. Sea Food	-0.51	-0.51
Other Foods	-0.28	-0.28
Beverages	-0.55	-0.55
Tobacco	-0.21	0.14
Natural Textiles	-0.19	0.19
Chemical Textiles	-0.91	0.11
Other Textiles	-0.14	-0.14
Wearing Apparel	-0.27	-0.27
Paper, Pulp	-0.19	-0.19
Basic, Int. Chems.	-0.56	-0.56
Final Chemicals	-0.86	-0.86
Petroleum Prods.	-0.34	-0.34
Coal Products	-0.57	-0.57
Rubber Products	-0.35	-0.35
Leather Products	-0.16	-0.16
Wood Products	0.07	0.37
Furniture	-0.19	-0.19
Cement	-0.19	-0.19
Other Ceramics	-0.40	-0.40
Iron Products	-0.61	1.07
Roll., Cast., Forg.	-0.69	-0.69
Aluminum	-0.59	-0.09
Oth. Nonfer. Metal	-0.16	0.36
Metal Products	-0.50	-0.50
Nonelect. Machinery	0.59	-0.59
Electrical Machinery	0.00	-0.56
Aircraft	-0.44	-0.44
Oth. Transp. Equip.	—	—
Automobiles	-0.16	-0.16
Instruments	-0.25	0.47
Misc. Manufactures	-0.37	-0.37
Unallocated	-0.93	-0.93
Weighted Average:	-0.33	-0.42

Notes: Short-run elasticities indicate the responsiveness of export prices
to exchange rate changes in the first year; long-run elasticities summarize
the cumulative change, including lagged adjustment. Dashes indicate the
price equation has no exchange rate term.

Table 5.15
Yen Appreciates 8%: Partial and Full Pass-Through Comparison

	YEAR 2		YEAR 6	
	PARTIAL	FULL	PARTIAL	FULL
JAPAN:				
Export Prices	-3.6	-2.0	-2.5	-1.8
Real Exports	-1.7	-2.9	-2.5	-3.9
Real Imports	1.1	0.8	0.9	0.6
Nominal Exports	-5.3	-4.9	-6.0	-5.7
Nominal Imports	-5.9	-6.3	-6.1	-6.3
Current Account ($b.)	3.6	5.7	0.8	2.9
Real GNE	-0.8	-1.1	-0.7	-0.9
Pers. Cons. Deflator	-1.4	-1.4	-1.7	-1.6
UNITED STATES:				
Import Price	1.0	1.4	1.1	1.7
Imp. Pr. from Japan	2.4	3.9	2.5	4.6
Real Imports	-0.7	-1.0	-1.2	-2.0
Real Imp. from Japan	-2.7	-3.9	-3.7	-5.8
Exports	0.1	0.1	-0.1	-0.2
Nominal Imports	0.3	0.4	-0.1	-0.3
Nominal Exports	0.3	0.4	0.5	0.6
Current Account ($b.)	-0.3	-0.5	4.2	6.9
Real GNP	0.2	0.2	0.3	0.5
Consumer Prices	0.1	0.2	0.5	0.8
WORLD:				
Nominal Exports	0.2	0.3	0.2	0.2
Real Exports	-0.2	-0.4	-0.5	-0.9
Export Price	0.5	0.8	0.7	1.1
GNP	0.01	0.10	0.02	0.03

Notes: Figures are percent differences from the baseline solution, unless otherwise indicated. The partial pass-through results shown here differ slightly from the simulation discussed earlier in the chapter, because they were run on a different baseline.

Table 5.16
Yen Appreciates 8%, Partial Pass-Through: Japan Industry Effects

	EXPORT PRICE	REAL EXPORTS		REAL OUTPUT	
	%DIF	DIF	%DIF	DIF	%DIF
General Crops	-7.2	0.4	2.1	-14.0	-0.2
Industrial Crops	-1.7	-0.4	-4.5	4.7	0.8
Livestock	-0.6	-0.1	-6.0	-12.8	-0.3
Forestry	0.1	-1.2	-6.6	-20.7	-1.5
Fisheries	-3.5	-0.5	-2.6	-5.1	-0.2
Coal Mining	-4.6	0.0	-2.4	4.9	1.8
Nonfer. Metal Ore	-14.7	0.3	10.3	0.0	0.0
Crude Petroleum	0.0	0.0	-6.5	0.0	0.0
Other Mining	-8.5	0.2	0.9	-28.4	-1.3
Meat, Dairy	-3.7	-0.4	-2.6	-2.4	0.0
Grain Products	0.0	-1.1	-5.5	6.5	0.2
Manuf. Sea Food	-5.0	-1.6	-0.8	-14.9	-0.5
Other Foods	-3.6	-1.2	-2.9	5.3	0.0
Beverages	-4.0	-0.4	-1.7	17.4	0.3
Tobacco	-0.6	-0.1	-3.4	6.9	0.3
Natural Textiles	0.0	-4.1	-6.6	-31.0	-3.5
Chemical Textiles	-1.0	-3.7	-5.7	-6.3	-1.5
Other Textiles	-2.1	-48.0	-4.6	-86.5	-1.3
Wearing Apparel	-3.0	-6.7	-6.3	-74.1	-1.2
Wood Products	2.1	-2.4	-9.0	-28.0	-0.5
Furniture	-2.2	-2.3	-5.2	-23.4	-0.6
Pulp, Paper	-6.0	-2.0	-0.8	-54.5	-0.7
Print., Publishing	-1.4	0.0	1.4	-41.3	-0.5
Leather Products	-4.2	-1.8	-3.2	-8.4	-1.6
Rubber Products	-5.6	-11.9	-1.9	-68.4	-2.5
Basic, Int. Chems.	-9.9	45.0	2.1	-84.2	-0.5
Final Chemicals	-8.8	30.6	1.4	-39.9	-0.3
Petroleum Prods.	-7.1	1.1	0.2	129.9	0.7
Coal Products	0.0	-2.9	-7.0	7.8	0.3
Cement	-3.5	-4.6	-3.3	-5.7	-0.5
Other Ceramics	-4.1	-16.8	-3.4	-54.2	-0.6
Iron Products	6.5	-2.2	-12.4	79.0	0.9
Roll., Cast., Forg.	-6.3	-23.2	-0.5	71.2	0.4
Aluminum	-2.3	-1.2	-4.0	0.0	0.0
Oth. Nonfer. Metal	0.8	-53.0	-8.8	-184.7	-2.5
Metal Products	-4.5	-27.2	-2.6	-103.6	-0.7
Nonelect. Machinery	-5.6	-112.1	-1.9	-794.5	-2.6
Electrical Machinery	-4.4	-325.0	-2.9	-802.0	-1.6
Automobiles	-4.5	-290.1	-3.1	-541.9	-1.9
Aircraft	0.0	-14.8	-20.2	0.0	0.0
Oth. Transp. Equip.	0.0	-192.7	-7.9	-280.2	-7.0
Instruments	3.3	-80.4	-7.0	-144.0	-3.2
Misc. Manufactures	-6.2	-8.5	-0.7	-88.8	-0.7
Unallocated	-7.7	43.0	2.0	-57.0	-0.5
Total	-4.1	-1124.0	-2.1	-4323.0	-0.6

Notes: Figures are differences and percent differences from the baseline solution for the second year of the simulation. Exports and output are measured in billions of 1980 yen. Omitted industries are unchanged from the baseline.

Table 5.17
Yen Appreciates 8%, Full Pass-Through: Japan Industry Effects

	EXPORT PRICE	REAL EXPORTS		REAL OUTPUT	
	%DIF	DIF	%DIF	DIF	%DIF
General Crops	-5.6	0.1	0.5	-13.8	-0.2
Industrial Crops	0.0	-0.5	-5.9	4.9	0.8
Livestock	-0.4	-0.1	-6.0	-13.5	-0.3
Forestry	0.0	-1.2	-6.3	-20.6	-1.5
Fisheries	-0.8	-0.9	-5.1	-5.8	-0.2
Coal Mining	0.0	0.0	-6.9	4.1	1.5
Nonfer. Metal Ore	33.5	-0.8	-29.3	0.0	0.0
Crude Petroleum	0.0	0.0	-6.5	0.0	0.0
Other Mining	-8.8	0.3	1.5	-33.3	-1.5
Meat, Dairy	-1.3	-0.7	-4.9	-2.4	0.0
Grain Products	0.0	-1.1	-5.4	6.6	0.2
Manuf. Sea Food	-1.9	-7.3	-3.9	-17.9	-0.6
Other Foods	-2.0	-1.8	-4.4	7.9	0.1
Beverages	0.2	-1.4	-5.8	22.4	0.4
Tobacco	-1.5	-0.1	-2.5	9.1	0.3
Natural Textiles	-1.2	-3.1	-5.1	-31.4	-3.5
Chemical Textiles	-0.3	-3.8	-5.9	-7.7	-1.9
Other Textiles	-1.3	-51.9	-4.9	-93.2	-1.4
Wearing Apparel	-1.2	-7.4	-7.0	-73.2	-1.2
Wood Products	-0.4	-1.9	-7.2	-37.9	-0.7
Furniture	-0.8	-2.8	-6.3	-31.4	-0.8
Pulp, Paper	-5.7	-1.7	-0.7	-67.4	-0.8
Print., Publishing	-1.1	0.0	1.2	-55.7	-0.7
Leather Products	-3.6	-1.9	-3.3	-8.1	-1.5
Rubber Products	-6.0	-9.5	-1.5	-64.0	-2.4
Basic, Int. Chems.	-10.6	69.9	3.3	-87.6	-0.5
Final Chemicals	-7.1	-1.9	-0.1	-82.7	-0.7
Petroleum Prods.	-6.8	-1.2	-0.2	116.8	0.6
Coal Products	0.0	-2.9	-7.0	-11.6	-0.5
Cement	-2.6	-5.3	-3.8	-12.8	-1.2
Other Ceramics	-1.7	-28.8	-5.8	-84.2	-1.0
Iron Products	-0.7	-1.0	-5.6	-47.7	-0.5
Roll., Cast., Forg.	-3.2	-151.8	-3.2	-149.7	-0.8
Aluminum	-1.8	-1.6	-5.4	0.0	0.0
Oth. Nonfer. Metal	-1.3	-34.5	-5.8	-225.3	-3.1
Metal Products	-1.2	-57.5	-5.5	-170.4	-1.2
Nonelect. Machinery	-3.9	-198.4	-3.3	-984.0	-3.2
Electrical Machinery	-0.2	-691.5	-6.2	-1507.0	-3.0
Automobiles	-4.1	-299.1	-3.2	-588.6	-2.1
Aircraft	0.0	-13.8	-18.9	0.0	0.0
Oth. Transp. Equip.	0.0	-184.6	-7.6	-275.8	-6.9
Instruments	-0.2	-52.8	-4.6	-120.4	-2.7
Misc. Manufactures	-5.6	-12.2	-1.0	-123.0	-1.0
Unallocated	-2.4	-66.7	-3.1	-171.3	-1.6
Total	-2.4	-1835.0	-3.4	-6257.0	-0.9

Notes: Figures are differences and percent differences from the baseline solution for the second year of the simulation. Exports and output are measured in billions of 1980 yen. Omitted industries are unchanged from the baseline.

Table 5.18
Yen Appreciates 8%, Partial Pass-Through: U.S. Industry Effects

	JAPAN	UNITED STATES				
	EXP. PRICE	IMP. PRICE	REAL IMPORTS		REAL OUTPUT	
	%DIF	%DIF	DIF	%DIF	DIF	%DIF
Natural Textiles	0.0	4.2	-0.01	-2.1	0.07	0.2
Chemical Textiles	-1.0					
Other Textiles	-2.1					
Wearing Apparel	-3.0	3.3	-0.02	-6.4	0.04	0.2
Wood Products	2.1	7.9	0.00	-7.2	0.14	0.5
Furniture	-2.2	4.0	0.00	-4.6	0.05	0.3
Pulp, Paper	-6.0	0.7	0.00	0.2	0.10	0.2
Leather Products	-4.2	1.7	0.00	-13.0	0.01	0.3
Rubber Products	-5.6	0.7	-0.01	-2.7	0.11	0.3
Basic, Int. Chems.	-9.9	-2.3	-0.03	-11.0	0.18	0.8
Final Chemicals	-8.8	-0.9	-0.03	-3.8	0.18	0.2
Cement	-3.5	2.8	0.00	0.0	0.01	0.4
Other Ceramics	-4.1	2.3	-0.02	-3.2	0.11	0.5
Iron Products	6.5	0.7	0.00	0.2	0.24	0.8
Roll., Cast., Forg.	-6.3					
Aluminum	-2.3	4.2	0.00	-2.4	0.02	1.1
Oth. Nonfer. Metal	0.8	6.9	-0.01	-11.9	0.25	0.6
Metal Products	-4.5	2.2	-0.01	-2.4	0.29	0.4
Nonelect. Machinery	-5.6	0.9	-0.19	-2.4	0.36	0.3
Electrical Machinery	-4.4	1.9	-0.34	-2.5	0.56	0.5
Automobiles	-4.5	1.9	-0.27	-3.2	0.68	0.7
Aircraft	0.0	5.9	-0.01	-25.6	0.14	0.6
Oth. Transp. Equip.	0.0	5.9	-0.07	-13.5	0.12	0.5
Instruments	3.3	9.2	-0.03	-1.7	0.02	0.1
Misc. Manufactures	-6.2	0.9	-0.01	-0.5	0.07	0.5
Total	-4.1	2.4	-1.07	-2.7	4.11	0.4

Notes: Figures are differences and percent differences from the baseline solution for the second year of the simulation. Imports and output are measured in billions of 1972 dollars. U.S. import price is a dollar index with 1972 = 100; Japan export price index is a yen index with 1980 = 100.

Table 5.19
Yen Appreciates 8%, Full Pass-Through: U.S. Industry Effects

	JAPAN	UNITED STATES					
	EXP. PRICE	IMP. PRICE	REAL IMPORTS		REAL OUTPUT		
	%DIF	%DIF	DIF	%DIF	DIF	%DIF	
Natural Textiles	-1.2	4.6	-0.01	-2.2	0.09	0.2	
Chemical Textiles	-0.3						
Other Textiles	-1.3						
Wearing Apparel	-1.2	4.9	-0.02	-6.5	0.06	0.2	
Wood Products	-0.4	5.4	0.00	-6.0	0.20	0.7	
Furniture	-0.8	5.2	0.00	-6.1	0.07	0.4	
Pulp, Paper	-5.7	1.0	0.00	0.5	0.14	0.3	
Leather Products	-3.6	2.4	0.00	-12.3	0.02	0.4	
Rubber Products	-6.0	-0.1	-0.01	-3.5	0.16	0.5	
Basic, Int. Chems.	-10.6	-3.1	-0.03	-11.9	0.27	1.1	
Final Chemicals	-7.1	0.5	-0.04	-5.5	0.28	0.3	
Cement	-2.6	3.6	0.00	0.0	0.01	0.6	
Other Ceramics	-1.7	4.5	-0.03	-5.9	0.16	0.7	
Iron Products	-0.7	3.3	-0.01	-1.5	0.36	1.3	
Roll., Cast., Forg.	-3.2						
Aluminum	-1.8	4.1	-0.01	-4.2	0.04	1.8	
Oth. Nonfer. Metal	-1.3	4.4	-0.01	-6.4	0.37	0.8	
Metal Products	-1.2	5.1	-0.03	-5.0	0.44	0.6	
Nonelect. Machinery	-3.9	2.1	-0.28	-3.4	0.53	0.4	
Electrical Machinery	-0.2	6.3	-0.66	-5.0	0.83	0.8	
Automobiles	-4.1	2.3	-0.28	-3.3	0.93	1.0	
Aircraft	0.0	5.9	-0.01	-23.8	0.20	0.8	
Oth. Transp. Equip.	0.0	5.9	-0.07	-13.8	0.15	0.6	
Instruments	-0.2	5.4	-0.01	-0.6	0.05	0.2	
Misc. Manufactures	-5.6	1.4	-0.02	-1.0	0.12	0.7	
Total	-2.4	3.9	-1.54	-3.9	5.96	0.5	

Notes: Figures are differences and percent differences from the baseline solution for the second year of the simulation. Imports and output are measured in billions of 1972 dollars. U.S. import price is a dollar index with 1972 = 100; Japan export price index is a yen index with 1980 = 100.

POLICY SIMULATIONS IN THE U.S.-JAPAN MODEL SYSTEM

One of the most important uses of econometric models is to evaluate the impact of policy changes on many dimensions of the economy. The NIRA-LINK model system provides a comprehensive, detailed, and consistent framework for policy evaluation. As our discussion in the previous chapters suggests, a model of a single country, lacking the feedbacks operating through the rest of the world, may not fully appraise policy effects. The extent and nature of the transmission to other countries affect the impact of a country's policy instruments. Moreover, policy actions in one country may have important positive or negative impacts on its trade partners. We have illustrated these interactions in the previous chapters. Here, we use the NIRA-LINK system to evaluate the effects of a variety of specific policy changes.

In the first section of the chapter we consider macro policies, extending our discussion of fiscal policies, already covered at length in Chapter 4. We compare these with monetary policies. In the second section of the chapter, we consider industrial policy aimed at improving economic performance in the United States. In the third section of the chapter, we treat tariff policies.

FISCAL AND MONETARY POLICY SIMULATIONS

A variety of fiscal and monetary policy tools are available. Although each policy measure may well have a unique set of consequences, which show up when large complex models like the present ones are utilized, we have restricted our analysis to a limited number of choices. These appeared to be the ones most appropriate for each country. The discussion of demand impacts in Chapter 4 was based on a fiscal policy stimulus, an increase of defense expenditures in the United States, and an increase in public investment spending in Japan. Our further study of fiscal policies in this chapter considers increases in personal and corporate income taxes intended to redress the imbalance in the U.S. budget. Our analysis of monetary policy deals with reductions in the key bank lending rates in each country.

Clearly any realistic evaluation of policies will need to take into account other policy measures, such as expenditure cuts or changes in value added or excise taxes. Moreover, serious study of policy would consider, in more detail than we do below, the possibility of judiciously combining policies in order to achieve a variety of policy objectives. The simulations presented here are intended to be illustrative of the international spillovers. They also illustrate the powerful potential of the model system for such analysis.

Fiscal Policy Simulations

The principal fiscal demand stimulus computations have already been presented in connection with our evaluation of international interdependence in Chapter 4. In that chapter, we postulated increases in government spending amounting to 1% of gross national product in the form of defense expenditures and in the form of public investment for the United States and for Japan, respectively. The results, summarized most conveniently in Tables 4.7 and 4.14, suggest that there are substantial multiplier effects of fiscal expansion in both the United States and Japan, but international transmission of economic activity is quite asymmetrical, with U.S. expansion providing a much stronger stimulus to Japan and the rest of the world than a comparable Japanese expansion.

In addition to the final demand simulations, we could have made equivalent changes in taxes, that is, reductions in taxes amounting either to 1% of GNP or, alternatively, tax cuts producing a reduction of demand of 1% of GNP. This type of calculation would have been quite academic however.

The critical macro-policy issue of the current economic situation is the continuation of the large U.S. federal budget deficit, amounting to approximately 4% of GNP in the United States. This deficit continues in our base simulations, in violation of the rules imposed by the Gramm-Rudman-Hollings legislation. In the macro-policy simulations that follow, we pose the question of what would be the impact on the U.S. economy and on the economies of Japan and the "rest of the world" countries of a systematic effort to bring down the deficit (Adams, 1988). Focusing on the medium- term horizon as we do here, we have not attempted to wipe out the deficit entirely. Bringing the federal deficit down to a value of $96 billion in 1992 means that allowing for the substantial surplus of state and local government, the overall deficit of all government operations combined is reduced to a manageable level (about $20 billion).[1] This represents a federal deficit reduction of approximately 1% of GNP in the terminal year.

Tax Increase, No Monetary Offset

Effective tax rates have been increased equally on personal and corporate income with the deficit reduction target outlined above. Money supply has been held at the baseline level, but interest rates adjust endogenously.

The results, shown in Table 6.1, can be summarized briefly as follows:

For the United States

- The impact of deficit reduction is a sharp slowdown on the demand side, resulting in less than 1% growth in 1989 and 1990. On the basis of quarterly data, this would show an absolute recession, two-quarters of negative growth, during the latter half of 1989 and early 1990.

- In 1991, real GNP is 2.0% below baseline, and unemployment is 1.3% higher.

- The economy shows a delayed recovery, as compared to the base solution; however, it does rebound to only 0.3% lower GNP than baseline in 1992.

- The improvement in the deficit of approximately $70 billion by 1992 is accompanied by a significant effect on the current account balance, a reduction of the latter deficit by almost $20 billion.

- In nominal terms, there is a $14 billion reduction in U.S. imports by 1991.

For Japan

- The readjustment of the U.S. fiscal balance has a slowing effect on the Japanese economy amounting to 0.3% lower GNE than in the baseline.

- This effect operates through a reduction of Japanese exports by some 1% in nominal terms.

For the Rest of the World

- The reduction of the U.S. deficit has only small impacts on the world economy. World GNP is affected by a maximum of 0.6% in 1991.

- World exports are reduced by only 0.8% to 0.9% overall, though the impact on the developing countries, particularly those of Asia (for example

Korea) is somewhat larger.

How do these results compare with the fiscal stimulus simulations considered in Chapter 4? The comparison is appropriate, since by 1992 the tax increase required is approximately 1% of GNP. At the same time, there have been no exogenous adjustments in monetary policy. A comparison for 1992 is shown in Table 6.2.

We would anticipate that the expenditure shock would have somewhat greater impact than the tax shock, with opposite signs, of course. In the simulations, the effect of the tax increase on nominal and real output is somewhat less than half as big as the expenditure shock. The impact on the budget is, however, comparable, in fact a little larger for the tax increase. Since the output effects of the tax policy are considerably smaller than for the comparable expenditure shock, international trade changes are more modest. The U.S. current account improves by less than one-third as much under the tax policy. The effect on world trade and output is also proportionately smaller.

More systematic differences would be apparent for industrial sectors, since the mix of products purchased for military purposes is quite different from that which would have been purchased by the private sector with higher after-tax income.

Tax Increase with Monetary Offset

The negative effects of the tax increase simulation, basically Keynesian effects, are not realistic policy outcomes in the absence of some adjustment of monetary policy. There is an internal adjustment of money supply in the model in response to lower levels of activity, but additional autonomous policy action is appropriate—a monetary policy offset. This simulation assumes an increase in taxes to reduce the deficit with a reduction of interest rates by the Federal Reserve. Significant reductions in interest rates have been achieved not only by allowing the endogenous mechanisms of the model to work, but also by autonomously increasing the money supply.

The results of this simulation, shown in Table 6.3, can be summarized briefly as follows:

For the United States

- An offsetting easing of monetary policy helps greatly to reduce the recessionary impact. There is still a significant slowdown in 1989, since monetary policies have lagged effects on the U.S. economy, but the economy bounces back sharply with a rate of growth above the base solution in 1992. By 1992, the unemployment rate shows a slight improvement over the base solution.

- The improvement in the current account is much lower in this solution, and the effect on imports is very small over most of the simulation period, in fact showing a small increase over the base solution in 1992.

For Japan and the Rest of the World

- Since economic conditions in the United States are considerably better with the monetary offset and imports are well maintained, the negative impact on Japan and the world economy is considerably smaller than the small effect of the tax increase alone.

As we note in more detail below, the introduction of interest rate changes into the simulation should also call for direct financial links between the United States and Japan and, perhaps, reconsideration of the exchange rate assumptions. These means of transmission might alter the effects on Japan and other countries.

Monetary Policy Simulations

In this section, we evaluate the domestic and international transmission effects of monetary policies in the U.S. and Japan economies. The simulations described consist of 100 basis point reductions in the key bank lending rates in each economy, with other policies unchanged.[2] We find similar "multiplier" effects on domestic output in the two countries, with a much more inflationary response in the United States than in Japan. As in the case of fiscal expansion, a U.S. interest rate reduction has a much greater impact on the world economy than does a Japanese rate reduction. In addition to the country size and import elasticity, another explanation for this result is direct financial market linkages between U.S. interest rates and other national interest rates.

The overall effects of U.S. and Japanese monetary expansion are summarized in Tables 6.4 and 6.5. Paths of output and price response in the two economies are graphed in Figure 6.1. The 100 basis point reduction in U.S. short-term interest rates raises U.S. GNP 0.2% in the first year and 0.9% by 1993. The domestic activity effect of a similar Japanese interest rate reduction is somewhat stronger in percentage terms in the first few years—GNE is up 0.4% in 1988—but virtually identical to the U.S. scenario in the final three simulation years. As in the fiscal policy simulations discussed above, the U.S. monetary expansion is transmitted significantly to Japan, raising output by 0.3% by 1993, whereas the U.S. effects of a Japanese monetary expansion are almost negligible.

The inflationary effect of monetary expansion is much stronger in the

United States than in Japan.   Consumer prices rise 1.2% above base in the United States, but only 0.2% in Japan.

Before turning to the world effects of the monetary expansion policies, we compare, in Figure 6.2, the U.S. monetary expansion results with the results of the Social Science Research Council (SSRC) Model Comparison Project. Percent changes in U.S. GNP and the GNP deflator are graphed against the nine-model average from Adams and Klein (1991), as well as the results they report for the Wharton Quarterly Model. Our results show a considerably less expansionary path for both activity and prices than the Adams and Klein average, although our results are similar to those of the Wharton Quarterly Model. The Adams and Klein results found considerable variation across individual models, for example, the standard deviation of their 2.9% GNP deflator effect average for the third year is about 6%.

As in the case of fiscal expansion, U.S. monetary policy has a much larger effect on world trade and activity than Japanese policy. The Japanese interest rate reduction raises world GNP a nearly negligible 0.1% over the forecast horizon, whereas U.S. monetary expansion raises world GNP by 0.7%. World prices are little affected in either simulation. In addition to the familiar trade volume and price effects, U.S. monetary policy has direct "financial market" effects on some foreign economies. In particular, Canadian interest rates are directly tied to movements in U.S. rates, reflecting the notion of a competitive North American market for capital. As shown in Table 6.4, the 100 basis point reduction in U.S. interest rates results in a 50 basis point drop in Canadian rates, providing an additional stimulus to the Canadian economy over and above the gains from increased exports to the United States. In fact, Canadian GNP rises 1.7% above base by 1993, twice the 0.9% gain experienced in the United States.

There are no such direct financial market links between the U.S. and Japan models. This is certainly an important simplification. As it is, a drop of 100 basis points in interest rates of Japan or the United States elicits no comparable decline in the partner-country rates. Were such a channel of transmission in place, the bilateral impact of the interest rate reductions would presumably be much larger.

Another financial transmission channel that is neglected in the present simulations would operate through the endogenous adjustment of exchange rates. Barring a direct competitive decline in partner-country interest rates, the rise in the bilateral interest rate differential resulting from a sharp interest rate reduction should set up an incipient depreciation of the local currency in order to maintain uncovered interest parity.   The resulting improvement in domestic competitiveness would stimulate exports and improve the current account, while increasing inflationary pressures at home. These exchange rate effects would reinforce the expansionary impact of monetary policy on the home country and reduce the transmission of activity abroad.

Within the current modeling framework, the companion monetary policy simulations show remarkably similar U.S. and Japanese activity effect of interest rate reductions. As expected, price effects in the U.S. model are considerably stronger than in Japan, and the U.S. rate reduction casts a considerably longer shadow on the world economy. The limitations of the present analysis with respect to international financial linkages and exchange rate determination suggest caution be taken in interpreting these results.

INDUSTRIAL POLICY SIMULATIONS

The lag in U.S. industrial productivity and competitiveness has become a matter of concern to economists and policy makers in the United States and Japan alike. In this section, we consider some industrial policies to address this problem, focusing first on an exogenous improvement in industrial performance and then on the effect of investment incentives.

Productivity Improvement in U.S. High-Tech Industries

In order to represent the consequences of sector-specific industrial policy in the United States, we have introduced improvements in productivity in the high-technology industries.[3] These improvements, which are assumed to result from technological change stimulated by industrial policies, amount to a reduction in employment, relative to the baseline solution, of approximately 2% per year over a five year simulation period. The following two simulations have been run:

- Higher Productivity—Higher productivity is assumed in the high-technology industries, with no offsetting changes.

- Higher Productivity with a Demand Stimulus—This consists of the same higher productivity assumption as above, with the addition of a demand stimulus introduced by increasing defense expenditures.

A brief explanation of the two simulations is required. The increases in productivity represent technical change of a labor-saving kind. The result is not translated immediately into higher worker incomes, and there is insufficient demand to absorb the product that can be produced. For a period of time, this demand shortfall produces a somewhat higher unemployment rate. In order to prevent increased unemployment, we have introduced in the second simulation a demand stimulus in the form of increased defense expenditures sufficient to maintain the unemployment rate at approximately its baseline level.

The results of these simulations are shown in Tables 6.6-6.9, and can be summarized as follows:

For the United States

- The improvement in labor productivity in the simulation with no fiscal offset has the result of reducing labor demand and increasing the unemployment rate by up to 0.5%. GNP remains near baseline and begins to increase moderately above the baseline level (by 0.4% in 1992).

- The improvement in productivity has a favorable impact on the price level of up to 0.7% in 1992.

- There is only a moderate improvement in the current account of $7 billion in 1992, but that reflects the fact that the productivity improvement has been limited, by assumption, to five industries.

- The demand stimulus offset produces a 0.6 to 0.7% improvement of GNP with respect to the baseline. With the adverse demand effects eliminated, the full benefit of increased worker productivity is felt.

- With the fiscal offset, the improvement in the deflator is wiped out by the increased demand, and the balance of payments deteriorates slightly below the baseline.

For Japan

- U.S. industrial policy has only a modest impact on Japan, reducing the level of real GNE by 0.2%.

- There is only a small reduction of exports (0.7% in real terms), and there is a very small decline in the current account balance.

- The application of a demand stimulus in the United States largely wipes out the adverse impact on the Japanese economy at the aggregate level.

- There are perceptible impacts, of course, at the level of the specific industries that have been favored in the United States including, for example, electrical machinery, other transportation equipment, and chemicals.

For the Rest of the World

- The impact on the world GNP is not of perceptible magnitude. There is a small reduction in world trade.

- The U.S. demand stimulus offsets the negative effect on trade. World GNP remains unaffected as compared to the baseline.

Long-Run Forecast and Investment Stimulus

Economic phenomena involving structural change and policies seeking structural adaptation call for a long-term time perspective. For the analysis of such policies, we need to simulate the world model system over a period of many years.

Long-Run Baseline

The integrated forecast using the Japan and U.S. models and the country models of Project LINK has been extended to the end of the century (1999). As has been indicated above, such a forecast, which seeks a feasible noninflationary full employment growth path, is different from the medium-term outlook, dominated by the business cycle. The long-term solution uses as a basis a more recent LINK forecast, and as a consequence, the long-term base solution differs somewhat from our original base solution even for the 1988-1992 period. The principal dimensions of the baseline long-run path shown in Tables 6.10-6.15 are:

For the United States

- Growth of real GNP during the 1994-1999 period at an average 2.9% annual rate. This means average productivity gains of almost 2% per year. This forecast implies an improvement in the rate of overall productivity gains, since the growth of the labor force will be considerably reduced during the coming decade, whereas output growth will remain close to past trends. The inflation rate is between 3% and 4% per year. Unemployment varies in the 7% to 9% range.

- A slow fiscal deficit reduction to an average deficit of $76 billion for the 1994-1999 period. Including the state and local surplus, the overall public budget is almost in balance by the end of the 1990s.

- A continued deficit on current account, exceeding $150 billion and near recent peaks.   This pattern reflects significant improvement in the merchandise trade balance, particularly in real terms, which is offset by rapidly rising debt service payments. (It suggests that further devaluation of the dollar may be required beyond 1992. We assume a fixed exchange rate in the 1992-1999 period.)

For Japan

- During the 1994-1999 period, the forecast is very similar to the stand-alone base solution of the Japanese model, an increase in GNE at a 4.6% annual rate. Inflation will be maintained at approximately 2.1%, as measured by the deflator.

- A continuation of trends in the manufacturing sectors of the economy. At the end of the century, manufacturing has maintained its share of GNP in real terms, but accounts for significantly less employment as a result of the differences in productivity trends between the manufacturing and the service sectors.

- Japanese exports continue to increase more rapidly than imports in real terms but not in nominal terms. Japan will continue to have a current account surplus amounting to around $50 billion.

For the Rest of the World

- The world economy is projected to grow at an annual rate of 2.9%.

- The developing countries as an aggregate grow at 5.4% per year. The Asian NIEs show a 5.9% growth rate.

- World trade (real exports) is projected to grow at approximately 4.9 percent per year.

Against this long-term baseline forecast, we simulate the effect of increased tax incentives for U.S. investment.

Investment Incentives

It has been assumed that an investment tax credit is introduced at a rate of 5%. This alternative illustrates a realistic policy response that may be suitable for addressing the U.S. productivity slowdown.

The results shown in Tables 6.16-6.18 can be summarized as follows:

For the United States

- The investment incentive simulation shows an increase in business fixed investment of 3.1% and an improvement of real GNP of 0.9% (1999).

- Employment, however, also grows, and there is no perceptible improvement in productivity. (Demand effects of increased investment appear to be dominant.)

- There is no gain on the trade side, since improvements in exports are more than offset by gains in imports, reflecting the high sensitivity of imports in the U.S. economy.

- Initially, industries enjoying the biggest stimulus from the investment tax credit are the capital-intensive industries of autos and the metals industries, and residential construction. By 1999, the distribution of output gains is quite different because of substantial changes in imports and exports by industry.

For Japan

- Not surprisingly, given the relatively small impact on trade, the effect of improved investment and productivity performance in the United States on the Japanese economy is quite small, only 0.4% of GNE. (The impact is positive because of demand effects.)

For the Rest of the World

- The improvements in U.S. investment give only a small stimulus to world economic activity, just 0.4%.

- World trade is affected by 0.8% in real terms.

Long-term simulations such as this one pose some difficult problems of analysis, since both demand and supply side forces operate. It is not always possible to disentangle their relative impacts. On the other hand, there are opportunities in this model framework to study some of the most important current long-run economic issues and to evaluate alternative policy responses.

BILATERAL TARIFF ELIMINATION SIMULATIONS

The effect of U.S.-Japan tariff reductions was analyzed through long-term forecast simulations of the NIRA-LINK model. In order to give the analysis some realism, we have assumed tariff reductions that would be similar to those making up part of a Free Trade Area (FTA) agreement. The simulation involves elimination of industry-specific tariffs on imports from the partner country (either the United States or Japan), while maintaining existing tariff rates on imports from the ROW. Nontariff trade policies of the United States and Japan, trade policies of other countries, and national macroeconomic policies are assumed unchanged throughout.

The baseline tariff rates assumed in the analysis are post-Tokyo Round offer rates compiled from General Agreement on Tariff and Trade (GATT) data by the Office of the U.S. Trade Representative (USTR) during the Tokyo Round negotiations, as reported by Whalley (1985). Whalley has aggregated from more detailed USTR data to the twenty-four semi-aggregate commodity groupings of his four-region world model system. The tariff rates reported in Whalley (1985) are used in lieu of rates computed for the precise disaggregation scheme of the present model.[4]

Tariff rates, as applied to the trade categories of the NIRA-LINK model, are given in Table 6.19. Our model is slightly more disaggregated than the Whalley study, so that it was necessary in several cases to apply a single reported tariff rate to more than one model category. The tariff schedule shows a higher average tariff rate for Japanese imports than for the United States.

Apart from the imperfect correspondence between the rates reported in the Whalley study and the industrial classification of the present model, the tariff rates used suffer from two shortcomings because of their age. First, although tariff rates agreed to in the Tokyo Round have become fully effective only recently, so that the overall pattern of tariffs should be fairly up to date, Japan has taken additional substantial unilateral tariff reductions on a wide range of industrial products and has eliminated tariffs on some goods. The rates used here exclude these recent cuts, and so will overestimate the effect of tariff eliminations on Japanese imports. Second, semi-aggregate tariff rates were computed from data at the tariff line level, using 1976 trade weights. Current average tariff rates might be different because of changes in the composition of trade since 1976.

To implement the tariff reduction simulation, changes were made to two sets of tariff parameters in the U.S. and Japan models. Tariff rates on imports from the partner country were reduced to zero from the post-Tokyo Round rates reported in the source study.[5] Tariff rates on overall imports (from all countries) were then reduced by a proportion of the bilateral tariff reduction, the proportion being the share of partner-country exports in total imports. The model was then solved with these tariff changes imposed, and the simulation results were compared to the original baseline solution. The tariff changes simulated are given in Table 6.20.

Macroeconomic Effects

The effects of a bilateral tariff elimination by the United States and Japan are summarized in Table 6.21-6.31. The simulation shows a small rise in U.S. GNP of slightly less than 0.1% of the baseline level in the first year, with GNP above base for the next several years, and declining after 1990-91. U.S. GNP is down by about 1972$ 8 billion by 1999, or about 0.3%. The price level is down slightly by about 0.3% by 1999. The current account deteriorates steadily to about $13 billion below baseline levels.

Japanese economic activity is up 0.1% in year one, and 0.5% in year twelve. Consumer prices decline very little. The Japanese current account improves steadily, up about $5 billion by 1999.

The rest of the world sees a small decline in nominal exports and real GNP in the first several years of the simulation, as U.S. and Japanese demand shifts toward the partner country. Exports are down less than 0.1% in the first year, and GNP is down 0.1%. After several years, ROW exports and activity rebound to above baseline levels as a result of strong demand in the United States. We will discuss this point below. ROW exports are up $15 billion by 1999. The effects on ROW GNP are quite modest, with real GNP up 0.1% after eleven years.

Looking more closely at the macroeconomic response of the U.S. economy (Table 6.21), the deflationary effect of the tariff cut pulls down interest rates relative to the baseline, resulting in the strongest initial real spending gains in inventories, durable goods, and residential investment. Investment remains above base much longer than consumption expenditure, dropping below base levels in the mid-1990s. Interest rate stimulus would be even larger were it not for an endogenous monetary policy response in the U.S. model, under which monetary authorities reduce the money supply $400 million in 1988 and $40 billion by 1999.

The federal budget deficit rises $2 billion in the first year of the simulation and $17 billion by 1999. Part of the increase—$5.6 billion in 1993—is due to the loss of tariff revenues (not shown); the balance is due to the shrinking tax base under the economic recession. The real U.S. trade balance improves in 1988, but declines relative to baseline thereafter. The nominal trade balance is below base in 1988, resulting from a decline in U.S. export prices of 0.2% in 1988. Finally, note that exchange rates are held fixed in the simulation.

In Japan (Table 6.22), as we have seen, the tariff reductions are modestly expansionary over the entire forecast horizon. The investment components of aggregate demand experience the strongest gains. Unlike in the United States, however, the strong investment response is not due to declining interest rates—which stay virtually flat through the simulation—but rather to the procyclical nature of demand in these sectors. The Japanese government budget surplus declines by ¥393 billion by 1999, with domestic revenue gains partly compensating for lost tariff revenues, which are down by ¥796 billion (not shown).

The trade effects of the FTA tariff reductions on the ROW are summarized in the trade flow matrices of Table 6.23. Initially, the "trade diversion" effect of changes in tariff-inclusive relative import prices reduces U.S. and Japanese imports from the ROW, even while imports from the partner country rise. United States imports from the ROW are down 0.06% in nominal dollars in 1988, whereas U.S. imports from Japan are up 2.75%. Japan's imports from the ROW fall 0.61%, whereas its imports from the United States rise 3.7%. Japan's imports from the ROW remain below baseline levels throughout the simulation, but U.S. imports from the ROW rebound to 0.38% above base in 1999, because of the large rise in overall U.S. imports. U.S. import expansion swamps the Japanese import reductions, so that the ROW countries as a whole see net gains in exports by the later years. Loosely speaking, "trade creation" more than compensates the ROW for the "trade diversion" causes by the tariff reductions.

Tables 6.24 and 6.25 provide regional details for the global effects of the tariff reductions. Table 6.24 gives nominal dollar exports and trade balances for groups of industrialized, developing, and the centrally planned economies, as well as for the United States and Japan. All country groups except Japan experience trade balance deteriorations in the first year of the simulation, although rising U.S. import demand results in trade balance gains for most regions by 1993. The notable exceptions are the developed Pacific economies of Australia and New Zealand and the less-developed countries of Africa, both of which suffer export losses over the entire simulation horizon, but for different reasons. New Zealand and Australia are heavily dependent on exports to Japan, which remain depressed throughout. The African countries are primarily exporters of nonmanufactures; U.S. imports of these goods fall during the simulation, so African countries suffer export losses.

The effects on ROW GNP (Table 6.25) are very small, with most regions experiencing almost immeasurably small declines in GNP in the first years and very slight gains in the last half of the simulation period. Canada and the Asian NIEs suffer the largest GNP declines in early years because of their large manufacturing trade with the United States. For the same reason, they experience substantial real output gains in later years. Output in the Asian NIEs is up 0.34% by 1999; Canadian output is up 0.53%, a greater percentage gain than experienced by Japan.

Industry Effects

Although the macroeconomic effects of the bilateral tariff elimination are modest, the variation in tariff rates and differences in demand characteristics across industries suggest that effects at the industry level may vary widely. This is in fact the case. First, however, differences in trade response at the broad four-category level of Project LINK are indicated by the data in Table 6.26. For the United States, manufactures are the only category of imports to grow under the tariff reduction. This is because U.S. tariff reductions are limited to manufactures, since imports from Japan of nonmanufactures are insignificant.[6] Without a terms-of-trade gain, imports in nonmanufactures decline as overall U.S. activity falls below baseline levels.

For Japan, imports are significantly above base in all categories of goods. The large tariff reductions in food and beverages stimulate the largest initial rise in imports among the four groups, but raw materials and manufactures are also up about 1% by 1999. Manufactures are the only goods of which Japan exports significant quantities; manufacturing exports rise 1.8% by 1999. U.S. exports rise about 2% above base in food and beverages and raw materials as a result of the large rise in Japanese demand for these goods.

Turning to the industry level, Tables 6.27 and 6.28 give, for the United States and Japan, respectively, real imports by industry in 1988 and 1999. Total industry imports are broken down into imports from the partner country and from the ROW. The response of imports in a particular industry is the net result of several factors, including the extent of the tariff-inclusive relative import price decline, the sensitivity of behavioral imports to the price decline (price elasticity of import demand), and the sensitivity of import demand to total demand for industry output (activity elasticity of import demand).[7] The share of imports from the partner country likewise depends on the relative change in the tariff-inclusive price of imports from the partner and the price elasticity of the bilateral import demand.[8]

For overall import demands, tariff-inclusive relative import price changes are generally much smaller than the bilateral tariff reductions. In the United States, for example, the extent and pattern of declines in tariff-inclusive prices of total imports are much different from that of prices of imports from Japan, depending on the shares of Japanese goods in overall U.S. imports.[9] For this reason, the pattern of change in overall imports differs greatly from that of imports from Japan. In Table 6.27, note particularly the large percentage increase in leather product (32.6%) and aircraft (12.4%) imports from Japan, whereas overall imports of these goods rise little (0.1% and 0.4%, respectively).

The importance of price elasticities in import response is evident from an examination of overall imports of textiles and instruments. These categories, which experience the greatest overall tariff declines (2.83% for textiles and

2.48% for instruments), see unremarkable changes in overall import volume. This is the product of their small import price elasticities: 0.54 for textiles and 0.0 for instruments, for which the estimated relative price term was not significantly different from zero. By comparison, transportation equipment has a particularly large import price elasticity (-4.49) and so experiences a large rise (2.0%) in the first simulation year. Activity elasticities are similarly important, illustrated by the eventual decline in the instrument category, where the high income elasticity of 2.29 pulls down imports below baseline levels as overall activity in the economy falls.[10]

Overall, the largest percentage increases in U.S. imports occur in the chemical categories, the metal products industries (excluding iron and steel), electrical machinery and the transportation categories. In absolute terms, increases in electrical machinery are more than twice as large as the next biggest category, motor vehicles. Imports decline the most (in absolute terms) in iron and steel, apparel, and other nonferrous metals.

Imports from Japan rise substantially in percentage terms in two of the three categories seeing very large bilateral tariff reductions; imports are up 12% (in 1988) in textiles and 33% in leather products, although the latter is, of course, on a small volume. Apparel is flat because the equation was fitted without a relative price term. After several years, substantial percentage gains are realized in imports from Japan of chemicals, rubber and plastics, metals, motor vehicles, and miscellaneous manufactures. As was the case for overall imports, the largest absolute rises are in electrical machinery and motor vehicles.

Table 6.28 provides industry detail for Japanese imports. As in the United States, responses of categories of imports to the tariff reductions vary substantially. For overall imports, large percentage increases are experienced in agricultural goods, rubber and plastics, leather, chemicals, and the machinery categories, where overall tariff rates decline substantially.[11] Overall imports are also higher in industries with more modest tariff changes, including autos, aircraft and iron and steel. In absolute terms, the largest import increase is (not surprisingly) in crude petroleum, which expands by ¥11 billion in 1988 and by ¥97 billion in 1999 as the general Japanese economy expands. Other large absolute increases are in electrical machinery, petroleum products, chemicals, and agricultural goods.

Imports from the U.S. increase substantially in percentage terms in agricultural goods and food products, where the largest tariff reductions are concentrated. Japanese imports of U.S. industrial crops, livestock, fish, and processed seafood are all up over 15% by 1999.[12] Large increases are also seen in U.S. exports to Japan of textiles and leather products. In absolute terms, the largest increases are in agricultural products and food, chemicals, nonferrous metals, machinery, and non-auto transportation equipment. U.S. tobacco exports to Japan do not benefit from the removal of their 54% tariff because they are exogenous (in nominal dollars) in the model.[13]

With respect to the industry-level effects of the tariff reductions on the rest of the world, ROW exports of agricultural and food products are down, as Japan diverts its import demand strongly toward U.S. exports. Japanese real imports from the ROW in general crops are down 3.8% by 1999, fishery imports are down 2.2%, with greater than 1% declines in livestock, forestry, grain products, seafood, and other foods. Recall that U.S. imports of these goods (modeled at the four-category LINK level—see Table 6.26) are also below baseline levels, causing the small sustained decline in GNP of the agricultural export-dependent African countries.

Among ROW manufacturing exports, textile exports are down to both the U.S. and Japanese markets. For most other industries, U.S. and Japanese real imports from the ROW move in opposing directions. For example, industrial chemical demand from the ROW is up sharply in the United States, but is down somewhat in Japan; rubber and plastic imports are down 15% in the United States, but are up 4.5% in Japan. Table 6.29 reports the 1999 changes in nominal dollars to facilitate comparison. In all cases, the change in U.S. imports from the ROW is of greater magnitude than the change in Japanese imports. ROW exports to the combined U.S.-Japan market rise by more than $7 billion in chemicals, over $5 billion in automobiles, and about $2 billion in electrical machinery. ROW exporters experience net losses in textiles, apparel, rubber and plastics, iron and steel, other nonferrous metals, and instruments.

At this point, we should reiterate that industry-level demand and price effects are not modeled for ROW imports from the United States and Japan. The non-U.S.-Japan countries and regions of the LINK system have trade modeled at the four-category level, and U.S. and Japan exports to the ROW at the industrial level are computed as fixed historical shares of the broader trade categories. For these simulations, this limitation may not be particularly important, since the significant autonomous (tariff-inclusive) relative price changes are limited to the U.S. and Japanese import markets.

The effect of the tariff eliminations on U.S. and Japanese overall real exports, imports, and output by industry is summarized in Tables 6.30 and 6.31. In the United States, in 1988, the sharp increase in Japanese imports from the U.S. of agricultural goods, food, textiles, and apparel results in appreciable expansion of output in the corresponding U.S. industries. Large import increases in miscellaneous manufactures and electrical machinery result in output declines (relative to base) in these industries in 1988, and hold down output gains in such sectors as nonelectrical machinery, rubber and plastics, and automobiles. By 1999, substantial import growth in most manufacturing industries more than outweighs gains in exports to Japan. Output declines by more than 4% in industrial chemicals and aircraft, with measurable losses in electrical machinery, metals industries, and automobiles. Only textiles remain above baseline levels. Agriculture declines despite the 2% increase in real exports.[14]

Included in Tables 6.30 and 6.31 is industry output detail for "nontraded" industries.[15] Output changes in these industries reflect changes in overall demand conditions, as well as changes in the indirect demands of traded goods industries, transmitted through the input-output matrix. Note that waterborne transportation is the only positive service sector in 1999, benefiting from the large increase in import and export flows.

In Japan, 1988 output is significantly higher in those industries benefiting from U.S. import growth (textiles, rubber and plastics, machinery, and autos), and unchanged or lower in industries seeing large Japanese import increases (agricultural goods, forestry, tobacco and leather). A number of manufacturing industries see substantial growth in both imports and exports, with net exports and output little changed. Note that aluminum and aircraft output is fixed exogenously in the current version of the Japan model.

By 1999, all Japanese industries but general crops and apparel have output above baseline levels, but output gains are tempered by import growth, especially in forestry, coal mining, textiles, chemicals, and instruments.

CONCLUSIONS

Because the average level of existing tariffs is low, the macroeconomic effects of the bilateral tariff reductions are small. Japan experiences modest output gains, although the United States sees a slight decline in economic activity. This difference stems from the (by now familiar) structural differences of a larger U.S. economy and greater U.S. import responsiveness. Among industries that are significantly affected are those subject to large initial tariffs, including textiles, apparel, agriculture, and foods. Noteworthy changes also occur in industries that are heavily traded, such as automobiles and chemicals, or that are particularly sensitive to relative price changes, such as rubber and plastics, and transportation equipment. Some sectors that supply intermediate output to these industries also show significant effects from the tariff reductions.

Figure 6.1
Interest Rate Reductions in the U.S. and Japan:
Domestic Output and Price Effects

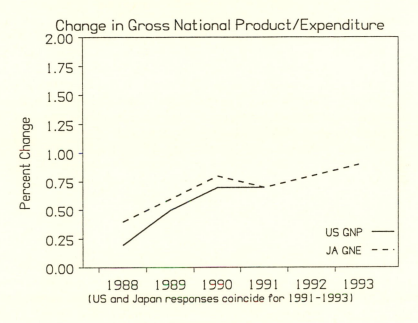

Change in Gross National Product/Expenditure

US GNP ——
JA GNE – – ·

(US and Japan responses coincide for 1991-1993)

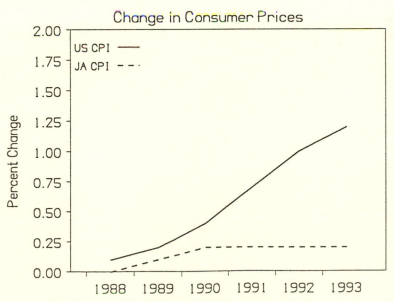

Change in Consumer Prices

US CPI ——
JA CPI – – ·

Figure 6.2
U.S. Interest Rate Simulation Results in Several Models

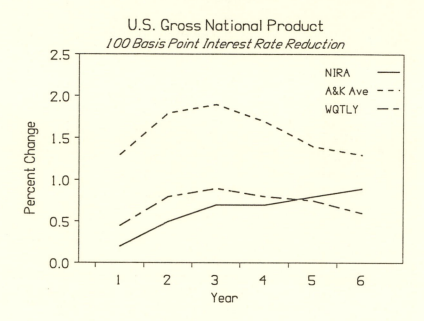

U.S. Gross National Product
100 Basis Point Interest Rate Reduction

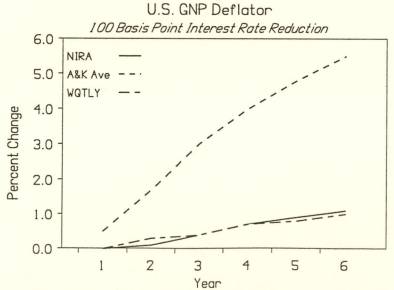

U.S. GNP Deflator
100 Basis Point Interest Rate Reduction

Source: A&K average and Wharton Quarterly Model results are from Adams and Klein (1991).

Table 6.1
U.S. Personal and Corporate Taxes Increased, No Monetary Accommodation: U.S., Japan, World Macro Summary

	1989	%DIF	1990	%DIF	1991	%DIF	1992	%DIF
UNITED STATES:								
GNP (72$ billion)	-31.9	-1.7	-31.0	-1.6	-39.3	-2.0	-6.3	-0.3
Nominal GNP ($b.)	-91.2	-1.7	-123.5	-2.2	-196.8	-3.3	-151.6	-2.4
GNP Deflator	-0.2	-0.1	-1.7	-0.6	-4.0	-1.3	-6.5	-2.1
Nominal Net Exports ($b.)	11.3	10.1	13.9	14.1	20.2	19.5	12.0	11.5
Nominal Exports	-1.0	-0.2	-2.8	-0.5	-5.4	-0.9	-7.1	-1.1
Nominal Imports	-12.3	-2.0	-16.7	-2.5	-25.6	-3.6	-19.1	-2.5
Current Account ($b.)	11.3	7.4	13.9	9.7	20.2	13.3	12.0	7.7
Consumer Prices	-1.0	-0.3	-3.0	-0.7	-5.9	-1.4	-8.2	-1.9
Employment (thous.)	-775.0	-0.1	-1252.0	-1.1	-1743.0	-1.5	-1327.0	-1.1
Unemployment Rate (%)	0.6	9.8	1.0	13.0	1.3	19.1	0.8	12.4
3-Month CD Rate (%)	-1.2	-10.8	-1.7	-17.0	-2.7	-30.2	-2.3	-27.6
Fed. Budget Surplus ($b.)	24.0	14.0	46.0	22.5	68.0	39.7	69.6	41.3
JAPAN:								
GNE (80¥ billion)	-512.0	-0.2	-796.0	-0.2	-1118.0	-0.3	-811.0	-0.2
Nominal GNE (¥b.)	-383.0	-0.1	-729.0	-0.2	-1110.0	-0.3	-1086.0	-0.2
GNE Deflator	0.1	0.1	0.1	0.1	0.1	0.0	0.0	0.0
Nominal Net Exports (80¥b.)	-183.3	-1.8	-229.2	-2.4	-317.4	-3.4	-177.2	-2.0
Nominal Exports	-239.9	-0.6	-346.8	-0.8	-531.7	-1.1	-437.4	-0.9
Nominal Imports	-56.6	-0.2	-117.6	-0.3	-214.3	-0.6	-260.2	-0.6
Current Account ($b.)	-1.5	-1.9	-1.9	-2.5	-2.6	-3.6	-1.5	-2.1
Consumer Prices	0.0	0.0	0.0	0.0	0.0	0.0	-0.1	-0.1
Employment (thous.)	-10.6	0.0	-23.7	0.0	-37.7	-0.1	-40.5	-0.1
Unemployment Rate (%)	0.0	0.1	0.0	0.2	0.0	0.3	0.0	0.2
Bank Lending Rate (%)	0.0	0.0	0.0	0.0	0.0	0.0	0.0	0.0
WORLD:								
Nominal Exports ($b.)	-12.3	-0.4	-19.7	-0.6	-32.5	-0.9	-30.5	-0.8
Developing Countries	-3.9	-0.6	-5.8	-0.9	-9.6	-1.3	-8.6	-1.1
Korea	-0.4	-0.6	-0.6	-0.8	-1.0	-1.3	-0.9	-1.1
Taiwan	-0.5	-0.8	-0.7	-1.1	-1.3	-1.7	-1.2	-1.5
Real Exports (70$b.)	-3.5	-0.4	-4.6	-0.5	-6.9	-0.8	-4.9	-0.5
Gross Natl. Prod. (70$b.)	-31.4	-0.5	-32.6	-0.5	-43.1	-0.6	-13.2	-0.2

Note: Figures are differences and percent differences from the baseline solution.

Table 6.2
Comparison of Macroeconomic Effects of Expenditure and Tax Shocks

	EXPENDITURE INCREASE		TAX INCREASE	
	DIF	%DIF	DIF	%DIF
GNP (72$ billion)	16.9	0.8	-6.3	-0.3
Nominal GNP ($b.)	335.6	5.2	-151.6	-2.4
GNP Deflator	13.8	4.4	-6.5	-2.1
Consumer Prices	16.8	3.8	-8.2	-1.9
Employment (mil.)	2.0	1.7	-1.3	-1.1
Unemployment Rate (%)	-1.1	-15.6	0.8	12.4
3-Month CD Rate (%)	0.5	6.0	-2.3	-27.6
M2 ($b)	203.3	5.4	6.0	0.0
Federal Surplus ($b.)	-53.3	31.7	69.5	43.3
Current Account ($b.)	-42.3	27.1	12.0	-7.7
W.Ave. $ Exch. Rate	0.0	0.0	0.0	0.0
Personal Consumption	22.1	1.7	-27.1	-2.0
Durable Goods	5.3	2.3	-6.0	-2.6
Nondurable Goods	6.9	1.5	-9.0	-1.9
Services	9.8	1.6	-12.1	-1.9
Gross Private Investment	-6.9	-1.9	15.0	4.1
Fixed Investment	-4.0	-1.1	12.8	3.7
Nonresidential	0.2	0.1	2.2	0.5
Residential	-4.2	-6.5	10.0	16.4
Change in Bus. Inventories	-2.9	-19.9	2.1	14.5
Net Exports, Goods and Srvcs.	-16.1	54.9	5.9	-20.0
Exports	-0.9	-0.5	1.0	0.5
Imports	15.2	6.8	-4.8	-2.2
Government Purchases	17.9	4.8	0.0	0.0

Notes: Figures are differences from 1992 baseline values in billions of 1972 dollars and in percent, unless otherwise noted.

Table 6.3
U.S. Personal and Corporate Taxes Reduced, Monetary Offset: U.S., Japan, World Macro Summary

	1989	%DIF	1990	%DIF	1991	%DIF	1992	%DIF
UNITED STATES:								
GNP (72$ billion)	-25.4	-1.3	-13.8	-0.7	-10.0	-0.5	36.7	1.8
Nominal GNP ($b.)	-72.6	-1.4	-63.5	-1.1	-74.1	-1.2	63.9	1.0
GNP Deflator	-0.1	0.0	-1.2	-0.4	-2.2	-0.7	-2.5	-0.8
Nominal Net Exports ($b.)	9.2	8.2	7.5	7.6	7.5	7.2	10.5	10.1
Nominal Exports	-0.7	-0.1	-1.6	-0.3	-2.3	-0.4	-0.9	-0.1
Nominal Imports	-9.9	-1.6	-9.1	-1.4	-9.9	-1.4	9.6	1.2
Current Account ($b.)	9.2	6.0	7.5	5.3	7.5	4.9	10.5	6.7
Consumer Prices	-0.8	-0.2	-1.9	-0.5	-3.0	-0.7	-2.2	-0.5
Employment (thous.)	-617.0	-0.5	-735.0	-0.6	-724.0	-0.6	322.0	0.3
Unemployment Rate (%)	0.5	7.8	0.6	7.5	0.5	7.6	-0.4	-5.2
3-Month CD Rate (%)	-2.1	-19.5	-2.8	-27.3	-3.5	-39.7	-2.6	-32.4
Fed. Budget Surplus ($b.)	24.0	14.0	46.1	22.5	68.3	39.7	69.7	41.3
JAPAN:								
GNE (80¥ billion)	-396.8	-0.1	-420.9	-0.1	-320.6	-0.1	634.7	0.2
Nominal GNE (¥b.)	-297.5	-0.1	-419.4	-0.1	-399.6	-0.1	281.4	0.1
GNE Deflator	0.1	0.0	0.0	0.0	0.0	0.0	-0.1	-0.1
Nominal Net Exports (80¥b.)	-143.3	-1.4	-110.0	-1.2	-76.4	-0.8	254.4	2.8
Nominal Exports	-186.6	-0.4	-179.0	-0.4	-168.6	-0.4	246.9	0.5
Nominal Imports	-43.3	-0.1	-69.0	-0.2	-92.2	-0.2	-7.5	0.0
Current Account ($b.)	-1.2	-1.5	-0.9	-1.2	-0.6	-0.9	2.1	3.0
Consumer Prices	0.0	0.0	0.0	0.0	0.0	0.0	-0.1	-0.1
Employment (thous.)	-8.2	0.0	-14.4	0.0	-15.7	0.0	0.9	0.0
Unemployment Rate (%)	0.0	0.1	0.0	0.1	0.0	0.1	0.0	-0.1
Bank Lending Rate (%)	0.0	0.0	0.0	0.0	0.0	0.0	0.0	-0.1
WORLD:								
Nominal Exports ($b.)	-9.5	-0.3	-10.3	-0.3	-11.9	-0.3	8.4	0.2
Developing Countries	-3.0	-0.5	-3.0	-0.4	-3.6	-0.5	2.8	0.3
Korea	-0.3	-0.4	-0.3	-0.4	-0.4	-0.5	0.3	0.3
Taiwan	-0.4	-0.6	-0.4	-0.6	-0.5	-0.1	0.4	0.4
Real Exports (70$b.)	-2.7	-0.3	-2.2	-0.3	-2.1	-0.2	3.6	0.4
Gross Natl. Prod. (70$b.)	-24.4	-0.4	-14.5	-0.2	-11.5	-0.2	35.3	0.5

Note: Figures are differences and percent differences from the baseline solution.

Table 6.4
100 Basis Point Reduction in U.S. Interest Rates

	1988	1989	1990	1991	1992	1993
United States:						
3-Mo. CD Rate (%)	-1.0	-1.0	-1.0	-1.0	-1.0	-1.0
Gross National Product	4.5	9.4	13.6	13.4	16.1	17.7
Percent Difference	0.2	0.5	0.7	0.7	0.8	0.9
Consumer Prices (%Dif.)	0.1	0.2	0.4	0.7	1.0	1.2
Exports (%Dif.)	0.0	0.0	0.0	0.0	0.0	0.0
Import (%Dif.)	0.2	0.5	0.9	1.2	1.7	2.3
Current Account ($b.)	-1.4	-3.4	-5.9	-7.9	-11.9	-16.6
Japan:						
Bank Lending Rate (%)	0.0	0.0	0.0	0.0	0.0	0.0
Gross National Expend.	72.0	201.0	366.0	527.0	774.0	1069.0
Percent Difference	0.0	0.1	0.1	0.1	0.2	0.2
Pers. Cons. Defl. (%Dif.)	0.0	0.0	0.0	0.0	0.0	0.0
Exports (%Dif.)	0.1	0.2	0.3	0.4	0.6	0.8
Import (%Dif.)	0.0	0.1	0.1	0.1	0.2	0.2
Current Account ($b.)	0.2	0.5	0.9	1.3	1.9	2.6
World:						
World Exports	1.6	4.6	9.1	14.4	22.4	32.1
Percent Difference	0.1	0.2	0.3	0.4	0.6	0.7
World GNP	5.1	10.5	15.4	17.1	22.3	27.1
Percent Difference	0.1	0.2	0.2	0.3	0.3	0.4
World Exp. Pr. (%Dif.)	0.0	0.0	0.0	0.0	0.0	0.0
Canada:						
Interest Rate (%)	-0.5	-0.5	-0.5	-0.5	-0.5	-0.5
Gross Natl. Prod. (%Dif.)	0.1	0.2	0.4	0.6	1.1	1.7

Notes: Figures are absolute and percent differences from the baseline simulation. Unless otherwise indicated, U.S. figures are in billions of 1972 dollars, Japanese figures are in billions of 1980 yen, and world figures are in billions of 1970 dollars.

Table 6.5
100 Basis Point Reduction in Japanese Interest Rates

	1988	1989	1990	1991	1992	1993
Japan:						
Bank Lending Rate (%)	-1.0	-1.0	-1.0	-1.0	-1.0	-1.0
Gross National Expend.	1253.0	2050.0	2745.0	2682.0	3053.0	3518.0
Percent Difference	0.4	0.6	0.8	0.7	0.8	0.9
Pers. Cons. Defl. (%Dif.)	0.0	0.1	0.2	0.2	0.2	0.2
Exports (%Dif.)	-0.3	-0.6	-0.7	-0.6	-0.4	-0.2
Import (%Dif.)	0.3	0.5	0.6	0.6	0.6	0.6
Current Account ($b)	-0.4	-0.9	-1.5	-1.9	-2.3	-2.8
United States:						
3-Mo. CD Rate (%)	0.00	0.01	0.03	0.04	0.04	0.04
Gross National Product	0.4	1.1	1.7	1.9	1.7	1.2
Percent Difference	0.0	0.1	0.1	0.1	0.1	0.1
Consumer Prices (%Dif.)	0.0	0.0	0.1	0.1	0.1	0.1
Exports (%Dif.)	0.1	0.1	0.1	0.0	0.0	0.0
Import (%Dif.)	-0.1	-0.2	-0.2	-0.2	-0.2	-0.1
Current Account ($b)	0.0	0.2	0.7	1.3	1.7	1.9
World:						
World Exports	2.2	3.8	4.0	2.8	2.5	2.5
Percent Difference	0.1	0.1	0.1	0.1	0.1	0.1
World GNP	2.3	4.2	5.7	5.6	5.9	6.1
Percent Difference	0.0	0.1	0.1	0.1	0.1	0.1
World Exp. Pr. (%Dif.)	0.1	0.2	0.2	0.1	0.1	0.1
Canada:						
Interest Rate (%)	0.00	0.01	0.01	0.02	0.02	0.02
Gross Natl. Prod. (%Dif.)	0.0	0.0	0.0	0.0	0.0	0.0

Notes: Figures are absolute and percent differences from the baseline simulation. Unless otherwise indicated, U.S. figures are in billions of 1972 dollars, Japanese figures are in billions of 1980 yen, and world figures are in billions of 1970 dollars.

Table 6.6
Increased Productivity in U.S. High-Tech Industries: U.S., Japan, World Macro Summary

	1987	%DIF	1988	%DIF	1989	%DIF	1990	%DIF	1991	%DIF	1992	%DIF
UNITED STATES:												
GNP (72$ billion)	-1.8	-0.1	-1.6	-0.1	-1.1	-0.1	0.6	0.0	2.7	0.1	7.7	0.4
Nominal GNP ($b.)	-8.8	-0.2	-16.0	-0.3	-25.1	-0.5	-32.0	-0.6	-36.3	-0.6	-22.5	-0.4
GNP Deflator	-0.2	-0.1	-0.6	-0.2	-1.2	-0.4	-1.8	-0.6	-2.2	-0.7	-2.3	-0.7
Net Exports (72$b.)	0.3	-1.0	0.6	-3.1	1.3	-5.4	2.1	-10.0	3.1	-11.6	4.0	-13.7
Exports	0.0	0.0	0.2	0.1	0.4	0.3	0.7	0.4	0.9	0.5	1.2	0.6
Imports	-0.2	-0.1	-0.4	-0.2	-0.8	-0.4	-1.3	-0.7	-2.2	-1.0	-2.9	-1.3
Current Account ($b.)	0.6	0.4	1.0	0.7	1.9	1.2	3.0	2.1	5.3	3.5	7.4	4.8
Consumer Prices	-0.4	-0.1	-0.8	-0.2	-1.4	-0.4	-2.0	-0.5	-2.4	-0.6	-2.1	-0.5
Employment (thous.)	-171.0	-0.2	-357.0	-0.3	-524.0	-0.5	-654.0	-0.6	-790.0	-0.7	-713.0	-0.6
Unemployment Rate (%)	0.1	1.9	0.3	4.0	0.4	5.8	0.5	6.2	0.5	8.1	0.5	7.0
3-Month CD Rate (%)	-0.1	-1.1	-0.1	-1.4	-0.2	-1.8	-0.2	-2.1	-0.2	-2.1	0.0	-0.5
M2 ($b.)	-3.5	-0.1	-7.9	-0.3	-12.8	-0.4	-17.2	-0.5	-20.3	-0.6	-16.1	-0.4
Fed. Budget Surplus ($b.)	-2.1	-1.4	-2.6	-1.8	-2.6	-1.5	-1.0	-0.5	0.6	0.3	6.6	3.9
JAPAN:												
GNE (80¥ billion)	-43.8	0.0	-116.0	0.0	-221.6	-0.1	-367.1	-0.1	-568.4	-0.2	-766.8	-0.2
Nominal GNE (¥b.)	-33.3	0.0	-97.0	0.0	-193.0	-0.1	-331.6	-0.1	-527.6	-0.1	-746.4	-0.2
GNE Deflator	0.0	0.0	0.0	0.0	0.0	0.0	0.0	0.0	0.1	0.0	0.1	0.1
Net Exports (80¥b.)	-22.3	-1.0	-61.6	-1.7	-131.5	-4.5	-223.0	-5.6	-346.4	-5.7	-465.7	-5.3
Exports	-25.4	0.0	-63.2	-0.1	-130.3	-0.2	-223.8	-0.4	-356.9	-0.5	-492.2	-0.7
Imports	-3.0	0.0	-1.7	0.0	1.2	0.0	-0.8	0.0	-10.4	0.0	-26.6	0.0
Current Account ($b.)	-0.1	-0.2	-0.2	-0.3	-0.5	-0.6	-0.8	-1.0	-1.3	-1.7	-1.7	-2.5
Consumer Prices	0.0	0.0	0.0	0.0	0.0	0.0	0.0	0.0	0.0	0.0	-0.1	-0.1
Employment (thous.)	-1.1	0.0	-3.1	0.0	-5.8	0.0	-9.4	0.0	-13.8	0.0	-18.0	0.0
Unemployment Rate (%)	0.0	0.0	0.0	0.0	0.0	0.0	0.0	0.1	0.0	0.1	0.0	0.2
Bank Lending Rate (%)	0.0	0.0	0.0	0.0	0.0	0.0	0.0	0.0	0.0	0.0	0.0	0.0
WORLD:												
Nominal Exports ($b.)	-1.0	0.0	-2.8	-0.1	-5.9	-0.2	-10.3	-0.3	-16.3	-0.5	-22.2	-0.6
Industrial Countries	-0.7	0.0	-2.1	-0.1	-4.4	-0.2	-7.8	-0.3	-12.2	-0.5	-16.6	-0.6
Developing Countries	-0.3	-0.1	-0.7	-0.1	-1.4	-0.2	-2.4	-0.4	-3.9	-0.5	-5.3	-0.6
Real Exports (70$b.)	-0.2	0.0	-0.4	0.0	-0.7	-0.1	-1.3	-0.1	-2.2	-0.2	-3.1	-0.3
Gross Natl. Prod. (70$b.)	-1.8	0.0	-2.1	0.0	-2.3	0.0	-1.7	0.0	-1.3	0.0	1.7	0.0

Note: Figures are differences and percent differences from the baseline solution.

Table 6.7
Increased Productivity in U.S. High-Tech Industries: Effects on Industry Real Output, Selected Industries

	1987	%DIF	1988	%DIF	1989	%DIF	1990	%DIF	1991	%DIF	1992	%DIF
UNITED STATES:												
High-Tech Industries												
Electrical Machinery	-0.05	-0.1	0.03	0.1	0.18	0.4	0.44	0.9	0.79	1.5	1.30	2.4
Nonelect. Machinery	-0.04	-0.1	0.04	0.1	0.16	0.3	0.37	0.6	0.64	1.0	1.02	1.4
Instruments	-0.01	-0.1	0.00	0.0	0.03	0.2	0.06	0.4	0.11	0.6	0.18	0.9
Nonauto. Transp. Eq.	-0.03	-0.2	0.00	0.0	0.07	0.3	0.18	0.9	0.33	1.6	0.57	2.7
Chemicals	-0.03	-0.1	-0.01	0.0	0.08	0.2	0.24	0.6	0.51	1.2	0.90	2.1
Misc. Manufactures	-0.01	-0.1	0.00	0.0	0.02	0.3	0.04	0.6	0.07	0.9	0.10	1.4
Selected Other Industries												
Mining	-0.02	-0.1	-0.01	0.0	0.00	0.0	0.02	0.1	0.07	0.3	0.14	0.6
Iron, Steel	-0.04	-0.3	-0.04	-0.3	-0.02	-0.1	0.03	0.3	0.08	0.7	0.19	1.6
Aluminum	0.00	-0.3	0.00	-0.3	0.00	-0.2	0.00	0.0	0.00	0.1	0.00	0.5
Rubber, Plastics	-0.02	-0.2	-0.02	-0.1	-0.01	-0.1	0.01	0.0	0.03	0.2	0.10	0.6
Textiles	-0.02	-0.2	-0.03	-0.2	-0.02	-0.2	-0.01	-0.1	0.00	0.0	0.05	0.4
Contract Construction	-0.15	-0.2	-0.05	-0.1	0.02	0.0	0.13	0.2	0.16	0.3	0.38	0.6
JAPAN:												
Selected Industries												
Natural Textiles	-0.28	0.0	-0.79	-0.1	-1.45	-0.2	-2.26	-0.2	-3.13	-0.3	-3.75	-0.4
Chemical Textiles	-0.09	0.0	-0.25	-0.1	-0.48	-0.1	-0.79	-0.2	-1.17	-0.3	-1.51	-0.3
Industrial Chemicals	-3.80	0.0	-9.00	-0.1	-21.60	-0.1	-45.00	-0.3	-88.10	-0.5	-143.90	-0.8
Iron Products	0.80	0.0	11.86	0.1	32.71	0.4	54.70	0.6	81.59	0.9	104.03	1.0
Metal Products	0.46	0.0	11.60	0.1	36.64	0.2	67.36	0.4	102.85	0.5	139.33	0.7
Nonelect. Machinery	-11.25	0.0	-22.91	-0.1	-39.34	-0.1	-58.29	-0.2	-81.60	-0.2	-92.80	-0.2
Electr. Machinery	-11.00	0.0	-42.30	-0.1	-98.80	-0.2	-186.30	-0.3	-305.20	-0.5	-443.20	-0.7
Automobiles	-9.98	0.0	-22.82	-0.1	-39.52	-0.1	-56.70	-0.2	-78.80	-0.2	-88.07	-0.2
Oth. Transportation	-4.73	-0.1	-11.42	-0.3	-20.13	-0.5	-32.79	-0.8	-49.61	-1.1	-70.93	-1.4
Wholesale, Retail	-3.89	0.0	-10.44	-0.1	-18.94	0.0	-29.75	0.0	-43.75	-0.1	-56.19	-0.1

Notes: Figures are differences and percent differences from the baseline solution. U.S. figures are in billions of 1972 dollars; Japan figures are in billions of 1980 yen.

Table 6.8

Increased Productivity in U.S. High-Tech Industries, Monetary and Fiscal Offset: U.S., Japan, World Macro Summary

	1987	1988	%DIF	1989	%DIF	1990	%DIF	1991	%DIF	1992	%DIF
UNITED STATES:											
GNP (72$ billion)	12.2	12.2	0.6	13.1	0.7	13.6	0.7	12.4	0.6	14.8	0.7
Nominal GNP ($b.)	27.5	34.8	0.7	47.8	0.9	60.2	1.1	62.6	1.0	80.5	1.3
GNP Deflator	-0.2	0.2	0.1	0.6	0.2	1.1	0.4	1.3	0.4	1.7	0.5
Govt. Purchases G&S	5.4	5.4	1.6	5.4	1.6	5.4	1.5	5.4	1.5	5.4	1.4
Real Net Exports ($b.)	-0.6	-0.7	-3.4	-0.8	-3.5	-0.9	-4.2	-0.7	-2.6	-0.8	-2.7
Real Exports	0.2	0.4	0.2	0.5	0.3	0.7	0.4	0.8	0.5	1.0	0.5
Real Imports	0.9	1.1	0.6	1.4	0.7	1.6	0.8	1.5	0.7	1.8	0.8
Current Account ($b.)	-3.3	-4.1	-2.8	-5.0	-3.3	-5.5	-3.9	-5.2	-3.4	-6.1	-3.9
Consumer Prices	-0.2	0.4	1.0	1.1	0.3	1.7	0.4	2.1	0.5	3.0	0.7
Employment (thous.)	232.0	183.0	0.2	121.0	0.1	42.0	0.0	-118.0	-0.1	-100.0	-0.1
Unemployment Rate (%)	-0.2	-0.2	-2.5	-0.1	-1.5	0.0	-0.1	0.1	2.1	0.0	2.1
3-Month CD Rate (%)	0.0	0.0	0.0	0.0	0.0	0.0	0.0	0.0	0.0	0.0	0.0
M2($b.)	13.5	19.8	0.7	26.5	0.8	33.9	1.0	37.4	1.0	45.0	1.2
Fed. Budget Surplus ($b.)	-7.2	-7.1	-4.8	-6.4	-3.7	-6.7	-3.3	-8.1	-4.7	-5.3	-3.2
JAPAN:											
GNE (80¥ billion)	185.1	265.1	0.1	267.9	0.1	242.1	0.1	168.8	0.0	167.4	0.0
Nominal GNE (¥b.)	154.3	280.6	0.1	345.6	0.1	380.5	0.1	373.3	0.1	410.2	0.1
GNE Deflator	0.0	0.0	0.0	0.0	0.0	0.0	0.0	0.1	0.1	0.1	0.1
Real Net Exports (80¥b.)	59.3	54.1	1.5	43.7	1.5	27.4	0.7	-24.5	-0.4	-51.2	-0.6
Real Exports	100.0	120.2	0.2	132.5	0.2	131.1	0.2	95.5	0.1	93.1	0.1
Real Imports	40.7	66.1	0.1	88.8	0.2	103.7	0.2	120.0	0.2	144.2	0.2
Current Account ($b.)	0.5	0.7	0.9	0.8	1.1	0.9	1.2	0.7	1.0	0.8	1.1
Consumer Prices	0.0	0.0	0.0	0.0	0.0	0.0	0.0	0.0	0.0	0.0	0.0
Employment (thous.)	4.1	8.8	0.0	12.3	0.0	14.8	0.0	16.0	0.0	18.0	0.0
Unemployment Rate (%)	0.0	0.0	-0.1	0.0	-0.1	0.0	-0.1	0.0	0.0	0.0	0.0
Bank Lending Rate (%)	0.0	0.0	0.0	0.0	0.0	0.0	0.0	0.0	0.0	0.0	0.0
WORLD:											
Nominal Exports ($b.)	3.4	4.7	0.2	5.9	0.2	7.0	0.2	6.9	0.2	8.1	0.2
Real Exports (70$b.)	1.2	1.6	0.2	2.1	0.2	2.4	0.3	2.6	0.3	3.0	0.3
Gross Natl. Prod. (70$b.)	12.0	12.1	0.2	13.6	0.2	14.3	0.2	13.3	0.2	15.7	0.2

Note: Figures are differences and percent differences from the baseline solution.

Table 6.9

Increased Productivity in U.S. High-Tech Industries, Monetary and Fiscal Offset: Effects on Industry Real Output, Selected Industries

	1987	1988	%DIF	1989	%DIF	1990	%DIF	1991	%DIF	1992	%DIF
UNITED STATES:											
High-Tech Industries											
Electrical Machinery	0.94	1.03	2.1	1.23	2.4	1.43	2.8	1.61	3.0	1.98	3.6
Nonelect. Machinery	0.63	0.69	1.1	0.84	1.4	0.96	1.6	1.05	1.6	1.28	1.8
Instruments	0.17	0.19	1.2	0.22	1.3	0.24	1.4	0.25	1.4	0.29	1.6
Nonauto. Transp. Eq.	0.81	0.73	2.5	0.73	2.6	0.72	2.6	0.70	2.5	0.81	2.8
Chemicals	0.25	0.30	0.8	0.39	1.0	0.50	1.3	0.64	1.5	0.92	2.2
Misc. Manufactures	0.05	0.07	1.0	0.09	1.3	0.10	1.4	0.10	1.4	0.12	1.6
Selected Other Industries											
Iron, Steel	0.29	0.25	1.9	0.24	1.9	0.20	1.8	0.14	1.2	0.17	1.4
Aluminum	0.02	0.01	1.1	0.00	0.4	-0.01	-0.9	-0.02	-3.0	-0.04	-4.6
Oth. Nonfer. Metal	0.17	0.09	0.6	0.01	0.1	-0.14	-0.9	-0.39	-2.7	-0.65	-4.4
Rubber, Plastics	0.13	0.13	0.8	0.15	0.9	0.15	1.0	0.14	0.8	0.17	1.0
Textiles	0.11	0.10	0.8	0.11	0.9	0.11	0.9	0.08	0.7	0.11	0.9
Petr., Coal Refining	0.06	0.06	0.7	0.07	0.9	0.08	1.0	0.08	1.0	0.11	1.2
Services	0.83	1.01	0.4	1.26	0.5	1.43	0.5	1.41	0.5	1.62	0.6
Wholesale, Retail	1.62	1.72	0.5	2.06	0.6	2.20	0.6	1.96	0.6	2.41	0.7
JAPAN:											
Selected Industries											
Natural Textiles	0.56	0.64	0.1	0.42	0.0	0.21	0.0	-0.16	0.0	-0.20	0.0
Chemical Textiles	0.25	0.29	0.1	0.31	0.1	0.26	0.1	0.16	0.0	0.16	0.0
Industrial Chemicals	13.01	3.61	0.0	5.66	0.0	-21.54	-0.1	53.95	-0.3	-90.78	-0.5
Coal Products	5.47	7.36	0.3	11.65	0.5	13.23	0.5	16.49	0.7	19.15	0.7
Iron Products	29.45	43.70	0.5	71.18	0.8	83.57	0.9	105.28	1.1	122.86	1.2
Metal Products	32.61	61.02	0.3	90.54	0.5	120.96	0.6	149.54	0.8	183.54	0.9
Oth. Nonfer. Metal	7.02	16.50	0.2	23.71	0.3	33.79	0.5	51.16	0.7	79.00	1.0
Nonelect. Machinery	46.57	50.81	0.2	60.18	0.2	64.86	0.2	60.13	0.2	79.50	0.2
Electr. Machinery	20.40	16.10	0.0	-15.50	0.0	-65.10	-0.1	136.20	-0.2	-208.50	-0.3
Automobiles	28.80	38.32	0.1	41.81	0.1	44.87	0.1	45.36	0.1	63.12	0.2
Oth. Transportation	47.85	84.01	2.3	99.79	2.5	107.57	2.5	103.11	2.2	113.68	2.2
Instruments	7.51	10.83	0.2	14.06	0.3	15.49	0.3	16.63	0.3	20.42	0.4
Wholesale, Retail	18.91	32.25	0.0	37.50	0.1	41.88	0.1	41.94	0.1	49.06	0.1

Notes: Figures are differences and percent differences from the baseline solution. U.S. figures are in billions of 1972 dollars; Japan figures are in billions of 1980 yen.

Table 6.10
U.S.–Japan-LINK Long-Term Baseline: U.S. Macro Summary

	1988	%CHG	1989	%CHG	1990	%CHG	1991	%CHG	1992	%CHG	1993	%CHG	AVE %CHG 1988-1993
							Selected Economic Indicators						
GNP (72$ billion)	1851.1	3.7	1884.0	1.8	1914.1	1.6	1968.5	2.8	2019.0	2.6	2066.2	2.3	2.5
Nominal GNP ($b.)	4845.9	8.5	5206.0	7.4	5586.6	7.3	5983.0	7.1	6343.7	6.0	6731.0	6.1	7.1
GNP Deflator	261.8	4.6	276.3	5.6	291.9	5.6	303.9	4.1	314.2	3.4	325.8	3.7	4.5
Consumer Prices	368.4	5.1	389.3	5.7	411.3	5.7	428.4	4.1	443.6	3.5	460.8	3.9	4.7
Employment (mil.)	113.1	1.9	114.6	1.3	114.9	0.2	117.3	2.1	118.3	0.9	119.2	0.8	1.2
Unemployment Rate (%)	6.6	-4.5	6.6	0.7	7.7	16.1	7.0	-8.3	7.3	3.3	7.6	5.1	7.1 *
3-Month CD Rate (%)	9.3	13.2	10.3	10.4	8.8	14.0	6.9	21.4	6.2	11.3	5.8	-6.2	7.9 *
M2 ($b.)	2988.1	6.1	3189.0	6.7	3409.7	6.9	3651.8	7.1	3872.1	6.0	4091.1	5.7	6.4
Federal Surplus ($b.)	-151.1	-2.5	-156.3	-3.5	-172.0	10.1	-117.7	31.6	-97.5	17.2	-92.2	5.5	-131.1 *
W. Ave. $ Exch. Rate	96.1	6.5	99.7	3.8	102.0	2.3	101.6	-0.4	101.2	-0.4	100.8	-0.4	1.9
Current Account ($b.)	-150.2	-2.5	-145.1	3.4	-133.1	8.3	-143.3	-7.7	-154.3	-7.7	-156.1	-1.1	-147.0 *
						Real Gross National Product by Category (72$ billion)							
Personal Consumption	1200.6	3.4	1229.0	2.4	1261.1	2.6	1281.4	1.6	1306.2	1.9	1333.5	2.1	2.3
Business Investment	250.8	3.9	255.7	1.9	252.6	-1.2	267.4	5.9	285.1	6.6	297.1	4.2	3.6
Residential Investment	71.0	4.9	62.7	11.7	62.4	-0.4	64.7	3.6	67.0	3.6	66.2	-1.2	3.7
Change in Bus. Inventories	15.2	10.6	12.6	17.0	0.6	95.2	14.3	99.9	14.2	-0.7	15.4	8.4	38.4
Net Exports, Goods and Srvcs.	-20.6	19.9	-18.5	10.3	-13.8	25.5	-19.6	42.1	-23.1	17.6	-24.7	-7.3	-20.1 *
Exports	167.0	6.3	173.2	3.7	182.2	5.1	188.0	3.2	197.2	4.9	205.0	3.9	4.5
Imports	187.7	2.6	191.8	2.2	196.0	2.2	207.6	5.9	220.3	6.1	229.7	4.3	3.9
Government Purchases	334.2	2.2	342.6	2.5	351.2	2.5	360.4	2.6	369.6	2.5	378.7	2.5	2.5

	1994	%CHG	1995	%CHG	1996	%CHG	1997	%CHG	1998	%CHG	1999	%CHG	AVE %CHG 1994-1999
					Selected Economic Indicators								
GNP (72$ billion)	2126.8	2.9	2181.6	2.6	2250.1	3.1	2302.0	2.3	2368.9	2.9	2446.4	3.3	2.9
Nominal GNP ($b.)	7164.2	6.4	7639.2	6.6	8191.5	7.2	8723.1	6.5	9322.1	6.9	9948.0	6.7	6.7
GNP Deflator	336.9	3.4	350.2	3.9	364.0	4.0	378.9	4.1	393.5	3.8	406.6	3.3	3.8
Consumer Prices	477.2	3.6	497.1	4.2	517.3	4.1	538.6	4.1	559.8	3.9	579.8	3.6	3.9
Employment (mil.)	120.4	1.0	121.5	0.9	123.1	1.3	124.0	0.8	124.9	0.7	125.7	0.7	0.9
Unemployment Rate (%)	7.7	1.1	7.8	1.8	7.7	-2.3	8.0	4.1	8.4	5.7	8.9	5.9	8.1 *
3-Month CD Rate (%)	5.7	-1.7	5.7	1.1	5.8	1.5	5.6	-3.0	5.5	-2.2	5.4	-1.8	5.6 *
M2 ($b.)	4334.5	6.0	4576.9	5.6	4867.0	6.3	5136.9	5.5	5445.7	6.0	5802.2	6.5	6.0
Federal Surplus ($b.)	-81.7	11.3	-77.5	5.2	-64.6	16.6	-70.8	-9.5	-76.1	-7.5	-85.9	12.9	-76.1 *
W. Ave. $ Exch. Rate	100.4	-0.4	100.0	-0.4	99.6	-0.4	99.2	-0.4	98.8	-0.4	98.4	-0.4	-0.4
Current Account ($b.)	-161.1	-3.2	-164.7	-2.3	-168.2	-2.1	-166.8	0.8	-166.9	0.0	-157.9	5.4	-164.3 *
					Real Gross National Product by Category (72$ billion)								
Personal Consumption	1366.7	2.5	1399.0	2.4	1438.6	2.8	1473.3	2.4	1513.4	2.7	1557.5	2.9	2.6
Business Investment	310.8	4.6	323.7	4.1	340.1	5.1	353.8	4.0	368.3	4.1	382.0	3.7	4.3
Residential Investment	72.0	8.7	73.4	2.0	77.6	5.6	74.1	-4.4	79.0	6.6	87.2	10.4	4.8
Change in Bus. Inventories	16.0	4.2	17.0	6.4	18.4	7.9	18.1	-1.4	19.2	6.1	21.8	13.4	6.1
Net Exports, Goods and Srvcs.	-26.8	-8.4	-28.9	-7.7	-31.6	-9.5	-34.4	-8.7	-38.3	11.4	-40.1	-4.7	-33.3 *
Exports	213.1	4.0	221.0	3.7	228.5	3.4	235.7	3.2	242.5	2.8	250.4	3.3	3.4
Imports	239.9	4.4	249.9	4.2	260.1	4.1	270.1	3.9	280.7	3.9	290.5	3.5	4.0
Government Purchases	388.1	2.5	397.4	2.4	407.1	2.5	417.1	2.5	427.4	2.5	437.9	2.5	2.5

Notes: Figures are long-term baseline values in billions of 1972 dollars and annual growth rates, unless otherwise noted.

* Average level of indicated series.

Table 6.11

U.S.-Japan-LINK Long-Term Baseline: U.S. Gross Output by Industry

	1988		1993		AVE %CHG 1988-1993	1999		AVE %CHG 1994-1999
	LEVEL	%CHG	LEVEL	%CHG		LEVEL	%CHG	
Agric., For., Fish.	113.5	4.4	115.6	0.9	1.1	124.0	0.8	1.2
Metal Mining	4.6	3.0	4.7	3.9	0.9	5.6	3.1	3.0
Coal Mining	8.1	3.2	8.3	1.7	0.9	11.5	8.0	5.7
Oil Extraction	11.9	-1.4	10.8	-2.1	-1.8	9.9	-1.3	-1.5
Natural Gas Extract.	3.3	-1.1	3.1	-1.1	-1.1	2.9	-1.1	-1.1
Nonmetal Mining	4.6	2.5	4.6	1.5	0.3	5.1	2.4	1.9
Resid. Construction	56.8	5.3	53.5	-1.0	4.1	71.9	10.7	5.2
Nonres. Construction	52.5	2.7	58.0	2.2	2.2	68.3	2.4	2.8
Other Construction	40.1	4.0	45.7	3.3	2.9	55.5	2.9	3.3
Food and Beverages	136.2	2.3	148.2	1.4	1.8	163.8	1.7	1.7
Tobacco	6.5	1.6	6.0	-0.2	-0.9	5.8	-0.7	-0.5
Textiles	41.3	4.5	41.6	1.2	0.9	48.0	3.3	2.4
Apparel	26.1	4.3	27.3	0.7	1.5	30.5	2.6	1.9
Paper, Pulp	49.5	3.6	54.3	2.0	2.1	62.2	2.7	2.3
Printing, Publish.	46.2	3.0	51.0	1.7	2.2	58.1	2.4	2.2
Industrial Chemicals	23.2	2.9	24.6	2.2	1.5	27.7	2.4	2.0
Nonind. Chemicals	81.3	4.4	91.6	2.2	2.7	103.4	2.4	2.0
Petr., Coal Refining	33.4	2.5	34.6	0.5	1.0	35.8	0.7	0.5
Rubber, Plastics	33.8	4.6	38.0	2.5	2.8	45.7	3.6	3.1
Leather	4.2	2.3	3.9	-1.1	-0.8	4.0	2.0	0.4
Lumber, Wood Prod.	31.5	7.1	32.7	1.1	1.8	41.1	6.7	3.9
Furniture	14.9	3.7	16.6	2.4	2.5	20.5	4.7	3.6
Cement	1.5	4.4	1.6	1.4	1.7	1.8	3.3	2.0
Oth. Stone, Clay, Gl.	23.0	4.9	24.6	1.1	2.0	28.3	3.7	2.3
Iron, Steel	30.3	-0.3	26.6	0.7	-2.1	29.4	2.6	1.6
Aluminum	2.4	8.8	2.2	1.2	0.3	2.3	3.9	0.5
Oth. Nonfer. Metal	46.3	1.9	44.1	0.9	-0.4	44.7	-0.3	0.3
Fabr. Metal Products	68.3	4.3	74.7	2.3	2.2	87.6	3.3	2.7
Nonelect. Machinery	129.7	5.9	165.0	5.3	5.1	239.6	8.4	6.4

Electrical Machinery	104.2	5.8	120.6	2.4	3.4	141.6	3.6	2.7
Aircraft	25.0	0.4	24.8	3.7	-0.1	29.7	3.9	3.1
Oth. Transp. Equip.	25.9	3.5	27.0	1.9	1.3	30.7	2.5	2.2
Motor Vehicles	101.0	6.3	101.1	1.8	1.1	116.9	2.2	2.5
Instruments	31.4	4.9	37.8	3.2	3.9	45.5	3.2	3.1
Misc. Manufactures	15.6	4.4	17.7	3.4	2.9	22.6	4.7	4.2
Rail Transportation	14.8	6.1	16.2	2.7	2.6	19.6	3.6	3.2
Passenger Transport.	4.4	3.0	4.8	1.7	1.8	5.5	2.4	2.2
Truck Transport.	41.8	4.7	47.1	2.5	2.8	56.0	3.1	2.9
Water Transport.	7.3	2.3	7.5	1.0	1.0	7.7	0.5	0.5
Air Transport.	22.0	5.0	26.2	3.2	3.8	32.3	3.6	3.6
Pipeline Transport.	2.1	2.2	2.1	0.2	0.6	2.2	0.6	0.5
Transport. Services	3.2	2.9	3.5	2.0	2.1	4.0	2.4	2.3
Communications	98.7	5.5	121.7	3.8	4.5	162.0	5.2	4.9
Electrical Utilities	49.6	3.3	54.5	2.0	2.2	63.0	2.3	2.5
Water, Sewer	14.4	3.6	16.3	2.1	2.7	18.7	2.2	2.4
Wholesale, Retail	454.7	3.3	501.3	1.9	2.2	574.3	2.5	2.3
Fin., Ins., Real Estate	433.9	3.0	500.3	2.9	2.9	599.9	3.2	3.1
Oth. Nonmed. Servs.	300.1	3.3	337.6	2.3	2.6	394.9	2.8	2.6
Medical Services	103.3	3.7	120.9	2.5	3.3	143.1	3.0	2.9
Federal Enterprise	15.2	3.5	16.8	1.9	2.3	19.1	2.2	2.1
St., Local Enterprise	15.9	3.7	18.1	2.3	2.8	20.9	2.5	2.5
Manufacture Total	1132.7	4.2	1238.3	2.3	2.2	1467.4	3.6	2.9

Notes: Figures are long-term baseline values in billions of 1972 dollars and annual growth rates. Includes indirect business taxes.

Table 6.12
U.S.-Japan-LINK Long-Term Baseline: Japan Macro Summary

	1988	%CHG	1989	%CHG	1990	%CHG	1991	%CHG	1992	%CHG	1993	%CHG	AVE %CHG 1988-1993
	Selected Economic Indicators												
GNE (80¥ billion)	323549.0	5.1	336068.0	3.9	347868.0	3.5	361985.0	4.1	378663.0	4.6	398269.0	5.2	4.4
Nominal GNE (¥b.)	346567.0	5.7	365912.0	5.6	384547.0	5.1	405458.0	5.4	428933.0	5.8	456593.0	6.4	5.7
GNE Deflator	116.5	1.4	119.1	2.2	121.4	1.9	123.4	1.7	125.2	1.5	127.6	1.9	1.8
Pers. Cons. Deflator	106.4	0.2	108.5	2.0	110.7	2.0	113.2	2.3	115.7	2.1	119.0	2.9	1.9
Employment (mil.)	58.2	0.6	58.6	0.8	59.0	0.6	59.3	0.6	59.8	0.7	60.4	1.0	0.7
Unemployment Rate (%)	2.8	0.8	2.8	1.0	2.8	1.5	2.9	1.5	2.9	1.2	2.9	0.9	2.8 *
Bank Lending Rate (%)	5.8	0.1	5.9	1.1	5.9	0.3	5.9	-0.2	5.8	-0.2	5.9	0.2	5.8 *
Govt. Surplus (¥b.)	23067.0	13.7	24498.0	-6.2	26175.0	-6.8	28105.0	-7.4	29915.0	-6.4	31441.0	-5.1	27200.2 *
Current Account ($b.)	76.7	47.3	75.7	-1.3	69.7	-8.0	61.9	11.1	56.3	-9.1	41.2	26.8	63.6 *
¥/$ Exchange Rate	128.8	11.0	123.8	-3.9	121.4	-2.0	121.5	0.1	121.8	0.3	121.8	0.0	0.9
	Real Gross National Product by Category (80¥ billion)												
Private Consumption	182868.0	4.3	189952.0	3.9	196742.0	3.6	203485.0	3.4	210468.0	3.4	217547.0	3.4	3.7
Nonprofit Consumption	1649.0	0.3	1655.0	0.3	1660.0	0.3	1666.0	0.3	1671.0	0.3	1677.0	0.3	0.3
Government Consumption	29672.0	3.0	30562.0	3.0	31479.0	3.0	32423.0	3.0	33396.0	3.0	34398.0	3.0	3.0
Business Investment	48908.0	3.8	51842.0	6.0	54329.0	4.8	57532.0	5.9	61568.0	7.0	67666.0	9.9	6.2
Residential Investment	23624.0	4.9	24098.0	2.0	24078.0	-0.1	24348.0	1.1	24960.0	2.5	25605.0	2.6	2.2
Government Investment	30569.0	11.8	31990.0	4.6	33467.0	4.6	35003.0	4.6	36600.0	4.6	38262.0	4.5	5.8
Priv. Inventory Invest.	2873.0	11.8	2939.0	2.3	2701.0	-8.1	2927.0	8.4	3574.0	22.1	4335.0	21.3	9.6
Govt. Inventory Invest.	306.0	0.0	306.0	0.0	306.0	0.0	306.0	0.0	306.0	0.0	306.0	0.0	0.0
Net Exports	3080.0	43.0	2725.0	11.5	3108.0	14.0	4296.0	38.2	6121.0	42.5	8474.0	38.4	4634.0 *
Exports	56755.0	9.0	59959.0	5.6	62395.0	4.1	65459.0	4.9	69526.0	6.2	74561.0	7.2	6.2
Imports	53675.0	7.5	57234.0	6.6	59287.0	3.6	61163.0	3.2	63404.0	3.7	66087.0	4.2	4.8

	1994	%CHG	1995	%CHG	1996	%CHG	1997	%CHG	1998	%CHG	1999	%CHG	AVE %CHG 1994-1999
Selected Economic Indicators													
GNE (80¥ billion)	416558.0	4.6	435313.0	4.5	457407.0	5.1	482723.0	5.5	500906.0	3.8	521527.0	4.1	4.6
Nominal GNE (¥b.)	486994.0	6.7	520891.0	7.0	556132.0	6.8	594243.0	6.9	626898.0	5.5	661233.0	5.5	6.4
GNE Deflator	130.6	2.3	135.4	3.7	137.5	1.6	139.4	1.4	142.5	2.2	144.7	1.5	2.1
Pers. Cons. Deflator	122.5	2.9	126.7	3.4	129.9	2.6	133.0	2.4	136.6	2.7	139.9	2.4	2.7
Employment (mil.)	61.0	1.0	61.8	1.3	62.6	1.3	63.6	1.5	64.4	1.4	65.4	1.5	1.3
Unemployment Rate (%)	3.0	1.5	3.0	2.0	3.1	2.1	3.2	2.1	3.3	3.5	3.4	4.0	3.2 *
Bank Lending Rate (%)	5.9	0.5	5.9	1.0	5.9	-0.3	5.9	-1.1	5.9	0.4	5.9	0.1	5.9 *
Govt. Surplus (¥b.)	33041.0	-5.1	34125.0	-3.3	35535.0	-4.1	36374.0	-2.4	38084.0	-4.7	40080.0	-5.2	36206.5 *
Current Account ($b.)	44.3	7.7	48.6	9.6	51.7	6.3	51.5	-0.3	54.1	5.1	60.1	11.1	51.7 *
¥/$ Exchange Rate	121.8	0.0	121.8	0.0	121.8	0.0	121.8	0.0	121.8	0.0	121.8	0.0	0.0
Real Gross National Product by Category (80¥ billion)													
Private Consumption	224775.0	3.3	231986.0	3.2	239651.0	3.3	248036.0	3.5	255726.0	3.1	263187.0	2.9	3.2
Nonprofit Consumption	1682.0	0.3	1687.0	0.3	1693.0	0.3	1698.0	0.3	1704.0	0.3	1709.0	0.3	0.3
Government Consumption	35429.0	3.0	36492.0	3.0	37587.0	3.0	38715.0	3.0	39876.0	3.0	41072.0	3.0	3.0
Business Investment	72601.0	7.3	77777.0	7.1	84993.0	9.3	93903.0	10.5	97732.0	4.1	102954.0	5.3	7.3
Residential Investment	26239.0	2.5	26741.0	1.9	27523.0	2.9	28840.0	4.8	29400.0	1.9	29346.0	-0.2	2.3
Government Investment	39989.0	4.5	41786.0	4.5	43655.0	4.5	45599.0	4.5	47620.0	4.4	49723.0	4.4	4.5
Priv. Inventory Invest.	4516.0	4.2	4661.0	3.2	5161.0	10.7	5940.0	15.1	5184.0	12.7	5373.0	3.6	8.3
Govt. Inventory Invest.	306.0	0.0	306.0	0.0	306.0	0.0	306.0	0.0	306.0	0.0	306.0	0.0	0.0
Net Exports	11019.0	30.0	13875.0	25.9	16838.0	21.3	19686.0	16.9	23357.0	18.6	27857.0	19.3	18772.0 *
Exports	79588.0	6.7	85310.0	7.2	91357.0	7.1	97886.0	7.1	104520.0	6.8	111894.0	7.1	7.0
Imports	68569.0	3.8	71435.0	4.2	74519.0	4.3	78199.0	4.9	81163.0	3.8	84037.0	3.5	4.1

Note: Figures are long-term baseline values in billions of 1980 yen and annual growth rates, unless otherwise noted.

*Average level of indicated series.

Table 6.13

U.S.-Japan-LINK Long-Term Baseline: Japanese Real Output by Industry

	1988		1993		AVE %CHG	1999		AVE %CHG
	LEVEL	%CHG	LEVEL	%CHG	1988-1993	LEVEL	%CHG	1994-1999
General Crops	8787.9	-0.4	7849.1	-1.3	-1.9	6828.9	-0.9	-2.3
Industrial Crops	584.8	4.8	699.9	3.1	3.9	838.4	3.2	3.1
Livestock, Textiles	0.4	-8.4	0.2	-8.4	-8.4	0.1	-8.4	-8.4
Livestock	4465.8	1.4	4676.1	4.0	1.0	5262.4	1.9	2.0
Forestry	1428.9	-2.9	1269.1	-2.2	-2.5	1092.1	-2.7	-2.5
Fisheries	2970.9	-0.5	3069.2	1.2	0.5	3085.1	0.2	0.1
Coal Mining	272.9	7.2	259.4	-0.9	0.4	251.3	-0.6	-0.5
Iron Ores	1.1	10.2	0.6	10.2	10.2	0.3	10.2	10.2
Nonfer. Metal Ore	97.4	-4.4	77.8	-4.4	-4.4	59.3	-4.4	-4.4
Crude Petroleum	18.0	-3.7	14.9	-3.7	-3.7	11.9	-3.7	-3.7
Natural Gas	74.3	0.0	74.3	0.0	0.0	74.3	0.0	0.0
Other Mining	2103.1	5.7	2413.0	-0.1	3.3	3123.1	3.6	4.4
Meat, Dairy	5483.3	2.5	5839.1	4.9	1.5	6903.9	2.5	2.8
Grain Products	4007.9	-0.8	3822.8	-0.6	-0.9	3781.8	-0.6	-0.2
Manuf. Sea Food	2992.2	1.2	3385.0	2.4	2.3	3720.2	1.4	1.6
Other Foods	11942.0	0.9	12948.0	3.2	1.6	13421.0	1.3	0.6
Beverages	5288.4	7.7	5890.5	1.8	3.1	6658.1	1.8	2.1
Tobacco	2760.8	4.8	2888.4	0.4	1.6	3037.7	0.7	0.8
Natural Textiles	868.3	-1.0	978.2	3.5	1.9	1116.6	2.3	2.3
Chemical Textiles	391.4	-1.1	435.5	3.8	1.6	534.8	4.0	3.5
Other Textiles	6253.4	-0.8	6977.4	3.3	1.7	7958.9	2.4	2.2
Wearing Apparel	6020.6	3.3	7138.5	4.4	3.5	8585.9	2.6	3.1
Wood Products	5595.2	6.1	6874.3	6.8	4.5	8883.0	3.1	4.4
Furniture	3820.4	2.8	4390.8	3.8	2.8	5275.9	2.6	3.1
Pulp, Paper	7920.1	2.0	8652.3	4.5	1.9	9710.3	1.8	2.0
Print., Publish.	7876.4	2.3	8434.9	3.3	1.6	9668.1	2.0	2.3
Leather Products	526.1	1.1	561.2	1.0	1.3	548.4	-0.4	-0.4
Rubber Products	2585.2	1.6	3120.0	3.4	3.5	3331.6	-0.5	1.1
Basic, Int. Chems.	15509.0	4.6	18980.0	6.9	4.2	23604.0	3.8	3.7
Final Chemicals	11007.0	5.0	15031.0	13.6	6.2	19088.0	3.9	4.1
Petroleum Prods.	17500.0	6.5	21606.0	3.3	4.7	27652.0	3.9	4.2

Coal Products	2361.1	11.5	2636.4	3.4	3.8	3109.7	2.3	2.8
Cement	1036.3	7.0	1204.1	-2.9	3.8	1631.0	3.9	5.2
Other Ceramics	8117.0	5.4	8729.1	-6.5	2.2	11348.0	3.6	4.5
Iron Products	9176.6	16.0	9866.5	2.8	3.9	10945.0	0.9	1.8
Roll., Cast., Forg.	17613.0	4.9	19759.0	2.8	2.8	22859.0	2.0	2.5
Aluminum	1444.2	6.9	2014.9	6.9	6.9	3004.8	6.9	6.9
Oth. Nonfer. Met.	7007.2	5.2	8273.9	4.6	3.7	9844.6	1.6	3.0
Metal Products	13996.0	5.2	18128.0	6.5	5.3	24912.0	4.1	5.5
Nonel. Machinery	29626.0	1.8	39593.0	8.4	5.3	58363.0	6.3	6.7
Electr. Machinery	45769.0	10.0	70070.0	10.4	9.1	118835.0	8.3	9.2
Automobiles	26790.0	6.1	35707.0	5.4	6.0	47319.0	4.3	4.8
Aircraft	730.6	7.7	1061.0	7.7	7.7	1660.4	7.7	7.7
Oth. Transp. Equip.	3659.6	4.1	5152.2	7.9	6.6	8272.4	8.1	8.2
Instruments	4410.9	0.4	5513.2	6.6	3.9	7892.5	5.8	6.2
Misc. Manufs.	11625.0	4.5	15430.0	14.1	5.7	18777.0	2.9	3.3
Housing	22005.0	4.9	23881.0	2.5	2.2	27331.0	0.1	2.3
Indus. Construction	20996.0	4.1	26310.0	6.3	4.5	35709.0	4.2	5.2
Public Construction	15629.0	8.5	18679.0	3.8	4.5	23300.0	3.7	3.8
Oth. Construction	15907.0	4.1	19132.0	5.1	3.8	24854.0	3.7	4.5
Electric Power	11140.0	2.1	13220.0	4.6	3.3	16269.0	3.2	3.5
Gas	1465.4	-0.2	1695.7	4.0	2.4	2023.4	2.5	3.0
Water, Sanitary	3868.1	1.3	4190.9	2.2	1.6	4674.4	1.7	1.8
Wholesale, Retail	65810.0	3.3	76724.0	6.3	3.2	93044.0	3.3	3.3
Real Estate	33504.0	4.8	41033.0	4.2	4.3	51438.0	3.4	3.9
Railways	3416.3	0.3	3531.8	1.2	0.6	3681.2	0.5	0.7
Trucks, Buses	10505.0	1.9	11537.0	3.6	1.9	13070.0	1.9	2.1
Oth. Transport.	7437.1	2.4	6587.1	16.5	4.2	7799.9	2.0	2.9
Communications	6425.5	2.0	7238.7	3.6	2.3	8771.7	3.0	3.3
Finance, Insurance	22966.0	4.4	26990.0	3.8	3.5	32629.0	2.9	3.2
Govt. Services	17761.0	1.6	19253.0	1.6	1.6	21227.0	1.6	1.6
Public Services	39102.0	2.9	47336.0	3.8	3.8	59491.0	3.6	3.9
Other Services	50048.0	3.7	58800.0	4.4	3.3	68039.0	2.0	2.5
Unallocated	10172.0	5.8	12670.0	5.4	4.7	16724.0	4.4	4.7
Total	680673.0	4.2	820305.0	5.0	3.9	1042956.4	3.7	4.1

Notes: Figures are long-term baseline values in billions of 1980 yen and annual growth rates.

Table 6.14
U.S.-Japan-LINK Long-Term Baseline: World Trade by Region (f.o.b.)

	1988	%CHG	1989	%CHG	1990	%CHG	1991	%CHG	1992	%CHG	1993	%CHG	AVE %CHG 1988-1993
United States													
Exports	305.3	22.5	342.2	12.1	377.5	10.3	409.5	8.5	442.5	8.1	480.4	8.6	11.7
Imports	444.2	8.1	471.7	6.2	497.0	5.4	551.4	10.9	617.9	12.1	670.8	8.6	8.6
Balance	-138.9		-129.4		-119.5		-141.9		-175.4		-190.4		-149.3
Japan													
Exports	254.8	13.4	279.9	9.9	296.3	5.9	314.0	5.9	337.2	7.4	365.0	8.2	8.5
Imports	145.3	12.4	158.8	9.3	172.2	8.4	186.6	8.4	203.2	8.9	221.7	9.1	9.4
Balance	109.5		121.1		124.1		127.3		134.0		143.3		126.6
Other Industr. Countries													
Exports	1428.4	12.3	1556.0	8.9	1696.0	9.0	1846.6	8.9	2032.5	10.1	2201.9	8.3	9.6
Imports	1404.2	12.8	1550.5	10.4	1710.4	10.3	1855.8	8.5	2031.4	9.5	2195.6	8.1	9.9
Balance	24.2		5.5		-14.4		-9.3		1.1		6.3		2.2
EC													
Exports	1040.9	11.4	1135.4	9.1	1243.0	9.5	1350.8	8.7	1489.1	10.2	1611.9	8.2	9.5
Imports	1025.1	13.0	1136.5	10.9	1257.9	10.7	1372.6	9.1	1512.1	10.2	1641.1	8.5	10.4
Balance	15.8		-1.1		-14.9		-21.8		-23.0		-29.3		-12.4
Developing Countries													
Exports	589.7	12.4	647.9	9.9	711.3	9.8	784.7	10.3	875.5	11.6	945.8	8.0	10.3
Imports	555.5	17.9	614.0	10.5	675.9	10.1	739.5	9.4	818.8	10.7	885.4	8.1	11.1
Balance	34.2		33.9		35.4		45.2		56.8		60.4		44.3
Asia Including China													
Exports	332.4	22.1	367.0	10.4	407.0	10.9	455.8	12.0	516.5	13.3	552.0	6.9	12.6
Imports	319.4	27.2	360.4	12.8	403.3	11.9	450.3	11.7	506.6	12.5	549.2	8.4	14.1
Balance	12.9		6.6		3.7		5.5		9.9		2.8		6.9
Asian NIEs													
Exports	221.6	26.1	242.8	9.5	269.4	11.0	301.8	12.0	342.0	13.3	362.8	6.1	13.0
Imports	197.7	32.8	222.0	12.3	249.3	12.3	280.1	12.4	317.9	13.5	350.3	10.2	15.6
Balance	23.9		20.8		20.2		21.7		24.1		12.4		20.5
CPEs Excluding China													
Exports	220.7	4.6	231.9	5.1	246.7	6.4	263.8	6.9	284.3	7.8	315.4	10.9	7.0
Imports	210.8	5.5	226.1	7.3	244.0	7.9	264.3	8.3	286.5	8.4	321.2	12.1	8.3
Balance	10.0		5.8		2.7		-0.5		-2.2		-5.8		1.7
World Exports	2798.9	12.8	3057.9	9.3	3327.8	8.8	3618.5	8.7	3972.0	9.8	4308.4	8.5	9.7
World Export Price	3.5	5.3	3.7	4.1	3.8	4.3	4.0	3.4	4.1	3.3	4.2	2.9	3.9
World Exports Real (70$b.)	792.1	7.1	831.1	4.9	867.5	4.4	912.2	5.2	969.0	6.2	1021.8	5.5	5.6

	1994	%CHG	1995	%CHG	1996	%CHG	1997	%CHG	1998	%CHG	1999	%CHG	AVE %CHG 1994-1999
United States													
Exports	519.7	8.2	562.2	8.2	608.6	8.2	658.6	8.2	708.4	7.6	766.7	8.2	8.1
Imports	730.7	8.9	791.1	8.3	854.3	8.0	921.3	7.8	989.2	7.4	1055.2	6.7	7.9
Balance	-211.0		-228.9		-245.7		-262.7		-280.8		-288.6		-253.0
Japan													
Exports	394.8	8.2	426.9	8.1	461.4	8.1	498.6	8.1	537.3	7.7	577.9	7.6	8.0
Imports	238.4	7.5	255.9	7.4	274.2	7.1	296.2	8.0	316.4	6.8	335.3	6.0	7.1
Balance	156.4		170.9		187.2		202.4		220.9		242.6		196.7
Other Industr. Countries													
Exports	2374.7	7.8	2561.6	7.9	2760.6	7.8	2978.7	7.9	3188.1	7.0	3432.9	7.7	7.7
Imports	2361.7	7.6	2544.7	7.8	2740.4	7.7	2953.6	7.8	3154.6	6.8	3403.8	7.9	7.6
Balance	13.0		16.9		20.2		25.1		33.5		29.1		23.0
EC													
Exports	1736.5	7.7	1872.6	7.8	2017.9	7.8	2176.8	7.9	2328.3	7.0	2510.8	7.8	7.7
Imports	1767.8	7.7	1908.4	8.0	2058.4	7.9	2221.9	7.9	2368.8	6.6	2553.0	7.8	7.7
Balance	-31.3		-35.8		-40.6		-45.1		-40.6		-42.1		-39.3
Developing Countries													
Exports	1020.1	7.9	1096.5	7.5	1176.5	7.3	1265.0	7.5	1355.1	7.1	1448.2	6.9	7.4
Imports	958.0	8.2	1034.8	8.0	1119.2	8.2	1209.9	8.1	1307.2	8.0	1408.4	7.7	8.0
Balance	62.1		61.8		57.4		55.1		47.9		39.8		54.0
Asia Including China													
Exports	589.7	6.8	629.8	6.8	672.4	6.8	719.4	7.0	766.5	6.6	816.2	6.5	6.8
Imports	596.1	8.5	645.9	8.4	700.4	8.4	759.2	8.4	821.1	8.1	884.2	7.7	8.3
Balance	-6.5		-16.2		-28.1		-39.8		-54.5		-68.0		-35.5
Asian NIEs													
Exports	385.1	6.1	408.8	6.2	434.0	6.2	461.8	6.4	489.5	6.0	518.5	5.9	6.1
Imports	383.5	9.5	419.1	9.3	457.4	9.2	498.0	8.9	539.7	8.4	582.8	8.0	8.9
Balance	1.6		-10.3		-23.4		-36.2		-50.3		-64.3		-30.5
CPEs Excluding China													
Exports	342.6	8.6	371.3	8.3	400.1	7.8	436.0	9.0	473.6	8.6	516.6	9.1	8.6
Imports	349.8	8.9	379.0	8.3	406.6	7.3	443.9	9.2	483.6	8.9	528.6	9.3	8.7
Balance	-7.2		-7.8		-6.5		-7.9		-10.0		-12.0		-8.6
World Exports	4651.9	8.0	5018.4	7.9	5407.1	7.7	5836.9	7.9	6262.5	7.3	6742.2	7.7	7.8
World Export Price	4.3	2.9	4.5	2.7	4.6	2.6	4.7	2.7	4.8	2.8	5.0	2.6	2.7
World Exports Real (70Sb.)	1072.4	5.0	1126.4	5.0	1182.5	5.0	1242.9	5.1	1297.6	4.4	1362.1	5.0	4.9

Notes: Figures are billions of U.S. dollars and growth rates. NIEs are newly industrializing economies; CPE refers to the centrally-planned economies. Statistical Discrepancy omitted.

Table 6.15
U.S.-Japan-LINK Long-Term Baseline: World GNP Growth by Region

	1988	1989	1990	1991	1992	1993	AVE.
U.S.	3.7	1.8	1.6	2.8	2.6	2.3	2.5
Japan	5.1	3.9	3.5	4.1	4.6	5.2	4.4
Other Industr. Countries	4.0	2.9	2.3	2.3	2.7	2.5	2.8
EC	2.9	2.7	2.2	2.5	2.8	2.6	2.6
Developing Countries	5.0	4.8	5.5	5.3	5.8	5.7	5.3
Asia Including China	9.6	7.9	7.4	7.2	7.3	7.0	7.7
Asian NIEs	10.1	6.4	7.1	7.7	9.1	5.8	7.7
Western Hemisphere	-1.1	-0.2	3.0	2.3	4.1	4.2	2.0
CPEs Excluding China	2.5	2.0	2.3	2.4	2.4	2.2	2.3
World Total	3.8	3.1	3.1	3.1	3.4	3.3	3.3

	1994	1995	1996	1997	1998	1999	AVE.
U.S.	2.9	2.6	3.1	2.3	2.9	3.3	2.9
Japan	4.6	4.5	5.1	5.5	3.8	4.1	4.6
Other Industr. Countries	2.1	2.2	2.2	2.3	1.8	1.9	2.1
EC	1.9	1.8	1.8	1.8	1.2	1.3	1.6
Developing Countries	4.9	5.6	5.4	5.5	5.5	5.2	5.4
Asia Including China	6.0	7.3	6.9	6.7	6.6	5.9	6.5
Asian NIEs	6.0	6.5	6.2	6.2	6.2	4.4	5.9
Western Hemisphere	3.7	3.9	3.6	4.0	4.5	4.7	4.1
CPEs Excluding China	2.4	2.5	-2.4	2.1	2.3	2.3	1.5
World Total	3.0	3.2	2.0	3.2	3.1	3.1	2.9

Notes: Figures are annual growth rates of real GNP, 1970 U.S. dollar basis. NIEs are newly industrializing economies; CPE refers to the centrally-planned economies.

Table 6.16
U.S. Investment Tax Credit Increased 5%: U.S., Japan, World Macro Summary

	1988	%DIF	1989	%DIF	1990	%DIF	1991	%DIF	1992	%DIF	1993	%DIF
UNITED STATES:												
GNP (72$ billion)	4.9	0.3	10.1	0.5	12.7	0.7	14.9	0.8	16.1	0.8	16.2	0.8
Bus. Fixed Investment	1.2	0.5	3.0	1.2	4.8	1.9	6.3	2.4	7.6	2.7	8.4	2.9
Nominal GNP ($b.)	13.5	0.3	33.1	0.6	53.8	1.0	79.6	1.3	105.5	1.7	128.1	1.9
Net Exports G&S (72$b.)	-0.3	1.3	-0.8	4.0	-1.4	8.6	-2.1	9.9	-3.0	12.0	-3.8	14.5
Exports	0.0	0.0	0.0	0.0	0.0	0.0	-0.2	-0.1	-0.3	-0.2	-0.5	-0.2
Imports	0.3	0.2	0.9	0.5	1.4	0.7	2.0	1.0	2.6	1.2	3.3	1.5
Current Account ($b.)	-1.4	0.9	-3.3	2.2	-4.8	3.5	-6.5	4.3	-8.3	5.2	-10.0	6.2
Consumer Prices	0.2	0.0	0.6	0.2	1.5	0.4	2.7	0.6	3.9	0.9	5.1	1.1
Employment (thous.)	117.2	0.1	315.8	0.3	498.3	0.4	658.3	0.6	786.7	0.7	860.7	0.7
Unemployment Rate (%)	-0.1	-1.4	-0.2	-3.5	-0.4	-4.8	-0.5	-6.4	-0.5	-7.0	-0.6	-7.0
3-Month CD Rate (%)	0.1	0.5	0.1	1.1	0.2	2.3	0.3	4.5	0.4	6.0	0.3	6.3
Fed. Budget Surplus ($b.)	-5.3	3.4	-10.9	6.5	-9.8	5.4	-8.4	6.4	-9.2	8.2	-11.5	10.7
JAPAN:												
GNE (80¥ billion)	67.0	0.0	191.5	0.1	314.9	0.1	452.9	0.1	616.9	0.2	780.4	0.2
Nominal GNE (¥b.)	44.3	0.0	136.5	0.0	252.7	0.1	390.7	0.1	557.4	0.1	748.0	0.2
Net Exports (80$b.)	26.9	0.9	74.1	2.7	124.9	4.0	199.1	4.7	290.8	4.8	380.4	4.6
Exports	38.6	0.1	103.7	0.2	169.0	0.3	256.5	0.4	362.0	0.5	466.6	0.6
Imports	11.7	0.0	29.6	0.1	44.2	0.1	57.3	0.1	71.2	0.1	86.2	0.1
Current Account ($b.)	0.1	0.2	0.4	0.5	0.6	0.9	0.8	1.3	1.1	1.9	1.3	3.3
Pers. Cons. Deflator	0.0	0.0	0.0	0.0	0.0	0.0	0.0	0.0	0.0	0.0	0.0	0.0
Employment (thous.)	1.4	0.0	5.0	0.0	9.8	0.0	15.4	0.0	21.5	0.0	27.9	0.0
Unemployment Rate (%)	0.0	0.0	0.0	0.0	0.0	-0.1	0.0	-0.1	0.0	-0.1	0.0	-0.2
Bank Lending Rate (%)	0.0	0.0	0.0	0.0	0.0	0.0	0.0	0.0	0.0	0.0	0.0	0.0
WORLD:												
Nominal Exports ($b.)	1.3	0.0	3.7	0.1	6.5	0.2	10.4	0.3	14.9	0.4	19.8	0.5
Industrial Countries	0.8	0.0	2.4	0.1	4.4	0.2	7.2	0.3	10.4	0.4	13.9	0.5
Developing Countries	0.4	0.1	1.2	0.2	1.9	0.3	3.0	0.4	4.2	0.5	5.5	0.6
Real Exports (70$b.)	0.4	0.0	1.0	0.1	1.5	0.2	2.1	0.2	2.8	0.3	3.6	0.3
Gross Nat'l. Prod. (70$b.)	4.9	0.8	10.4	0.2	13.9	0.2	17.1	0.3	19.6	0.3	21.1	0.3

Table 6.16—Continued

	1994	%DIF	1995	%DIF	1996	%DIF	1997	%DIF	1998	%DIF	1999	%DIF
UNITED STATES:												
GNP (72$ billion)	18.1	0.9	19.8	0.9	21.0	0.9	21.8	1.0	21.8	0.9	22.1	0.9
Bus. Fixed Investment	9.2	3.0	9.7	3.0	10.2	3.0	10.6	3.0	11.1	3.0	11.7	3.1
Nominal GNP ($b.)	156.6	2.2	185.9	2.5	217.2	2.7	248.9	2.9	279.4	3.1	310.2	3.2
Net Exports G&S (72$b.)	-4.7	16.9	-5.7	19.0	-6.7	20.5	-7.7	21.8	-9.0	22.8	-10.1	24.7
Exports	-0.6	-0.3	-0.7	-0.3	-0.7	-0.3	-0.8	-0.3	-0.9	-0.4	-0.9	-0.4
Imports	4.1	1.7	5.0	2.0	5.9	2.3	6.9	2.6	8.0	2.9	9.3	3.2
Current Account ($b.)	-12.6	7.5	-15.3	8.9	-18.4	10.5	-21.7	12.4	-25.8	14.7	-29.8	17.8
Consumer Prices	6.3	1.3	7.4	1.5	8.6	1.7	9.8	1.8	11.0	2.0	12.0	2.1
Employment (thous.)	943.5	0.8	1030.6	0.9	1107.7	0.9	1168.1	0.9	1204.2	1.0	1232.8	1.0
Unemployment Rate (%)	-0.6	-7.3	-0.6	-7.6	-0.7	-8.1	-0.7	-7.9	-0.7	-7.5	-0.7	-7.0
3-Month CD Rate (%)	0.3	6.1	0.3	5.3	0.3	4.7	0.3	4.6	0.2	4.2	0.2	3.7
Fed. Budget Surplus ($b.)	-12.0	12.2	-12.3	12.9	-12.9	15.3	-14.7	15.7	-17.7	17.5	-21.0	18.5
JAPAN:												
GNE (80¥ billion)	981.4	0.2	1202.8	0.3	1467.6	0.3	1763.0	0.4	2026.4	0.4	2321.6	0.4
Nominal GNE (¥b.)	968.4	0.2	1220.3	0.2	1519.7	0.3	1864.9	0.3	2180.4	0.3	2539.9	0.4
Net Exports (80¥b.)	492.7	4.6	609.9	4.5	738.0	4.5	877.4	4.6	1030.0	4.5	1200.6	4.4
Exports	597.8	0.8	736.7	0.9	891.1	1.0	1060.8	1.1	1239.3	1.2	1434.7	1.3
Imports	105.1	0.2	126.8	0.2	153.1	0.2	183.4	0.2	209.3	0.3	234.1	0.3
Current Account ($b.)	1.7	4.0	2.1	4.6	2.6	5.2	3.0	6.2	3.5	6.9	4.5	7.7
Pers. Cons. Deflator	0.1	0.0	0.1	0.1	0.1	0.1	0.1	0.1	0.1	0.1	0.1	0.1
Employment (thous.)	34.8	0.1	42.5	0.1	50.9	0.1	60.3	0.1	70.0	0.1	79.6	0.1
Unemployment Rate (%)	0.0	-0.2	0.0	-0.2	0.0	-0.2	0.0	-0.2	0.0	-0.2	0.0	-0.3
Bank Lending Rate (%)	0.0	0.0	0.0	0.0	0.0	0.0	0.0	0.0	0.0	0.0	0.0	0.0
WORLD:												
Nominal Exports ($b.)	25.8	0.7	32.4	0.6	39.2	0.7	47.0	0.8	54.1	0.9	64.7	1.0
Industrial Countries	18.1	0.6	22.7	0.6	27.6	0.7	33.2	0.8	37.9	0.9	45.2	1.0
Developing Countries	7.2	0.7	9.0	0.8	11.0	0.9	13.2	1.0	15.4	1.1	18.7	1.3
Real Exports (70$b.)	4.6	0.4	5.6	0.5	6.7	0.6	8.0	0.6	9.1	0.7	10.9	0.8
Gross Natl. Prod. (70$b.)	24.3	0.3	27.3	0.4	26.2	0.3	28.1	0.3	30.2	0.4	33.4	0.4

Note: Figures are differences and percent differences from the long-term baseline solution.

Table 6.17
U.S. Investment Tax Credit Increased 5%: Effects on U.S. Industry Output

	1988	%DIF	1989	%DIF	1990	%DIF	1993	%DIF	1999	%DIF
Agric., For., Fish.	0.31	0.3	0.64	0.6	0.80	0.7	0.93	0.8	1.48	1.3
Metal Mining	0.04	0.8	0.07	1.5	0.08	1.8	0.04	0.9	-0.05	-1.0
Coal Mining	0.04	0.5	0.09	1.2	0.12	1.6	0.16	1.9	0.22	1.9
Oil Extraction	0.00	0.0	0.00	0.0	0.00	0.0	0.00	0.0	0.00	0.0
Natural Gas Extract.	0.00	0.0	0.00	0.0	0.00	0.0	0.00	0.0	0.00	0.0
Nonmetal Mining	0.02	0.5	0.04	0.9	0.04	1.0	0.04	0.8	0.03	0.6
Resid. Construction	0.75	1.3	0.82	1.6	0.29	0.6	-0.86	-1.6	0.28	0.4
Nonres. Construction	0.16	0.3	0.38	0.7	0.57	1.1	0.86	1.5	0.86	1.3
Other Construction	0.12	0.3	0.28	0.7	0.41	1.0	0.57	1.3	0.63	1.1
Food and Beverages	0.26	0.2	0.62	0.4	0.87	0.6	1.22	0.8	1.81	1.1
Tobacco	0.04	0.6	0.08	1.3	0.09	1.5	0.09	1.5	0.13	2.2
Textiles	0.20	0.5	0.38	1.0	0.45	1.2	0.53	1.4	0.78	1.8
Apparel	0.15	0.6	0.27	1.0	0.32	1.2	0.40	1.5	0.51	1.7
Paper, Pulp	0.16	0.3	0.32	0.6	0.39	0.8	0.44	0.8	0.57	0.9
Printing, Publish.	0.12	0.3	0.26	0.6	0.35	0.7	0.45	0.9	0.66	1.1
Industrial Chemicals	0.07	0.3	0.14	0.6	0.16	0.7	0.14	0.6	0.12	0.4
Nonind. Chemicals	0.24	0.3	0.47	0.6	0.55	0.7	0.57	0.6	0.69	0.7
Petr., Coal Refining	0.09	0.3	0.20	0.6	0.27	0.7	0.42	1.2	0.73	2.1
Rubber, Plastics	0.14	0.4	0.28	0.8	0.36	1.0	0.44	1.2	0.56	1.2
Leather	0.02	0.6	0.05	1.1	0.06	1.4	0.08	2.0	0.11	2.7
Lumber, Wood Prod.	0.27	0.9	0.38	1.3	0.29	1.0	-0.02	-0.1	0.23	0.6
Furniture	0.06	0.4	0.14	0.9	0.19	1.2	0.22	1.3	0.20	1.0
Cement	0.01	0.5	0.01	1.0	0.02	1.0	0.01	0.7	0.01	0.7
Oth. Stone, Clay, Gl.	0.13	0.6	0.24	1.0	0.26	1.1	0.21	0.9	0.24	0.8
Iron, Steel	0.29	1.0	0.56	2.0	0.64	2.5	0.58	2.2	0.37	1.3
Aluminum	0.02	0.8	0.04	1.6	0.04	1.7	0.00	0.2	-0.15	-6.3
Oth. Nonfer. Metal	0.22	0.5	0.42	1.0	0.50	1.2	0.47	1.1	0.38	0.8
Fabr. Metal Products	0.38	0.6	0.73	1.1	0.85	1.3	0.90	1.2	1.00	1.1
Nonelect. Machinery	0.58	0.4	1.30	1.0	1.78	1.3	2.37	1.5	2.35	1.0
Electrical Machinery	0.43	0.4	0.93	0.9	1.20	1.1	1.27	1.1	0.16	0.1
Aircraft	0.14	0.5	0.28	1.1	0.32	1.4	0.23	0.9	0.15	0.5

Table 6.17—Continued

	1988	%DIF	1989	%DIF	1990	%DIF	1993	%DIF	1999	%DIF
Oth. Transp. Equip.	0.15	0.6	0.28	1.1	0.30	1.2	0.29	1.1	0.42	1.4
Motor Vehicles	1.17	1.2	2.26	2.3	2.47	2.6	2.77	2.8	1.74	1.5
Instruments	0.10	0.3	0.22	0.7	0.30	0.9	0.39	1.0	0.50	1.1
Misc. Manufactures	0.08	0.5	0.19	1.2	0.27	1.7	0.37	2.1	0.57	2.5
Rail Transportation	0.09	0.6	0.17	1.1	0.20	1.3	0.21	1.3	0.27	1.4
Passenger Transport.	0.01	0.3	0.03	0.7	0.05	1.0	0.06	1.3	0.10	1.8
Truck Transport.	0.16	0.4	0.33	0.8	0.42	1.0	0.55	1.2	0.81	1.5
Water Transport.	0.02	0.2	0.04	0.5	0.05	0.6	0.06	0.8	0.11	1.4
Air Transport.	0.06	0.3	0.14	0.6	0.20	0.8	0.29	1.1	0.47	1.5
Pipeline Transport.	0.00	0.2	0.01	0.4	0.01	0.5	0.02	0.8	0.03	1.2
Transport. Services	0.01	0.2	0.01	0.4	0.02	0.6	0.03	0.7	0.04	1.0
Communications	0.16	0.2	0.39	0.4	0.59	0.6	1.05	0.9	1.61	1.0
Electrical Utilities	0.11	0.2	0.25	0.5	0.37	0.7	0.64	1.2	1.15	1.8
Water, Sewer	0.02	0.1	0.04	0.3	0.07	0.4	0.11	0.7	0.17	0.9
Wholesale, Retail	1.34	0.3	2.88	0.6	3.82	0.8	5.41	1.1	8.25	1.4
Fin., Ins., Real Estate	0.43	0.1	0.93	0.2	1.27	0.3	2.01	0.4	3.63	0.6
Oth. Nonmed. Servs.	0.54	0.2	1.23	0.4	1.75	0.6	2.68	0.8	4.16	1.1
Medical Services	0.08	0.1	0.25	0.2	0.44	0.4	0.88	0.7	1.54	1.1
Federal Enterprise	0.04	0.2	0.08	0.5	0.11	0.7	0.15	0.9	0.20	1.1
St., Local Enterprise	0.03	0.2	0.07	0.4	0.10	0.6	0.15	0.8	0.23	1.1
Total Manufactures	5.51	0.5	11.04	1.0	13.26	1.2	14.84	1.2	14.84	1.0

Notes: Figures are differences from the long-term baseline in billions of 1972 dollars and percent. Includes indirect business taxes.

Table 6.18
U.S. Investment Tax Credit Increased 5%:   Effects on Japan Industry Output

	1988	%DIF	1989	%DIF	1990	%DIF	1993	%DIF	1999	%DIF
General Crops	0.1	0.0	0.2	0.0	0.5	0.0	0.7	0.0	0.9	0.0
Industrial Crops	0.1	0.0	0.2	0.0	0.4	0.1	0.9	0.1	2.1	0.3
Livestock, Textiles	0.0	0.0	0.0	0.0	0.0	0.0	0.0	0.0	0.0	0.0
Livestock	0.2	0.0	0.6	0.0	1.2	0.0	2.6	0.1	5.7	0.1
Forestry	0.0	0.0	0.0	0.0	0.0	0.0	0.1	0.0	0.3	0.0
Fisheries	0.1	0.0	0.1	0.0	0.2	0.0	0.5	0.0	1.2	0.0
Coal Mining	0.1	0.0	0.1	0.1	0.2	0.1	0.2	0.1	0.6	0.2
Iron Ores	0.0	0.0	0.0	0.0	0.0	0.0	0.0	0.0	0.0	0.0
Nonfer. Metal Ore	0.0	0.0	0.0	0.0	0.0	0.0	0.0	0.0	0.0	0.0
Crude Petroleum	0.0	0.0	0.0	0.0	0.0	0.0	0.0	0.0	0.0	0.0
Natural Gas	0.0	0.0	0.0	0.0	0.0	0.0	0.0	0.0	0.0	0.0
Other Mining	0.3	0.0	0.9	0.0	1.5	0.1	3.3	0.1	8.7	0.3
Meat, Dairy	0.2	0.0	0.6	0.0	1.2	0.0	2.7	0.0	6.1	0.1
Grain Products	-0.1	0.0	-0.2	0.0	-0.3	0.0	-0.7	0.0	-1.6	0.0
Manuf. Sea Food	0.1	0.0	0.2	0.0	0.3	0.0	0.8	0.0	2.7	0.1
Other Foods	0.4	0.0	0.5	0.0	1.1	0.0	1.4	0.0	-1.4	0.0
Beverages	0.5	0.0	1.1	0.0	1.4	0.0	2.8	0.0	7.1	0.1
Tobacco	0.2	0.0	0.3	0.0	0.4	0.0	0.7	0.0	1.4	0.0
Natural Textiles	0.2	0.0	0.6	0.1	1.0	0.1	2.5	0.3	4.4	0.4
Chemical Textiles	0.1	0.0	0.2	0.1	0.4	0.1	1.0	0.2	2.4	0.4
Other Textiles	1.4	0.0	3.2	0.0	5.1	0.1	11.0	0.2	21.5	0.3
Wearing Apparel	0.3	0.0	0.7	0.0	1.9	0.0	5.3	0.1	12.6	0.1
Wood Products	1.8	0.0	5.2	0.1	7.3	0.1	12.1	0.2	26.1	0.3
Furniture	0.8	0.0	2.0	0.1	3.1	0.1	6.8	0.2	18.0	0.3
Pulp, Paper	1.4	0.0	3.8	0.0	6.0	0.1	12.2	0.1	27.8	0.3
Print., Publish.	0.9	0.0	2.4	0.0	3.9	0.0	8.1	0.1	19.2	0.2
Leather Products	0.0	0.0	0.1	0.0	0.2	0.0	0.5	0.1	0.8	0.1
Rubber Products	3.0	0.1	7.8	0.3	11.8	0.4	24.7	0.8	46.6	1.4
Basic, Int. Chems.	3.0	0.0	8.2	0.1	13.1	0.1	30.2	0.2	68.5	0.3
Final Chemicals	1.9	0.0	5.5	0.0	9.4	0.1	28.5	0.2	77.6	0.4
Petroleum Prods.	2.2	0.0	6.0	0.0	9.5	0.0	22.8	0.1	68.4	0.2
Coal Products	1.9	0.1	3.6	0.2	4.4	0.2	4.8	0.2	6.5	0.2
Cement	0.2	0.0	0.8	0.1	1.5	0.1	2.6	0.2	6.0	0.4

Table 6.18—Continued

	1988	%DIF	1989	%DIF	1990	%DIF	1993	%DIF	1999	%DIF
Other Ceramics	1.5	0.0	4.4	0.1	7.3	0.1	15.9	0.2	42.8	0.4
Iron Products	10.1	0.1	20.0	0.2	24.8	0.3	23.5	0.2	22.7	0.2
Roll., Cast., Forg.	11.2	0.1	27.2	0.1	37.6	0.2	48.8	0.2	79.2	0.3
Aluminum	0.0	0.0	0.0	0.0	0.0	0.0	0.0	0.0	0.0	0.0
Oth. Nonfer. Met.	1.9	0.0	6.5	0.1	11.6	0.2	26.4	0.3	59.7	0.6
Metal Products	3.1	0.0	9.9	0.1	17.3	0.1	36.6	0.2	91.4	0.4
Nonel. Machinery	17.1	0.1	46.1	0.1	75.9	0.2	186.4	0.5	493.4	0.8
Electr. Machinery	10.5	0.0	34.5	0.1	65.1	0.1	233.6	0.3	893.8	0.8
Automobiles	29.7	0.1	81.3	0.3	126.1	0.4	309.1	0.9	913.6	1.9
Aircraft	0.0	0.0	0.0	0.0	0.0	0.0	0.0	0.0	0.0	0.0
Oth. Transp. Equip.	0.7	0.0	2.8	0.1	5.5	0.1	16.2	0.3	41.3	0.5
Instruments	2.7	0.1	7.9	0.2	13.5	0.3	31.5	0.6	69.8	0.9
Misc. Manufs.	2.1	0.0	6.3	0.1	10.8	0.1	29.5	0.2	73.8	0.4
Housing	5.0	0.0	15.6	0.1	23.1	0.1	34.7	0.1	88.5	0.3
Indus. Construction	3.1	0.0	10.1	0.0	17.4	0.1	39.8	0.2	114.4	0.3
Public Construction	0.1	0.0	0.4	0.0	0.8	0.0	1.7	0.0	5.0	0.0
Oth. Construction	1.6	0.0	5.4	0.0	9.3	0.1	21.0	0.1	61.0	0.2
Electric Power	2.3	0.0	5.9	0.1	9.0	0.1	19.1	0.1	37.4	0.2
Gas	0.1	0.0	0.4	0.0	0.7	0.0	1.8	0.1	4.5	0.2
Water, Sanitary	0.3	0.0	0.7	0.0	1.1	0.0	2.8	0.1	6.9	0.1
Wholesale, Retail	6.3	0.0	18.3	0.0	31.4	0.0	77.9	0.1	196.8	0.2
Real Estate	1.5	0.0	7.1	0.0	12.7	0.0	36.8	0.1	112.3	0.2
Railways	0.2	0.0	0.5	0.0	1.0	0.0	2.5	0.1	3.8	0.1
Trucks, Buses	1.3	0.0	3.3	0.0	5.4	0.1	12.0	0.1	29.2	0.2
Oth. Transport.	0.9	0.0	2.3	0.0	3.6	0.0	7.7	0.1	18.0	0.2
Communications	0.6	0.0	1.9	0.0	3.5	0.1	9.8	0.1	25.9	0.3
Finance, Insurance	3.5	0.0	9.6	0.0	15.3	0.1	35.4	0.1	90.0	0.3
Govt. Services	0.0	0.0	0.0	0.0	0.0	0.0	0.0	0.0	0.0	0.0
Public Services	2.0	0.0	6.6	0.0	11.1	0.0	29.4	0.1	85.7	0.1
Other Services	4.0	0.0	9.8	0.0	17.0	0.0	34.4	0.1	80.2	0.1
Unallocated	2.4	0.0	6.9	0.1	11.5	0.1	28.9	0.2	74.3	0.4
Total	147.4	0.0	407.3	0.1	656.4	0.1	1541.6	0.2	4255.5	0.4

Note: Figures are differences from the long-term baseline in billions of 1980 yen and percent.

Table 6.19
Assumed Baseline Tariff Rates

UNITED STATES		JAPAN	
Agric., For., Fish.	—	General Crops	14.5
		Industrial Crops	14.5
		Livestock,Textiles	14.5
		Livestock	14.5
		Forestry	5.7
		Fisheries	5.7
Metal Mining	—	Iron Ores	0.7
		Nonfer. Metal Ore	0.7
Coal Mining	—	Coal Mining	0.0
Petrol ., Nat. Gas	—	Crude Petroleum	0.0
		Natural Gas	0.0
Nonmetal Mining	—	Other Mining	0.7
Food and Beverages	—	Meat, Dairy	7.2
		Grain Products	8.4
		Manuf. Sea Food	8.4
		Other Foods	8.4
		Beverages	8.4
Tobacco	—	Tobacco	54.3
Textiles	15.9	Natural Textiles	8.0
		Chemical Textiles	8.0
		Other Textiles	8.0
Apparel	15.9	Wearing Apparel	8.0
Paper, Pulp	0.3	Pulp, Paper	1.4
Industrial Chemicals	3.9	Basic, Int. Chems.	4.8
Nonind. Chemicals	3.9	Final Chemicals	4.8
Petr., Coal Refining	—	Petroleum Prods.	1.4
		Coal Products	1.4
Rubber, Plastics	4.3	Rubber Products	6.6
Leather	15.9	Leather Products	8.0
Lumber, Wood Prod.	2.2	Wood, Products	0.5
Furniture	2.2	Furniture	0.5
Cement	3.2	Cement	2.2
Oth. Stone, Clay, Gl.	3.2	Other Ceramics	2.2
Iron, Steel	3.2	Iron Products	2.2
		Roll., Cast., Forg.	2.2
Aluminum	3.2	Aluminum	2.2
Oth. Nonfer. Metal	3.2	Oth. Nonfer. Met.	2.2
Fabr. Metal Products	3.2	Metal Products	2.2
Nonelect. Machinery	2.9	Nonel. Machinery	4.6
Electrical Machinery	4.2	Electr. Machinery	4.4
Aircraft	2.5	Aircraft	2.1
Oth. Transp. Equip.	2.5	Oth. Transp. Equip.	2.1
Motor Vehicles	2.5	Automobiles	2.1
Instruments	5.5	Instruments	5.3
Misc. Manufactures	4.7	Misc. Manufs.	6.4
Average	4.9		5.9
Weighted Average	4.0		5.7

Source: Post-Tokyo Round tariff rates (percent) from Whalley (1985), closest matching categories.

Note: Dashes indicate imports are not modeled at the industry level for this industry.

Table 6.20
Simulated Bilateral and Overall Tariff Reductions

| | U.S. IMPORTS FROM | | | JAPAN IMPORTS FROM | |
	JAPAN	OVERALL		U.S.	OVERALL
Agric., For., Fish.	—	—	General Crops	14.5	10.0
			Industrial Crops	14.5	3.0
			Livestock,Textiles	14.5	0.1
			Livestock	14.5	2.6
			Forestry	5.7	1.7
			Fisheries	5.7	1.0
Metal Mining	—	—	Iron Ores	0.7	0.0
			Nonfer. Metal Ore	0.7	0.1
Coal Mining	—	—	Coal Mining	0.0	0.0
Petrol., Nat. Gas	—	—	Crude Petroleum	0.0	0.0
			Natural Gas	0.0	0.0
Nonmetal Mining	—	—	Other Mining	0.7	0.1
Food and Beverages	—	—	Meat, Dairy	7.2	2.4
			Grain Products	8.4	3.3
			Manuf. Sea Food	8.4	0.8
			Other Foods	8.4	1.0
			Beverages	8.4	0.1
Tobacco	—	—	Tobacco	54.3	6.0
Textiles *	15.9	2.8	Natural Textiles	8.0	0.1
			Chemical Textiles	8.0	4.1
			Other Textiles	8.0	0.5
Apparel	15.9	0.4	Wearing Apparel	8.0	0.5
Paper, Pulp	0.3	0.0	Pulp, Paper	1.4	0.7
Industrial Chemicals	3.9	0.3	Basic, Int. Chems.	4.8	2.1
Nonind. Chemicals	3.9	1.1	Final Chemicals	4.8	1.2
Petr., Coal Refining	—	—	Petroleum Prods.	1.4	0.1
			Coal Products	1.4	0.7
Rubber, Plastics	4.3	1.4	Rubber Products	6.6	0.3
Leather	15.9	0.1	Leather Products	8.0	0.8
Lumber, Wood Prod.	2.2	0.1	Wood, Products	0.5	0.2
Furniture	2.2	0.1	Furniture	0.5	0.0
Cement	3.2	0.0	Cement	2.2	0.5
Oth. Stone, Clay, Gl.	3.2	0.6	Other Ceramics	2.2	0.4
Iron, Steel	3.2	0.6	Iron Products	2.2	0.6
			Roll., Cast., Forg.	2.2	0.2
Aluminum	3.2	0.6	Aluminum	2.2	0.6
Oth. Nonfer. Metal	3.2	0.1	Oth. Nonfer. Met.	2.2	0.3
Fabr. Metal Products	3.2	0.6	Metal Products	2.2	0.8
Nonelect. Machinery	2.9	1.1	Nonel. Machinery	4.6	3.4
Electrical Machinery	4.2	1.7	Electr. Machinery	4.4	1.9
Aircraft	2.5	0.1	Aircraft	2.1	1.3
Oth. Transp. Equip.	2.5	1.2	Oth. Transp. Equip.	2.1	0.5
Motor Vehicles	2.5	0.9	Automobiles	2.1	0.7
Instruments	5.5	2.5	Instruments	5.3	1.6
Misc. Manufactures	4.7	1.1	Misc. Manufs.	6.4	1.3
Average	4.9	0.8		5.9	1.3
Weighted Average	4.0	1.0		5.7	1.1

Source: Bilateral tariff rates (percent) from closest matching category in Whalley (1985).

Notes: Overall tariff reductions are computed using baseline Japan import shares. Dashes indicate imports are not modeled at the industry level.

Table 6.21
U.S.-Japan Bilateral Tariffs Removed: U.S. Macro Summary

	1988	%DIF	1989	%DIF	1990	%DIF	1991	%DIF	1992	%DIF	1993	%DIF
Selected Economic Indicators												
GNP (72$ billion)	1.2	0.1	0.6	0.0	0.1	0.0	-0.6	0.0	-1.2	-0.1	-1.7	-0.1
Nominal GNP ($b.)	-0.2	0.0	-1.1	0.0	-2.2	0.0	-4.4	-0.1	-7.9	-0.1	-12.0	-0.2
Consumer Prices	-0.1	0.0	-0.1	0.0	-0.1	0.0	-0.1	0.0	-0.2	0.0	-0.3	-0.1
Employment (thous.)	29.4	0.0	35.9	0.0	29.0	0.0	9.9	0.0	-14.2	0.0	-39.5	0.0
Unemployment Rate (%)	0.0	-0.4	0.0	-0.4	0.0	-0.2	0.0	0.0	0.0	0.2	0.0	0.4
3-Month CD Rate (%)	0.0	-0.4	0.0	-0.1	0.0	-0.1	0.0	-0.1	0.0	-0.3	0.0	-0.6
Money Supply, M2 ($b.)	0.4	0.0	-0.7	0.0	-1.2	0.0	-2.4	-0.1	-4.1	-0.1	-6.5	-0.2
Fed. Budget Surplus ($b.)	-1.8	1.2	-1.9	1.2	-2.4	1.4	-3.1	2.6	-4.1	4.2	-5.1	5.5
Current Account ($b.)	-0.6	0.4	-1.3	0.9	-2.0	1.5	-2.7	1.9	-3.3	2.1	-4.0	2.6
W. Ave. $ Exchange Rate	0.0	0.0	0.0	0.0	0.0	0.0	0.0	0.0	0.0	0.0	0.0	0.0
Real Gross National Product by Category (72$ billion)												
Personal Consumption	0.6	0.1	0.6	0.0	0.4	0.0	0.1	0.0	-0.2	0.0	-0.5	0.0
Durable Goods	0.4	0.2	0.3	0.1	0.2	0.1	0.0	0.0	-0.1	0.0	-0.2	-0.1
Business Fixed Investment	0.2	0.1	0.2	0.1	0.3	0.1	0.2	0.1	0.2	0.1	0.2	0.1
Residential Investment	0.2	0.3	0.0	0.0	-0.1	-0.1	-0.1	-0.2	-0.1	-0.2	-0.1	-0.2
Change in Bus. Inventories	0.1	0.9	0.0	0.3	-0.1	-9.4	-0.1	-1.0	-0.2	-1.4	-0.2	-1.3
Net Exports, Goods and Srvcs.	0.0	-0.2	-0.2	0.8	-0.4	3.1	-0.7	3.5	-0.9	3.8	-1.1	4.4
Exports	0.7	0.4	0.8	0.5	0.9	0.5	0.9	0.5	1.0	0.5	1.1	0.5
Imports	0.6	0.3	1.0	0.5	1.3	0.7	1.6	0.8	1.9	0.9	2.2	1.0
Government Purchases	0.0	0.0	0.0	0.0	0.0	0.0	0.0	0.0	0.0	0.0	0.0	0.0

Table 6.21—Continued

	1994	%DIF	1995	%DIF	1996	%DIF	1997	%DIF	1998	%DIF	1999	%DIF
						Selected Economic Indicators							
GNP (72$ billion)	-2.0	-0.1	-2.6	-0.1	-3.6	-0.2	-4.7	-0.2	-6.1	-0.3	-8.0	-0.3
Nominal GNP ($b.)	-16.1	-0.2	-22.0	-0.3	-30.1	-0.4	-40.6	-0.5	-54.7	-0.6	-73.8	-0.7
Consumer Prices	-0.5	-0.1	-0.6	-0.1	-0.9	-0.2	-1.2	-0.2	-1.6	-0.3	-2.1	-0.4
Employment (thous.)	-59.6	0.0	-86.2	-0.1	-121.9	-0.1	-167.6	-0.1	-223.7	-0.2	-297.1	-0.2
Unemployment Rate (%)	0.0	0.5	0.1	0.7	0.1	1.0	0.1	1.3	0.1	1.7	0.2	2.1
3-Month CD Rate (%)	0.0	-0.7	-0.1	-0.9	-0.1	-1.0	-0.1	-1.2	-0.1	-1.6	-0.1	-2.1
Money Supply, M2 ($b.)	-8.9	-0.2	-12.1	-0.3	-16.5	-0.3	-22.1	-0.4	-29.6	-0.5	-39.8	-0.7
Fed. Budget Surplus ($b.)	-5.9	7.2	-7.1	9.1	-8.8	13.5	-10.9	15.4	-13.7	18.0	-17.1	19.9
Current Account ($b.)	-5.1	3.1	-6.1	3.7	-7.4	4.4	-9.0	5.4	-11.3	6.8	-12.9	8.2
W. Ave. $ Exchange Rate	0.0	0.0	0.0	0.0	0.0	0.0	0.0	0.0	0.0	0.0	0.0	0.0
					Real Gross National Product by Category (72$ billion)								
Personal Consumption	-0.7	-0.1	-1.0	-0.1	-1.5	-0.1	-2.1	-0.1	-2.8	-0.2	-3.9	-0.3
Durable Goods	-0.2	-0.1	-0.3	-0.1	-0.5	-0.2	-0.7	-0.3	-1.0	-0.4	-1.4	-0.5
Business Fixed Investment	0.2	0.0	0.1	0.0	0.0	0.0	-0.1	0.0	-0.3	-0.1	-0.5	-0.1
Residential Investment	0.1	0.1	0.1	0.1	0.0	0.1	0.0	0.0	-0.1	-0.1	-0.1	-0.2
Change in Bus. Inventories	-0.2	-1.0	-0.2	-1.0	-0.2	-1.2	-0.3	-1.6	-0.4	-1.9	-0.5	-2.3
Net Exports, Goods and Srvcs.	-1.3	5.0	-1.6	5.5	-1.9	5.9	-2.2	6.4	-2.6	6.8	-2.9	7.2
Exports	1.2	0.6	1.4	0.6	1.5	0.6	1.6	0.7	1.9	0.8	2.1	0.9
Imports	2.6	1.1	3.0	1.2	3.4	1.3	3.8	1.4	4.5	1.6	5.0	1.7
Government Purchases	0.0	0.0	0.0	0.0	0.0	0.0	0.0	0.0	0.0	0.0	0.0	0.0

Note: Figures are differences from the long-term baseline solution in billions of 1972 dollars and percent, unless otherwise noted.

Table 6.22
U.S.-Japan Bilateral Tariffs Removed: Japan Macro Summary

	1988	%DIF	1989	%DIF	1990	%DIF	1991	%DIF	1992	%DIF	1993	%DIF
Selected Economic Indicators												
GNE (80¥ billion.)	356.2	0.1	635.7	0.2	819.4	0.2	967.0	0.3	1114.2	0.3	1244.4	0.3
Nominal GNE (¥b.)	69.8	0.0	316.7	0.1	515.7	0.1	692.1	0.2	845.6	0.2	1010.7	0.2
Consumer Prices	-0.1	-0.1	-0.2	-0.1	-0.1	-0.1	-0.1	-0.1	-0.1	-0.1	-0.1	-0.1
Employment (thous.)	4.9	0.0	16.3	0.0	24.9	0.0	31.8	0.1	37.4	0.1	42.6	0.1
Unemployment Rate (%)	0.0	-0.1	0.0	-0.1	0.0	-0.2	0.0	-0.2	0.0	-0.2	0.0	-0.2
Bank Lending Rate (%)	0.0	0.0	0.0	0.0	0.0	0.0	0.0	0.0	0.0	0.0	0.0	0.0
Govt. Budget Surplus (¥b.)	-265.1	1.1	-250.9	1.0	-239.2	0.9	-243.0	0.9	-259.1	0.9	-279.8	0.9
Current Account ($b.)	1.0	1.2	1.3	1.7	1.7	2.5	2.1	3.4	2.4	4.3	2.7	6.6
¥/$ Exchange Rate	0.0	0.0	0.0	0.0	0.0	0.0	0.0	0.0	0.0	0.0	0.0	0.0
Real Gross National Expenditure by Category (80¥ billion)												
Private Consumption	68.6	0.0	141.8	0.1	205.1	0.1	262.3	0.1	318.2	0.2	371.1	0.2
Business Investment	61.9	0.1	180.4	0.3	250.2	0.5	274.8	0.5	295.0	0.5	315.2	0.5
Residential Investment	46.9	0.2	87.5	0.4	89.4	0.4	86.2	0.4	88.7	0.4	92.3	0.4
Priv. Inventory Invest.	85.1	3.0	99.7	3.4	71.3	2.6	59.3	2.0	53.8	1.5	50.8	1.2
Net Exports	93.7	3.0	126.3	4.6	203.7	6.6	284.2	6.6	358.6	5.9	415.1	4.9
Exports	283.8	0.5	408.1	0.7	516.0	0.8	628.2	1.0	734.4	1.1	819.6	1.1
Imports	190.1	0.4	281.8	0.5	312.3	0.5	344.1	0.6	375.8	0.6	404.5	0.6
Government	0.0	0.0	0.0	0.0	0.0	0.0	0.0	0.0	0.0	0.0	0.0	0.0

Table 6.22—Continued

	1994	%DIF	1995	%DIF	1996	%DIF	1997	%DIF	1998	%DIF	1999	%DIF
	Selected Economic Indicators											
GNE (80¥ billion.)	1408.2	0.3	1575.3	0.4	1768.1	0.4	1977.4	0.4	2193.9	0.4	2405.9	0.5
Nominal GNE (¥b.)	1180.8	0.2	1381.9	0.3	1581.1	0.3	1812.7	0.3	2025.6	0.3	2277.2	0.3
Consumer Prices	-0.1	-0.1	-0.1	-0.1	-0.1	-0.1	-0.1	-0.1	-0.1	-0.1	-0.1	-0.1
Employment (thous.)	48.2	0.1	55.0	0.1	61.9	0.1	69.6	0.1	77.7	0.1	86.9	0.1
Unemployment Rate (%)	0.0	-0.2	0.0	-0.2	0.0	-0.1	0.0	-0.1	0.0	-0.1	0.0	-0.1
Bank Lending Rate (%)	0.0	0.0	0.0	0.0	0.0	0.0	0.0	0.0	0.0	0.0	0.0	0.0
Govt. Budget Surplus (¥b.)	-297.2	0.9	-311.3	0.9	-334.7	0.9	-356.1	1.0	-378.0	1.0	-393.4	1.0
Current Account ($b.)	3.1	6.9	3.3	6.8	3.6	7.0	3.9	7.6	4.4	8.0	4.7	7.9
¥/$ Exchange Rate	0.0	0.0	0.0	0.0	0.0	0.0	0.0	0.0	0.0	0.0	0.0	0.0
	Real Gross National Expenditure by Category (80¥ billion)											
Private Consumption	425.9	0.2	481.7	0.2	540.6	0.2	604.6	0.2	670.3	0.3	737.8	0.3
Business Investment	343.2	0.5	384.4	0.5	428.8	0.5	482.8	0.5	524.9	0.5	578.1	0.6
Residential Investment	98.2	0.4	105.5	0.4	113.8	0.4	124.0	0.4	133.4	0.5	140.4	0.5
Priv. Inventory Invest.	52.6	1.2	54.3	1.2	60.1	1.2	67.1	1.1	72.1	1.4	80.9	1.5
Net Exports	488.9	4.4	549.2	4.0	625.5	3.7	700.3	3.6	793.4	3.4	869.6	3.1
Exports	922.9	1.2	1008.9	1.2	1121.4	1.2	1236.1	1.3	1373.4	1.3	1494.4	1.3
Imports	434.0	0.6	459.8	0.6	495.9	0.7	535.9	0.7	580.0	0.7	624.8	0.7
Government	0.0	0.0	0.0	0.0	0.0	0.0	0.0	0.0	0.0	0.0	0.0	0.0

Note: Figures are differences from the long-term baseline solution in billions of 1980 yen and percent, unless otherwise noted.

Table 6.23
Bilateral Tariffs Removed: Changes in Merchandise Trade Flows

Year: 1988

EXP\IMP	U.S.	Japan	RoW	Total
U.S.	——	3.73	0.05	0.42
Japan	2.75	——	0.03	0.92
RoW	-0.06	-0.61	-0.03	-0.06
Total	0.47	0.31	-0.01	0.08

Year: 1993

EXP\IMP	U.S.	Japan	RoW	Total
U.S.	——	4.54	0.11	0.53
Japan	5.83	——	0.19	1.71
Row	0.38	-0.33	0.001	0.05
Total	1.18	0.67	0.03	0.24

Year: 1999

EXP\IMP	U.S.	Japan	RoW	Total
U.S.	——	4.76	0.19	0.65
Japan	6.42	——	0.21	1.74
Row	1.26	-0.33	0.10	0.27
Total	1.95	0.84	0.12	0.44

Note: Cell entries give changes from baseline levels for trade flowing from exporters (rows) to importers (columns) in billions of U.S. dollars.

Table 6.24
U.S.-Japan Bilateral Tariffs Removed: World Trade by Region (f.o.b.)

	1988	%DIF	1989	%DIF	1990	%DIF	1993	%DIF	1999	%DIF
United States										
Exports	1.29	0.4	1.69	0.5	1.88	0.5	2.54	0.5	5.02	0.7
Imports	2.06	0.5	3.24	0.7	4.43	0.9	7.91	1.2	21.06	2.0
Balance	-0.77		-1.55		-2.54		-5.38		-16.05	
Japan										
Exports	2.33	0.9	3.55	1.3	4.36	1.5	6.23	1.7	10.03	1.7
Imports	0.45	0.3	0.86	0.5	1.01	0.6	1.49	0.7	2.83	0.8
Balance	1.88		2.69		3.35		4.74		7.19	
Other Indust. Countries										
Exports	-0.77	-0.1	-0.55	0.0	-0.12	0.0	1.28	0.1	10.53	0.3
Imports	-0.28	0.0	-0.07	0.0	0.14	0.0	0.66	0.0	5.63	0.2
Balance	-0.49		-0.48		-0.26		0.62		4.90	
Canada										
Exports	-0.17	-0.1	-0.15	-0.1	-0.04	0.0	0.42	0.2	3.09	1.0
Imports	-0.01	0.0	-0.02	0.0	-0.03	0.0	-0.04	0.0	0.46	0.2
Balance	-0.16		-0.13		-0.01		0.47		2.64	
Australia, N.Z.										
Exports	-0.11	-0.3	-0.10	-0.2	-0.09	-0.2	-0.10	-0.2	-0.06	-0.1
Imports	-0.01	0.0	-0.01	0.0	-0.01	0.0	-0.02	0.0	-0.07	-0.1
Balance	-0.10		-0.09		-0.09		-0.08		0.01	
EC										
Exports	-0.36	0.0	-0.21	0.0	0.05	0.0	0.83	0.1	6.19	0.2
Imports	-0.21	0.0	-0.01	0.0	0.18	0.0	0.68	0.0	4.80	0.2
Balance	-0.16		-0.20		-0.14		0.15		1.39	
Rest of Industrialized										
Exports	-0.13	-0.1	-0.09	0.0	-0.04	0.0	0.13	0.0	1.31	0.2
Imports	-0.05	0.0	-0.03	0.0	-0.01	0.0	0.05	0.0	0.44	0.1
Balance	-0.08		-0.06		-0.03		0.08		0.87	
Developing Countries										
Exports	-0.58	-0.1	-0.47	-0.1	-0.28	0.0	0.33	0.0	3.86	0.3
Imports	-0.03	0.0	0.15	0.0	0.24	0.0	0.31	0.0	0.60	0.0
Balance	-0.56		-0.62		-0.51		0.02		3.26	

OPEC										
Exports	-0.01	0.0	0.01	0.0	0.02	0.0	0.04	0.0	-0.13	0.0
Imports	0.00	0.0	0.03	0.0	0.02	0.0	0.03	0.0	-0.02	0.0
Balance	-0.01		-0.02		0.00		0.01		-0.11	
Africa										
Exports	-0.02	-0.1	-0.02	-0.1	-0.02	-0.1	-0.02	0.0	-0.05	-0.1
Imports	-0.01	0.0	0.00	0.0	0.00	0.0	-0.01	0.0	-0.03	0.0
Balance	-0.02		-0.02		-0.01		-0.01		-0.02	
Asia Including China										
Exports	-0.45	-0.1	-0.40	-0.1	-0.27	-0.1	0.20	0.0	3.23	0.4
Imports	0.02	0.0	0.17	0.0	0.27	0.1	0.36	0.1	0.84	0.1
Balance	-0.47		-0.56		-0.54		-0.17		2.39	
Asian NIEs										
Exports	-0.22	-0.1	-0.20	-0.1	-0.10	0.0	0.29	0.1	2.76	0.5
Imports	-0.07	0.0	-0.04	0.0	-0.03	0.0	0.07	0.0	0.73	0.1
Balance	-0.15		-0.16		-0.08		0.23		2.03	
Middle East Nonoil										
Exports	-0.01	-0.1	-0.01	0.0	0.00	0.0	0.03	0.1	0.18	0.4
Imports	0.00	0.0	-0.01	0.0	-0.01	0.0	0.00	0.0	0.09	0.1
Balance	-0.01		0.00		0.01		0.03		0.09	
Western Hemisphere										
Exports	-0.09	-0.1	-0.06	-0.1	-0.01	0.0	0.09	0.1	0.63	0.3
Imports	-0.03	0.0	-0.04	0.0	-0.04	-0.1	-0.08	-0.1	-0.27	-0.2
Balance	-0.06		-0.03		0.03		0.17		0.90	
CPEs Excluding China										
Exports	-0.05	0.0	-0.04	0.0	-0.03	0.0	0.00	0.0	0.41	0.1
Imports	0.00	0.0	-0.01	0.0	-0.01	0.0	0.00	0.0	0.27	0.1
Balance	-0.04		-0.03		-0.02		0.00		0.14	
World Exports	2.22	0.1	4.17	0.1	5.81	0.2	10.38	0.2	29.84	0.4
World Export Price	0.00	0.0	0.00	0.0	0.00	0.0	0.00	-0.1	-0.01	-0.2
World Exports Real (70$b.)	0.90	0.1	1.41	0.2	1.89	0.2	3.25	0.3	8.14	0.6

Notes: Figures are differences from the long-term baseline simulation in billions of U.S. dollars and percent. NIEs are newly industrializing economies; CPE refers to the centrally-planned economies.

Table 6.25
U.S.–Japan Bilateral Tariffs Removed: World GNP by Region

	1988	%DIF	1989	%DIF	1990	%DIF	1993	%DIF	1999	%DIF
United States	1.09	0.07	0.58	0.03	0.12	0.01	-1.55	-0.08	-7.22	-0.33
Japan	0.48	0.11	0.85	0.19	1.09	0.24	1.66	0.31	3.22	0.46
Other Indust. Countries	-0.28	-0.01	-0.30	-0.01	-0.15	-0.01	0.45	0.02	3.29	0.12
Canada	-0.11	-0.06	-0.15	-0.07	-0.12	-0.06	0.17	0.08	1.43	0.53
Australia, N.Z.	-0.03	-0.05	-0.03	-0.05	-0.03	-0.04	-0.03	-0.04	-0.02	-0.02
EC	-0.12	-0.01	-0.11	-0.01	0.01	0.00	0.29	0.02	1.74	0.08
Rest of Industrialized	-0.01	-0.01	-0.01	-0.01	-0.01	0.00	0.02	0.01	0.15	0.05
Developing Countries	-0.15	-0.01	-0.23	-0.02	-0.27	-0.02	-0.21	-0.02	0.46	0.03
OPEC	-0.01	-0.01	0.00	0.00	0.00	0.00	0.01	0.00	-0.01	0.00
Africa	0.00	0.00	0.00	-0.01	0.00	0.00	0.00	0.00	-0.03	-0.04
Asia Including China	-0.14	-0.03	-0.21	-0.04	-0.27	-0.04	-0.25	-0.03	0.39	0.03
Asian NIEs	-0.05	-0.06	-0.06	-0.06	-0.05	-0.05	0.04	0.03	0.60	0.34
Middle East Nonoil	0.00	0.00	0.00	-0.01	0.00	0.00	0.01	0.01	0.06	0.08
Western Hemisphere	0.01	0.00	-0.01	0.00	0.00	0.00	0.02	0.01	0.04	0.01
CPEs Excluding China	0.00	0.00	0.00	0.00	0.00	0.00	0.00	0.00	1.42	0.11
World Total	1.14	0.02	0.89	0.01	0.79	0.01	0.35	0.00	1.17	0.01

Notes: Figures are differences from the long-term baseline solution in billions of 1970 dollars and percent. NIEs are newly industrializing economies; CPE refers to the centrally-planned economies.

Table 6.26
Bilateral Tariffs Removed: U.S. and Japan Nominal Trade by LINK Categories

	1988		1993		1999	
	DIF	%DIF	DIF	%DIF	DIF	%DIF
United States:						
Exports:						
0,1	0.29	0.9	0.69	1.8	1.15	1.7
2,4	0.48	2.1	0.83	2.3	1.44	1.8
3	0.01	0.1	0.03	0.2	0.05	0.2
5-9	0.51	0.2	0.98	0.3	2.37	0.4
Total	1.29	0.4	2.54	0.5	5.02	0.7
Imports:						
0,1	0.01	0.0	0.01	0.0	-0.09	-0.2
2,4	0.01	0.1	0.03	0.2	-0.08	-0.4
3	0.06	0.2	-0.13	-0.2	-1.35	-1.6
5-9	1.98	0.5	8.00	1.4	22.58	2.5
Total	2.06	0.5	7.91	1.2	21.06	2.0
Japan:						
Exports:						
0,1	0.00	0.0	0.00	0.0	0.00	0.0
2,4	0.01	0.4	0.02	0.7	0.01	0.2
3	0.00	0.0	0.00	0.0	0.00	-0.1
5-9	2.33	0.9	6.21	1.7	10.02	1.8
Total	2.33	0.9	6.23	1.7	10.03	1.7
Imports:						
0,1	0.12	0.6	0.27	0.7	0.50	0.9
2,4	0.01	0.0	0.30	0.8	0.56	1.0
3	0.04	0.1	0.18	0.3	0.41	0.5
5-9	0.28	0.4	0.74	0.8	1.37	0.9
Total	0.45	0.3	1.49	0.7	2.83	0.8

Notes: Figures are differences from the long-term baseline solution in billions of current dollars and percent; SITC 0,1 = food and beverages; 2,4 = raw materials; 3 = fuels; 5-9 = manufactures.

Table 6.27
U.S.–Japan Bilateral Tariffs Removed: U.S. Industry Imports

	1988						1999					
	TOTAL		FROM JAPAN		FROM ROW		TOTAL		FROM JAPAN		FROM ROW	
	DIF	%DIF	DIF	%DIF	DIF	%DIF	DIF	%DIF	DIF	%DIF	DIF	%DIF
Textiles	0.02	0.8	0.06	11.8	-0.04	-1.6	0.03	0.5	0.08	8.8	-0.05	-1.2
Apparel	0.02	0.1	0.00	0.1	0.02	0.1	-0.05	-0.2	0.00	-0.2	-0.05	-0.2
Paper, Pulp	0.00	0.0	0.00	0.3	0.00	0.0	0.00	-0.1	0.00	-0.3	0.00	-0.1
Industrial Chemicals	0.03	1.0	0.01	3.9	0.02	0.7	1.59	46.0	0.14	54.2	1.45	45.4
Nonind. Chemicals	0.02	0.8	0.02	2.7	0.00	0.0	0.10	2.3	0.08	6.4	0.02	0.7
Rubber, Plastics	0.02	1.6	0.02	5.9	0.00	-0.6	0.02	1.1	0.17	39.4	-0.16	-15.2
Leather	0.00	0.1	0.00	32.6	0.00	-0.2	0.00	0.2	0.02	199.5	-0.01	-1.6
Lumber, Wood Prod.	0.00	0.1	0.00	1.7	0.00	0.1	0.00	-0.2	0.00	3.2	0.00	-0.3
Furniture	0.00	0.2	0.00	1.7	0.00	0.0	-0.03	-0.9	0.00	1.4	-0.03	-1.0
Cement	0.00	0.0	0.00	0.0	0.00	0.0	0.00	0.0	0.00	0.0	0.00	0.0
Oth. Stone, Clay, Gl.	0.01	0.5	0.02	4.2	-0.01	-0.3	0.04	1.1	0.03	4.1	0.01	0.4
Iron, Steel	0.03	0.6	0.01	1.3	0.02	0.5	-0.13	-1.7	0.04	2.6	-0.17	-2.7
Aluminum	0.01	0.6	0.00	0.8	0.00	0.5	0.07	5.6	0.03	10.7	0.05	4.4
Oth. Nonfer. Metal	0.01	0.2	0.01	7.7	0.00	0.0	-0.09	-0.6	0.03	6.9	-0.11	-0.8
Fabr. Metal Products	0.02	0.5	0.01	0.9	0.01	0.4	0.04	0.5	0.00	0.0	0.04	0.5
Nonelect. Machinery	0.14	0.6	0.11	1.4	0.03	0.2	0.21	0.5	0.22	1.3	-0.01	0.0
Electrical Machinery	0.20	0.6	0.34	2.5	-0.13	-0.7	2.38	3.9	1.61	6.4	0.77	2.1
Aircraft	0.01	0.4	0.01	12.4	0.00	0.0	1.49	62.4	0.07	77.7	1.42	61.9
Oth. Transp. Equip.	0.02	2.0	0.01	2.0	0.01	2.0	0.35	11.1	0.16	11.1	0.19	11.1
Motor Vehicles	0.11	0.5	0.16	2.1	-0.05	-0.4	0.89	3.5	1.08	10.2	-0.19	-1.3
Instruments	0.01	0.1	0.04	1.8	-0.03	-1.2	-0.03	-0.3	0.05	1.1	-0.08	-1.8
Misc. Manufactures	0.12	1.2	0.17	7.4	-0.05	-0.7	0.14	1.2	0.33	13.1	-0.19	-2.2
Total	0.80	0.6	1.00	2.6	-0.20	-0.2	7.02	2.8	4.13	6.1	2.89	1.6

Note: Figures are differences from the long-term baseline solution in billions of 1972 dollars and in percent.

Table 6.28
U.S.-Japan Bilateral Tariffs Removed: Japan Industry Imports

	1988						1999					
	TOTAL		FROM U.S.		FROM ROW		TOTAL		FROM U.S.		FROM ROW	
	DIF	%DIF	DIF	%DIF	DIF	%DIF	DIF	%DIF	DIF	%DIF	DIF	%DIF
General Crops	30.0	1.8	51.4	4.9	-21.4	-3.4	31.3	0.8	90.9	4.0	-59.5	-3.8
Industrial Crops	5.0	0.4	38.5	15.2	-33.6	-3.4	30.5	1.8	46.2	17.2	-15.7	-1.1
Livestock, Textiles	1.7	0.9	0.7	46.6	1.0	0.5	1.1	0.5	0.4	47.6	0.7	0.3
Livestock	0.7	0.7	3.2	17.9	-2.5	-3.2	1.5	1.2	3.5	18.9	-2.0	-1.8
Forestry	8.7	0.6	16.8	3.2	-8.0	-0.8	30.5	0.9	36.8	3.8	-6.2	-0.3
Fisheries	0.0	0.0	0.0	0.0	0.0	0.0	2.3	0.4	12.8	20.3	-10.5	-2.2
Coal Mining	5.1	0.2	1.8	0.2	3.4	0.2	9.9	0.3	3.2	0.3	6.7	0.3
Iron Ores	3.4	0.4	0.0	****	3.4	0.4	2.2	0.2	0.0	****	2.2	0.2
Nonfer. Metal Ore	5.6	0.4	1.4	1.0	4.2	0.3	13.6	0.6	3.5	2.4	10.1	0.5
Crude Petroleum	10.8	0.1	0.0	0.0	10.8	0.1	97.2	0.4	0.0	0.0	97.2	0.4
Natural Gas	0.5	0.0	0.0	0.0	0.5	0.1	4.2	0.3	0.0	0.0	4.3	0.3
Other Mining	1.7	0.4	0.5	0.8	1.2	0.3	1.5	0.3	0.9	1.9	0.6	0.1
Meat, Dairy	4.8	0.4	13.1	3.6	-8.3	-1.0	11.6	0.5	26.9	3.9	-15.3	-0.9
Grain Products	0.0	0.1	0.3	3.5	-0.3	-2.1	0.1	0.5	0.4	4.2	-0.2	-1.6
Manuf. Sea Food	0.7	0.1	23.0	14.1	-22.3	-2.4	4.9	0.3	31.0	15.3	-26.1	-1.8
Other Foods	0.4	0.0	0.0	0.0	0.4	0.0	4.0	0.3	18.3	13.3	-14.3	-1.0
Beverages	1.2	0.2	0.0	0.0	1.2	0.2	3.5	0.4	0.0	-0.3	3.5	0.4
Tobacco	2.7	1.8	0.0	0.0	2.7	2.0	3.3	1.8	-0.1	-0.3	3.3	2.0
Natural Textiles	0.0	0.0	0.1	6.8	-0.2	-0.1	2.0	0.9	0.1	8.0	1.9	0.9
Chemical Textiles	0.0	0.6	0.0	0.6	0.0	0.6	0.1	0.8	0.5	6.3	-0.4	-9.8
Other Textiles	1.5	0.2	12.6	17.1	-11.1	-1.6	14.1	1.1	18.6	18.5	-4.5	-0.4
Wearing Apparel	-0.2	0.0	5.2	12.4	-5.4	-1.0	0.1	0.0	8.8	12.7	-8.8	-0.9
Wood Products	0.2	0.0	0.4	0.2	-0.4	-0.1	3.9	0.5	2.5	1.0	1.4	0.3
Furniture	0.2	0.2	0.0	0.2	0.2	0.2	1.4	0.6	0.2	1.7	1.2	0.6
Pulp, Paper	2.2	0.6	3.5	1.7	-1.3	-1.0	3.9	1.0	5.0	2.2	-1.1	-0.7
Print., Publish.	0.1	0.3	0.5	0.9	-0.3	-0.3	0.2	0.4	1.0	0.9	-0.7	1.6
Leather Products	1.1	1.2	2.0	12.3	-0.9	-1.2	3.6	3.0	3.0	14.6	0.6	0.6
Rubber Products	2.6	1.8	0.0	0.2	2.6	1.8	9.9	4.4	0.0	0.2	9.9	4.5
Basic, Int. Chems.	18.0	1.5	25.9	4.3	-7.9	-1.2	40.5	2.2	43.9	5.4	-3.5	-0.3
Final Chemicals	5.7	0.5	10.7	4.4	-5.0	-0.6	11.7	0.7	17.7	4.7	-6.0	-0.5

Table 6.28—Continued

	1988						1999					
	TOTAL		FROM U.S.		FROM ROW		TOTAL		FROM U.S.		FROM ROW	
	DIF	%DIF	DIF	%DIF	DIF	%DIF	DIF	%DIF	DIF	%DIF	DIF	%DIF
Petroleum Prods.	3.7	0.1	0.7	1.1	3.0	0.1	49.2	0.6	1.6	1.8	47.6	0.6
Coal Products	0.0	0.8	0.0	1.9	0.0	0.0	0.2	1.1	0.2	2.4	0.1	0.5
Cement	0.0	0.2	0.0	0.2	0.0	0.2	0.0	0.5	0.0	5.8	0.0	-0.9
Other Ceramics	0.6	0.4	0.0	0.2	0.6	0.4	1.8	0.6	0.0	0.2	1.8	0.7
Iron Products	0.1	0.1	0.5	2.3	-0.3	-0.2	1.2	0.4	0.6	3.1	0.6	0.2
Roll., Cast., Forg.	1.5	0.9	0.3	4.8	1.2	0.8	3.9	1.2	0.6	5.8	3.3	1.0
Aluminum	4.4	0.5	13.6	4.7	-9.1	-1.6	8.6	0.6	17.5	6.3	-8.9	-0.8
Oth. Nonfer. Met.	7.0	0.4	9.4	2.2	-2.3	-0.2	34.8	1.1	19.7	3.4	15.1	0.6
Metal Products	0.3	0.2	1.1	1.8	-0.8	-0.9	1.4	0.5	2.8	2.5	-1.4	-0.8
Nonel. Machinery	12.5	2.5	10.6	3.0	1.9	1.3	10.6	3.0	8.7	3.5	1.9	1.8
Electr. Machinery	16.3	1.2	21.5	4.0	-5.2	-0.7	52.8	1.9	58.0	5.1	-5.2	-0.3
Automobiles	0.9	0.4	2.9	3.6	-2.0	-1.5	11.2	3.0	8.3	6.5	2.9	1.2
Aircraft	5.1	1.7	9.2	2.5	-4.1	5.3	31.6	9.3	42.1	10.3	-10.5	15.1
Oth. Transp. Equip.	0.0	0.0	7.6	5.3	-7.6	-4.3	0.0	0.0	21.8	6.4	-21.8	-3.2
Instruments	8.8	2.0	6.2	4.1	2.5	0.9	16.4	2.3	11.0	4.5	5.4	1.1
Misc. Manufs.	12.0	1.6	6.9	3.5	5.2	0.9	20.1	1.8	10.9	3.8	9.1	1.1
Total	187.6	0.4	302.1	3.8	-114.4	-0.3	588.2	0.8	579.6	4.9	8.6	0.0

Notes: Figures are differences and percent differences from the long-term baseline solution in billions of 1980 yen.

Table 6.29
Bilateral Tariffs Removed: U.S., Japan Imports from the ROW

	UNITED STATES		JAPAN	
	DIF	%DIF	DIF	%DIF
General Crops	—	—	-0.55	-6.5
Industrial Crops	—	—	-0.21	-2.1
Livestock, Textiles	—	—	0.00	0.3
Livestock	—	—	-0.02	-2.1
Forestry	—	—	-0.05	-0.4
Fisheries	—	—	-0.09	-2.8
Coal Mining	—	—	0.03	0.3
Iron Ores	—	—	0.02	0.3
Nonfer. Metal Ore	—	—	0.05	0.5
Crude Petroleum	—	—	0.39	0.4
Natural Gas	—	—	0.02	0.3
Other Mining	—	—	0.01	0.2
Meat, Dairy	—	—	-0.09	-0.8
Grain Products	—	—	0.00	-1.6
Manuf. Sea Food	—	—	-0.13	-0.9
Other Foods	—	—	-0.11	-1.3
Beverages	—	—	0.04	0.8
Tobacco	—	—	0.04	2.4
Natural Textiles	-0.30	-2.4	0.01	0.7
Chemical Textiles			0.00	-6.3
Other Textiles			-0.03	-0.2
Wearing Apparel	-0.38	-0.6	-0.09	-1.0
Pulp, Paper	-0.05	-0.4	-0.01	-0.3
Basic, Int. Chems.	7.53	45.3	-0.05	-0.5
Final Chemicals	0.25	1.6	-0.09	-0.8
Rubber Products	-0.39	-9.0	0.10	4.2
Leather Products	-0.10	-2.2	0.02	1.5
Wood Products	-0.03	-0.7	0.00	0.0
Furniture	-0.14	-1.3	0.01	0.3
Print., Publish.	—	—	0.00	-1.5
Petroleum Prods.	—	—	0.16	0.5
Coal Products	—	—	0.00	0.1
Cement	-0.01	-0.3	0.00	-1.7
Other Ceramics	0.01	0.0	0.01	0.4
Iron Products	-0.82	-3.6	-0.01	-0.6
Roll., Cast., Forg.			0.02	0.6
Aluminum	0.22	4.1	-0.07	-0.9
Oth. Nonfer. Met.	-0.56	-1.3	0.12	0.6
Metal Products	0.05	0.2	-0.01	-0.8
Nonel. Machinery	-0.01	0.0	0.01	1.3
Electr. Machinery	2.03	2.6	-0.11	-0.7
Aircraft	5.58	61.0	0.15	7.5
Oth. Transp. Equip.	0.62	10.7	-0.19	-1.7
Automobiles	0.81	1.1	0.03	1.2
Instruments	-0.36	-2.7	0.04	0.9
Misc. Manufs.	-0.36	-1.2	0.08	1.0
Total	13.57	2.4	-0.53	-0.1

Notes: Figures are differences from long-term baseline solution in billions of current dollars and percent. Dashes indicate imports are not modeled at the industry level.

Table 6.30

U.S.–Japan Bilateral Tariffs Removed: U.S. Trade and Output by Industry

	1988 EXPORTS DIF	EXPORTS %DIF	IMPORTS DIF	IMPORTS %DIF	OUTPUT DIF	OUTPUT %DIF	1999 EXPORTS DIF	EXPORTS %DIF	IMPORTS DIF	IMPORTS %DIF	OUTPUT DIF	OUTPUT %DIF
Agric., For., Fish.	0.15	1.5	—	—	0.30	0.3	0.28	1.7	—	—	-0.05	0.0
Metal Mining	0.00	0.2	—	—	0.00	0.1	0.01	0.7	—	—	-0.06	-1.1
Coal Mining	0.00	0.1	—	—	0.01	0.1	0.00	0.1	—	—	-0.13	-1.2
Crude Oil Extraction	0.00	0.0	—	—	0.00	0.0	0.00	-0.1	—	—	0.00	0.0
Nat. Gas Extract.	—	—	—	—	0.00	0.0	—	—	—	—	0.00	0.0
Nonmetal Mining	0.00	0.2	—	—	0.00	0.1	0.01	0.7	—	—	-0.06	-1.1
Resid. Construction	—	—	—	—	0.19	0.3	—	—	—	—	-0.14	-0.2
Nonres. Construction	—	—	—	—	0.02	0.0	—	—	—	—	-0.13	-0.2
Other Construction	—	—	—	—	0.02	0.1	—	—	—	—	-0.16	-0.3
Food and Beverages	0.04	1.4	—	—	0.10	0.1	0.10	1.9	—	—	-0.42	-0.3
Tobacco	0.00	0.0	—	—	0.01	0.1	0.00	0.1	—	—	-0.04	-0.7
Textiles	0.13	4.0	0.02	0.8	0.23	0.6	0.22	3.6	0.03	0.5	0.07	0.2
Apparel	0.01	2.4	0.02	0.1	0.05	0.2	0.02	3.4	-0.05	-0.2	-0.11	-0.4
Paper, Pulp	0.00	0.3	0.00	0.0	0.04	0.1	0.02	0.5	0.00	-0.1	-0.22	-0.4
Printing, Publish.	—	—	—	—	0.03	0.1	—	—	—	—	-0.18	-0.3
Industrial Chemicals	0.03	0.8	0.03	1.0	0.02	0.1	0.08	2.0	1.59	46.0	-1.28	-4.6
Nonind. Chemicals	0.03	0.5	0.02	0.8	0.10	0.1	0.08	0.9	0.10	2.3	-0.39	-0.4
Petr., Coal Refining	0.00	0.2	—	—	0.03	0.1	0.00	0.3	—	—	-0.26	-0.7
Rubber, Plastics	0.00	0.0	0.02	1.6	0.01	0.0	0.00	0.5	0.02	1.1	-0.26	-0.6
Leather	0.00	0.9	0.00	0.1	0.01	0.2	0.00	1.3	0.00	0.2	-0.03	-0.6
Lumber, Wood Prod.	0.00	0.1	0.00	0.1	0.06	0.2	0.00	0.8	0.00	-0.2	-0.13	-0.3
Furniture	0.00	0.0	0.00	0.2	0.01	0.1	0.00	0.6	-0.03	-0.9	-0.05	-0.2
Cement	0.00	0.0	0.00	0.0	0.00	0.1	0.00	2.7	0.00	0.0	-0.01	-0.4
Oth. Stone, Clay, Gl.	0.00	0.0	0.01	0.5	0.02	0.1	0.01	0.5	0.04	1.1	-0.17	-0.6
Iron, Steel	0.00	0.2	0.03	0.6	0.02	0.1	0.00	0.9	-0.13	-1.7	-0.39	-1.3
Aluminum	0.01	2.6	0.01	0.6	0.01	0.6	0.02	3.6	0.07	5.6	-0.07	-2.9
Oth. Nonfer. Metal	0.00	0.4	0.01	0.2	0.03	0.1	0.01	1.2	-0.09	-0.6	-0.33	-0.7
Fabr. Metal Products	0.00	0.1	0.02	0.5	0.06	0.1	0.02	0.9	0.04	0.5	-0.54	-0.6
Nonelect. Machinery	0.05	0.3	0.14	0.6	0.06	0.0	0.22	0.7	0.21	0.5	-0.60	-0.2
Electrical Machinery	0.06	0.6	0.20	0.6	-0.01	0.0	0.26	1.6	2.38	3.9	-2.04	-1.4
Aircraft	0.02	0.3	0.01	0.4	0.04	0.2	0.13	1.5	1.49	62.4	-1.22	-4.1

Oth. Transp. Equip.	0.02	1.9	0.02	2.0	0.04	0.1	0.06	3.2	0.35	11.1	-0.32	-1.1
Motor Vehicles	0.02	0.3	0.11	0.5	0.19	0.2	0.10	0.7	0.89	3.5	-1.56	-1.3
Instruments	0.01	0.6	0.01	0.1	0.04	0.1	0.04	1.2	-0.03	-0.3	-0.07	-0.2
Misc. Manufactures	0.02	0.7	0.12	1.2	-0.04	-0.3	0.05	1.1	0.14	1.2	-0.16	-0.7
Rail Transportation	—	—	—	—	0.04	0.2	—	—	—	—	-0.08	-0.4
Passenger Transport.	—	—	—	—	0.00	0.1	—	—	—	—	-0.03	-0.5
Truck Transport.	—	—	—	—	0.06	0.1	—	—	—	—	-0.16	-0.3
Water Transport.	—	—	—	—	0.01	0.1	—	—	—	—	0.00	0.0
Air Transport.	—	—	—	—	0.02	0.1	—	—	—	—	-0.10	-0.3
Pipeline Transport.	—	—	—	—	0.00	0.0	—	—	—	—	-0.01	-0.3
Transport. Services	—	—	—	—	0.00	0.1	—	—	—	—	-0.01	-0.2
Communications	—	—	—	—	0.03	0.0	—	—	—	—	-0.33	-0.2
Electrical Utilities	—	—	—	—	0.03	0.1	—	—	—	—	-0.25	-0.4
Water, Sewer	—	—	—	—	0.00	0.0	—	—	—	—	-0.04	-0.2
Wholesale, Retail	—	—	—	—	0.38	0.1	—	—	—	—	-1.29	-0.2
Fin., Ins., Real Estate	—	—	—	—	0.12	0.0	—	—	—	—	-0.72	-0.1
Oth. Nonmed. Servs.	—	—	—	—	0.13	0.0	—	—	—	—	-1.04	-0.3
Medical Services	—	—	—	—	0.02	0.0	—	—	—	—	-0.26	-0.2
Federal Enterprise	—	—	—	—	0.01	0.1	—	—	—	—	-0.05	-0.3
St., Local Enterprise	—	—	—	—	0.01	0.0	—	—	—	—	-0.06	-0.3
Total Manuf.	0.63 *	0.7 *	0.80	0.6	1.18	0.1	1.78 *	1.2 *	7.02	2.8	-10.77	-0.7

NOTES: Figures are differences from the long-term baseline simulation in billions of 1972 dollars and percent; output includes indirect business taxes. Dashes indicate the variable is not modeled at the industry level or is exogenous in this simulation.

*Total is for all export industries.

Table 6.31
U.S.–Japan Bilateral Tariffs Removed: Japan Trade and Output by Industry

	1988						1999					
	EXPORTS		IMPORTS		OUTPUT		EXPORTS		IMPORTS		OUTPUT	
	DIF	%DIF	DIF	%DIF	DIF	%DIF	DIF	%DIF	DIF	%DIF	DIF	%DIF
General Crops	0.0	-0.3	30.0	1.8	-25.3	-0.3	-0.1	-0.7	31.3	0.8	-16.2	-0.2
Industrial Crops	0.0	0.3	5.0	0.4	-0.4	-0.1	0.0	0.2	30.5	1.8	10.5	1.3
Livestock, Textiles	—	—	1.7	0.9	—	—	—	—	1.1	0.5	—	—
Livestock	0.0	0.1	0.7	0.7	3.1	0.1	0.0	0.1	1.5	1.2	18.5	0.4
Forestry	0.1	0.3	8.7	0.6	-0.7	0.0	0.1	0.2	30.5	0.9	0.0	0.0
Fisheries	0.0	-0.1	0.0	0.0	2.6	0.1	0.0	0.0	2.3	0.4	3.9	0.1
Coal Mining	0.0	0.0	5.1	0.2	0.2	0.1	0.0	0.0	9.9	0.3	0.5	0.2
Iron Ores	0.0	0.3	3.4	0.4	—	—	0.0	0.2	2.2	0.2	—	—
Nonfer. Metal Ore	0.0	0.1	5.6	0.4	—	—	0.0	-0.2	13.6	0.6	—	—
Crude Petroleum	0.0	0.0	10.8	0.1	—	—	0.0	0.0	97.2	0.4	—	—
Natural Gas	—	—	0.5	0.0	—	—	—	—	4.2	0.3	—	—
Other Mining	0.1	0.6	1.7	0.4	1.5	0.1	0.0	-0.1	1.5	0.3	8.8	0.3
Meat, Dairy	0.0	0.1	4.8	0.4	6.0	0.1	0.0	0.1	11.6	0.5	31.6	0.5
Grain Products	0.0	0.0	0.0	0.1	2.6	0.1	0.0	0.1	0.1	0.5	2.6	0.1
Manuf. Sea Food	0.0	0.0	0.7	0.1	0.9	0.0	0.1	0.0	4.9	0.3	3.5	0.1
Other Foods	0.0	0.0	0.4	0.0	4.0	0.0	0.1	0.1	4.0	0.3	24.7	0.2
Beverages	0.0	0.0	1.2	0.2	7.8	0.1	0.0	0.0	3.5	0.4	18.2	0.3
Tobacco	0.0	0.0	2.7	1.8	-0.3	0.0	0.0	0.0	3.3	1.8	0.9	0.0
Natural Textiles	1.0	1.7	0.0	0.0	5.4	0.6	1.2	1.1	2.0	0.9	4.6	0.4
Chemical Textiles	1.2	1.9	0.0	0.6	2.6	0.7	1.8	1.4	0.1	0.8	4.2	0.8
Other Textiles	18.5	1.9	1.5	0.2	27.7	0.4	22.4	1.2	14.1	1.1	30.9	0.4
Wearing Apparel	0.1	0.1	-0.2	0.0	-9.4	-0.2	-0.1	-0.1	0.1	0.0	-7.0	-0.1
Wood Products	0.3	1.1	0.0	0.0	12.5	0.2	0.9	2.0	3.9	0.5	49.4	0.6
Furniture	0.3	0.7	0.2	0.2	5.7	0.1	0.5	0.6	1.4	0.6	18.2	0.3
Pulp, Paper	0.0	0.0	2.2	0.6	5.3	0.1	0.0	0.0	3.9	1.0	37.9	0.4
Print, Publish.	0.0	0.1	0.1	0.3	4.1	0.1	0.0	0.0	0.2	0.4	20.9	0.2
Leather Products	0.8	1.6	1.1	1.2	-0.4	-0.1	5.3	5.4	3.6	3.0	1.1	0.2
Rubber Products	10.8	1.9	2.6	1.8	24.8	1.0	64.5	6.1	9.9	4.4	90.1	2.7
Basic, Int. Chems.	7.2	0.4	18.0	1.5	17.0	0.1	85.9	2.0	40.5	2.2	196.8	0.8
Final Chemicals	8.2	0.4	5.7	0.5	11.9	0.1	33.7	0.7	11.7	0.7	68.8	0.4

Petroleum Prods.	-0.3	0.0	3.7	0.1	13.2	0.1	-2.4	-0.4	49.2	0.6	124.6	0.5
Coal Products	0.0	0.0	0.0	0.8	7.0	0.3	0.0	0.0	0.2	1.1	11.3	0.4
Cement	0.0	0.0	0.0	0.2	2.1	0.2	-0.2	-0.1	0.0	0.5	9.1	0.6
Other Ceramics	8.3	1.8	0.6	0.4	17.9	0.2	11.5	1.5	1.8	0.6	46.8	0.4
Iron Products	0.1	0.3	0.1	0.1	36.4	0.4	0.1	0.3	1.2	0.4	45.5	0.4
Roll., Cast, Forg.	8.3	0.2	1.5	0.9	39.7	0.2	28.1	0.3	3.9	1.2	114.6	0.5
Aluminum	0.1	0.5	4.4	0.5	—	—	2.7	6.0	8.6	0.6	—	—
Oth. Nonfer. Met.	9.4	1.6	7.0	0.4	21.9	0.3	37.5	2.6	34.8	1.1	80.1	0.8
Metal Products	2.0	0.2	0.3	0.2	8.4	0.1	1.4	0.1	1.4	0.5	86.1	0.3
Nonel. Machinery	24.1	0.4	12.5	2.5	53.9	0.2	49.5	0.4	10.6	3.0	295.5	0.5
Electr. Machinery	100.2	1.0	16.3	1.2	200.8	0.4	502.2	2.0	52.8	1.9	1024.1	0.9
Automobiles	50.5	0.6	0.9	0.4	75.4	0.3	468.7	2.5	11.2	3.0	658.0	1.4
Aircraft	5.9	8.4	5.1	1.7	—	—	62.7	46.4	31.6	9.3	—	—
Oth. Transp. Equip.	5.9	0.3	0.0	0.0	10.3	0.3	111.1	2.0	0.0	0.0	147.8	1.8
Instruments	9.8	0.9	8.8	2.0	3.0	0.1	15.6	0.6	16.4	2.3	24.2	0.3
Misc. Manufs.	21.9	2.0	12.0	1.6	26.1	0.2	45.6	2.0	20.1	1.8	111.7	0.6
Housing	—	—	—	—	38.9	0.2	—	—	—	—	116.6	0.4
Indus. Construction	—	—	—	—	13.2	0.1	—	—	—	—	132.2	0.4
Public Construction	—	—	—	—	0.5	0.0	—	—	—	—	5.7	0.0
Oth. Construction	—	—	—	—	6.6	0.0	—	—	—	—	69.3	0.3
Electric Power	—	—	—	—	10.9	0.1	—	—	—	—	53.1	0.3
Gas	—	—	—	—	-0.3	0.0	—	—	—	—	3.0	0.1
Water, Sanitary	—	—	—	—	1.2	0.0	—	—	—	—	7.2	0.2
Wholesale, Retail	—	—	0.4	0.0	26.0	0.0	—	—	4.0	0.3	237.8	0.3
Real Estate	—	—	—	—	9.6	0.0	—	—	—	—	157.0	0.3
Railways	—	—	0.0	0.0	-0.2	0.0	—	—	0.0	0.0	1.9	0.1
Trucks, Buses	—	—	0.1	0.1	5.4	0.1	—	—	0.6	0.2	28.9	0.2
Oth. Transport.	—	—	0.4	0.0	5.9	0.1	—	—	5.4	0.4	26.9	0.3
Communications	—	—	0.0	0.1	4.1	0.1	—	—	0.3	0.5	36.3	0.4
Finance, Insurance	—	—	0.6	0.2	15.6	0.1	—	—	4.3	0.5	103.2	0.3
Public Services	—	—	—	—	28.3	0.1	—	—	—	—	132.8	0.2
Other Services	—	—	0.3	0.0	18.4	0.0	—	—	3.2	0.2	125.4	0.2
Unallocated	-0.1	0.0	5.7	0.4	12.5	0.1	2.2	0.1	25.2	0.8	81.3	0.5
Total	294.6	0.6	195.2	0.4	822.0	0.1	1552.4	1.4	631.2	0.8	4720.9	0.5

Notes: Figures are differences from the long-term baseline solution in billions of 1980 yen and percent.   Dashes indicate the variable is exogenous in the simulation.

CONCLUDING REMARKS AND DIRECTIONS FOR FURTHER RESEARCH

This volume has attempted to provide a more complete picture of international transmission relationships, particularly the trading relationship between the United States and Japan in the setting of the entire world economy. The goal has been to combine elements of aggregate macroeconomic modeling, input-output industry analysis, and disaggregated estimates of trade elasticities to construct an integrated model of macroeconomic and industry-level relationships. The resulting model system sheds light on causes and consequences of macroeconomic conditions, as well as the distribution of macro effects across industries in the United States and Japan, recognizing the feedback interactions of the entire world economy.

This project has seen the development of a broad, yet disaggregated (for the U.S. and Japan), econometric model. The principal steps of the research effort can be summarized as follows:

- Elaboration of the U.S. model to integrate sectorally disaggregated trade distinguishing between flows between the United States and Japan and the rest of the world.

- Construction and further development of a highly disaggregated model of Japan, including a corresponding trade disaggregation.

- Linkage of the two models through bilateral trade equations at the industry level.

- Integration of the models into Project LINK. The models operate in a complete world model, with trade and price feedbacks from seventy-nine separate countries and country blocks.

- Preparation of baseline forecast solutions for the medium term to 1992 and extension for the long term to 1999.

- Application of the model to numerous policy simulations to examine the impact of: demand shocks in the United States, Japan, and the rest of the world; alternative fiscal and monetary policies; exchange rate variations; industrial policy stimulus in the United States; tariff reduction policies in Japan and the United States.

At the macroeconomic level, the picture that emerges is of a U.S. economy that—even in 1990—exerts a much greater impact on the economies of Japan and the rest of the world than they exert on it.   The effect of U.S. economic expansion on Japan is about ten times as great, in percentage terms, as that of a Japanese expansion on the United States; it is at least twice as great as the larger country size would suggest.   The reason for this asymmetry lies in the greater response of imports in the United States than in Japan.   Interestingly, this greater import response comes not from larger activity elasticities, but from a strong substitution of U.S. demand toward imports in response to induced inflation in domestic goods prices.   The effect of U.S. expansion is also much more widely distributed in the world economy than an expansion in Japan or the other major industrialized countries because of the more extensive pattern of U.S. trade—America buys from everyone.

At the industry level, the distribution of gains and losses from macroeconomic events is quite diverse.   Domestic macroeconomic policies that affect output or price, or international fluctuations that affect trade prices and values directly, create varied responses in industries depending on spending propensities, trade income and price elasticities, and interindustry structure.   For some industries, changes in intermediate demand are more important than changes in final demand in determining the overall effect on output of an economic event.

Some specific results are as follows:

- There is a marked imbalance between the effect of a U.S. stimulus on Japan and a Japanese stimulus on the United States.   A 1% demand stimulus on the United States has significant impact on Japan (0.8%).   A 1% stimulus in Japan has only a very small impact (0.1%) in the United States.   This reflects differences in the import elasticities, differences in the responses of the economies to demand stimulus, and differences in trade patterns.

- The impact on the world economy of a 1% of GNP stimulus in the United States and Japan is approximately 0.8% for U.S. stimulus, and 0.15% for Japanese stimulus.

- In turn, the impact of 1% of GNP changes in economic activity in the other major industrialized countries on the economies of Japan and the United States is approximately 0.1% in both cases.

- The macro policy simulations are directed toward reducing the imbalance of the U.S. fiscal budget. The simulation of reduction in the budget without monetary offset shows significant slowdown in the U.S. economy during 1989 and 1990 followed by a recovery in 1991. The impact on the Japanese economy is negative. The simulation that assumes an offsetting monetary stimulus still shows some slowdown in 1989, but indicates that monetary measures might substantially reduce the short-term impact of budget balancing on the U.S. economy and would sharply stimulate the U.S. economy in the last year of the medium-term simulation period. This also means that there is less impact on U.S. imports and little impact on Japanese exports and economic activity.

- The exchange rate simulations show that exchange rate adjustments have substantial impact on specific industries (though with great variation among sectors) and on overall economic activity. An 8% appreciation of the yen reduces U.S. real imports by 1.3% resulting in a 0.4% positive effect on U.S. GNP, and a negative effect of 0.7% on Japanese activity. A 10% appreciation of the dollar causes an initial J-curve deterioration of the U.S. balance of payments, which is, however, reversed after a couple of years. U.S. exports and imports change by about 2% positively for exports and negatively for imports, causing an increase in U.S. economic activity of 0.8% and a decline in Japanese activity of 0.5%. The exchange rate mechanism also has significant indirect effects through third countries.

- An industrial policy simulation of increased productivity growth in U.S. high-technology industries was performed. The reduced labor demand pulls down U.S. economic activity initially, but higher output in affected sectors and lower prices overall spur economic growth in later years. Japan's economy is only marginally affected, except in the specific industries targeted.

- Long-term simulation exercises were carried out to 1999. The results indicated average growth rates during 1994 to 1999 of 2.9% for the United States and 4.6% for Japan. An alternative simulation of a 5% investment tax credit resulted in an increase in GNP by 0.9% for the United States and 0.4% for Japan during the same period.

- Trade liberalization between the United States and Japan was simulated with the removal of existing tariffs on their bilateral trade. Because the average level of existing tariffs is low, macroeconomic effects are small, but there are sizable impacts on industrial sectors.

FURTHER WORK

The integration of very large-scale econometric models of Japan and the United States in the LINK model of the world economy represents a considerable step forward in closely linking the two economies at the sectoral level and introducing world economy feedback into their relationship. There remain numerous possibilities for further developing and improving the model system. The following are some priorities for our research.

Further Model Disaggregation

We have noted above that the LINK system lacks the sector disaggregation that we have included in the U.S. and Japan models. We have had to use the LINK disaggregation rather than our more detailed sectoral disaggregation to deal with the rest of the world group of countries. Unfortunately, this means that we do not have the detailed relationships determining trade by sector that operate in the U.S.-Japan system, and we do not model competitiveness on the sectoral level in the relationship among the United States, Japan, and other countries as fully as would be desirable. Further disaggregation poses some massive problems that represent an agenda for additional large-scale research. The following elements would be involved for providing additional disaggregation to particular countries (somewhat similar problems but on an even more massive scale are involved if disaggregation is sought for additional blocks of countries, like the EC):

- The need for a set of detailed trade matrixes, prices, and quantities, as a basis for measuring competitiveness relationships among the countries involved. Current calculations have divided imports into the United States into those from Japan and those from other countries, and similarly imports into Japan into those from the United States and those from other countries. The data required here would serve to provide additional breakdowns for other competitors. Note that third-country imports would then have to be split up into those from the United States, Japan, and from other third countries, providing the competitiveness factor between the United States and Japan that we are seeking.

- The need for disaggregated models for other countries. Presently, only the models of the United States and Japan are sectorally disaggregated. We would require sectorally disaggregated models with sectoral outputs, prices, exports, and imports for other countries integrated into the system.

- The problem of integration of these sectorally disaggregated systems in the trade matrix of LINK, so that the present LINK system would continue to function for those countries that remain on an aggregated basis.

Although there is no doubt that it would be useful to establish further bilateral linkages, particularly with countries where the United States and Japan compete and with countries that serve as primary sources for the United States (Canada, for example) and Japan (Korea, for example), it is apparent that significant difficulties will have to be overcome to enlarge the system further.

Extension into Service and Capital Flows and Exchange Rates

LINK and the bilateral linkage of the U.S. and the Japan models deal only with trade flows of goods. Increasingly, services have become an important component of international trade flows. It is still difficult to develop a multilateral linkage in service flows largely because of statistical deficiencies. The statistical basis for developing bilateral flows among the United States, Japan, and the "rest of the world," however, is available, and services would make an interesting addition to the linked model system. A disaggregation of service flows into tourism, transportation, insurance and finance, and related services, earnings on foreign assets, and debt service would provide some interesting insights into U.S. and Japanese service flows.

International capital flows pose even more serious data problems on a multilateral basis. Not only is the required data matrix not available, but the underlying statistics cannot even be reconciled. On the other hand, it should be possible to deal with the bilateral relationship between the United States and Japan, and with the aggregate of the "rest of the world," so that an integration of capital flows into the system would be possible.

Finally, given the components of the balance of current accounts including services and an analysis of capital flows, it should be possible to introduce these data into an improved treatment of exchange rates. Current LINK methodology rests on a purchasing power parity basis, with important short-run influences of trade flows and interest rate differentials. A more structured approach recognizing explicitly the trade, service, and capital flows (and stocks) would be a useful and interesting elaboration of the system.

Additional Simulation Exercises

The model system has been constructed for purposes of simulation. In our discussion above, we have illustrated the capabilities of the system with a variety of applications. But, we are far from exhausting its potential. An important priority in a further phase of this project would be additional model simulations aimed at current issues in the U.S.-Japan economic relationship. Many such simulations can be carried out on the basis of the model system as it stands.[1] Others may require elaboration of the model or some "side calculations" to develop the appropriate inputs for the model system. We might consider, for example, further simulations, along the following lines:

- Alternative baseline calculations. A number of alternative baseline scenarios might be visualized, particularly into the long-run future. These might be termed optimistic or pessimistic scenarios, but more logically, they would involve alternative approaches to economic priorities and policies. For example, we may want to show a scenario with more restrictive fiscal and monetary policy to bring the U.S. economy to a lower rate of inflation and a reduced current account deficit. On the opposite side, we may want to provide additional stimulus to reduce the unemployment rate further even at the risk of higher inflation and other economic imbalances.

- Macro- and micro-policy coordination studies. The strategic impediments initiative (SII) talks provide an example of international policy discussions dealing with issues on the macro and micro level. The NIRA-LINK system is an appropriate instrument for alternative SII proposals making adjustments at the aggregate and the sectoral level. Similarly, we may consider a redirection of Japanese demand toward higher levels of consumption or housing.

- Additional industrial policy simulations. There are many alternative possibilities for investigating industrial policies in Japan and in the United States. As described in Adams and Klein (1983), and Adams (1985), these policies can take the form of general stimulus to investment, education, research, and development, or they may take the form of sector-specific policies, as illustrated above. A variety of policy measures can be tested. A particular concern should be the competitiveness of advanced technology industries in both countries.

- Wage and price policies. Wage and price policies significantly affect the international competitiveness of many industries. There are interesting possibilities to consider: the impact of minimum wage policies in the United States, for example, and wage offensive in Japan.

- Readjustment scenarios, and experiments to investigate various ways to wipe out current international and internal disequilibrium. Can the United States and Japan develop coordinated policies that will achieve adjustment and that will maintain internal and external equilibrium?

- Exchange rate scenarios. Alternative approaches to exchange rates with respect to the dollar, the yen, and the exchange rates of competing countries can be further examined.

- The impact of technological and social trends. The long-term simulations offer the opportunity to examine more deeply the impact of long-term trends in technology, for example the productivity slowdown in the United States or the transfer of technology to competing countries. Social trends, such as the aging of the population, also bear further study.

- Sectoral disturbances. The system can also serve to examine the impact of sectoral disturbances, such as the movement of oil prices or the effect of large-scale labor disputes, natural disasters, and so forth.

The model system presented in this volume represents a contribution to the modeling of the U.S.-Japan-World economy by providing an integrated treatment of macroeconomic change and trade and production developments at the industry level. Refinements of the system would help provide a more complete picture of the interdependence of the U.S., Japan, and the rest of the world economies.

NOTES

CHAPTER 1

1. The LINK model is described in Ball (1973), Sawyer (1979), Waelbroeck (1976), and Klein, Pauly, and Voisin (1982).

CHAPTER 2

1. Detailed descriptions of the models can be found in Wharton Econometric Forecasting Associates (1982), Preston (1972), Economic Planning Agency (1985), and Shishido, Harada, and Matsumura (1990).

2. For a discussion of the relevant issues and for empirical studies of exchange rate pass-through, see Gangnes (1990) and Marquez (1991).

3. The average is dominated by the low estimates for autos and electrical and nonelectrical machinery, which together account for about 75% of U.S. manufacturing imports.

4. See Houthakker and Magee (1969). For a recent study using spectral methods, see Haynes and Stone (1983). Overall income elasticities from Houthakker and Magee (1969) are 1.51 for the United States and 1.23 for Japan.

5. On the other hand, the trend terms may account for shifts in export supply that are not otherwise captured by the equations. However, the use of lagged dependent variables in several equations (including automobiles) is problematic for another reason. The lagged dependent variable introduces an inertia into the equations' responses to price or activity shocks that may be unrealistic.

6. Stern, Francis, and Schumacher (1976) (as cited in Ethier, 1988) report estimates of U.S. import price elasticities ranging from -0.4 to -3.00, with a "best guess" value of -1.66. Petri (1984) reports a range of elasticity estimates from more recent studies of -0.41 to -2.25.

7. See, for instance, Shishido, Harada and Matsumura (1990), Economic Planning Agency (1985), Kinoshita et al. (1982), and Ueno and Muto (1975).

8. See Shishido et al. (1986).

9. See Shishido, Harada, and Matsumura (1990) for the static version on a larger I-O coefficient matrix.

10. See note 4, above.

CHAPTER 3

1. See Gangnes (1990) and Marquez (1988).

2. For a recent discussion of Project LINK, see Bodkin, Klein, and Marwah (1991) and Hickman, Klein, and Pauly (forthcoming). For earlier descriptions and applications of the LINK model, see Ball (1973), Sawyer (1979), Waelbroeck (1976), and Klein, Pauly, and Voisin (1982).

CHAPTER 4

1. Interestingly, the baseline simulation has a faster rate of increase in U.S. nominal imports from Canada than from Japan. As a result, although the U.S. imports more from Japan in 1987 ($78.6 billion, compared with $65.6 billion for Canada), by 1992 imports from Canada ($11.5 billion) exceed those from Japan ($103.5 billion). This appears to be a price effect resulting from lower inflation in Japanese exports than in overall world exports.

2. The difference in instruments makes the two simulations not exactly comparable, since government investment and defense spending play somewhat different roles in the Japan and U.S. models. In both cases, the instrument used is the fiscal instrument of choice of the source-country modeling group.

3. As Helliwell (1988) points out, country size affects international transmission in two ways: an equal percentage fiscal stimulus will be a smaller absolute increase in Japan than in the United States, and the resulting change in trade flows will be a smaller percentage of U.S. GNP than of Japan's GNP. Since Japan's GNP is roughly one-half as large as U.S. GNP, we would therefore expect a bilateral transmission of Japanese activity 1/4th as large as for a U.S. expansion, if multipliers and propensities to import were equal. So the relative effect of Japan expansion on the United States found here (1/10th) is only about half as strong as expected based on these simple calculations. The source of the remaining difference is the smaller import response in Japan.

4. Recent data suggest that such a change may be occurring.

5. Extensive empirical work on this topic is reported in Marquez (1988, 1990, 1991).

6. The percent changes in manufacturing imports shown in this table are not directly comparable to the percent changes in aggregate imports of Table 4.7, repeated as the last line in this table. This is due to a significant constant adjustment used to bridge between the industrially detailed manufacturing categories and the aggregate trade data. In particular, the 10.6% increase in manufacturing imports reported in the second column is roughly equivalent to the 6.9% increase in the aggregate import volume, and does not

indicate that manufacturing imports grew by more than nonmanufactures.

7. The remaining 2.8% rise in imports appears high if the weighted average activity elasticity, 0.57, is applied to the average percent rise in GNP of about 2.5% in the first several years. In fact, manufacturing output rises about 5% during this period, explaining the strong stimulus in imports from the activity side. This illustrates the point made in Chapter 2 that with respect to income, the elasticity is close to one.

8. Interestingly, the early year transmission effects are much higher than those reported a few years earlier in the Oudiz and Sachs (1984) paper, discussed below.

9. The twelve models in the Brookings study showed an average 1.12% appreciation in the first year and 1.33% by year six. Only one model, the Wharton World model, showed a substantial dollar depreciation following the U.S. fiscal expansion. The LINK model shows a very small (0.3%) depreciation under the fiscal expansion.

10. Oudiz and Sachs (1984) have argued that this asymmetrical behavior may be due to the low interest elasticity of money demand in the U.S. economy and disproportionately high marginal propensity to hold dollar-denominated assets. Foreign investors are willing to accumulate the excess U.S. foreign debt so that a depreciation is not necessary to maintain portfolio equilibrium.

Such asymmetrical exchange rate behavior is far from an established fact, however. The more recent analysis by Helliwell (1988) finds currency appreciations following fiscal expansions for both the United States and Japan in the MCM and EPA Models, with the only depreciation occurring with a U.S. fiscal expansion under the OECD Model.

11. The expression is not a closed form; the final double sum, which captures second-order (and third-order) effects of other industry demand, includes a set of X terms.

The closed form is, of course, obtained from inversion of the basic input-output relationship of Chapter 2:

$$AX + (Hg + N) = X$$

where N, the net export vector, is now split out from the other components of final demand.

The inverse is given by

$$X = (I - A)^{-1} (Hg + N)$$

which can be written less compactly as

$$X = \Sigma_j b_{ij} (\Sigma_l h_{jl} g_l + E_j + M_j)$$

where g_l represents the macro-domestic final expenditure categories, which are allocated across industries according to the ratios h_{jl}, and b_{ij} are elements of the inverse of the technical coefficients matrix A. Industry output depends on trade $(E_j\text{-}M_j)$ of this and other industries, as well as the intermediate demand $(h_{jl}g_l)$ of other industries.

12. Since a comparable disaggregated macro model of U.S.-Japan trade does not exist, it is difficult to find other industry-level transmission effects with which to compare these results. A comparison with Petri's (1984) "direct effects" of a U.S. fiscal expansion (effects on Japanese industries after product markets have cleared, but before effects on

terms of trade and income levels have occurred) shows uniformly larger results for the NIRA-LINK model but a somewhat similar ranking by industries:

	Petri	NIRA-LINK
•Transport Equipment	0.05%	0.15%
•Machinery, Instruments	0.02	0.08
•Electrical Machinery	0.02	0.12
•Misc. Manufactures	0.013	0.014
•Iron, Steel	0.008	0.06
•Textiles, Apparel	0.003	0.013
•Chemicals	0.002	0.04
•Metal Products	-0.001	0.02
•Wood, Paper	-0.005	0.013
•Stone, Clay, Glass	-0.012	0.02

The numbers given are percent changes from baseline Japan real GNE. Some of Petri's direct effects are negative, since world prices may rise to clear world markets. Except for textiles/apparel and transportation equipment, the full general equilibrium effects are negative.

13. Some of the service industries are indeed traded, but such links have not (yet) been established in the model system.

14. The other Big Seven countries are the United Kingdom, France, Canada, Italy and the Federal Republic of Germany.

The simulation performed here is somewhat different from those performed for the U.S. and Japan economies. Here, government consumption is raised 1% above the base level in each year of the simulation (the absolute size of the shock rises over the simulation period), whereas in the U.S. and Japan simulations a constant absolute change equal to 1% of first-year GNP was applied in each simulation year. Therefore, the policies implemented here are somewhat larger than those applied in the U.S. and Japanese simulations.

CHAPTER 5

1. The particular changes simulated were chosen for pragmatic and policy considerations. The 8% yen appreciation is the change needed to bring the yen/dollar rate to about 120 ¥/$, a "magic number" in policy discussions. In the case of the dollar depreciation, only the currencies of the other Big Seven countries (including Japan) were altered. Other currencies are assumed to be tied to the U.S. dollar.

2. The $/¥ exchange value index of the Japan model is raised 8% above its exogenous baseline path. Since the dollar is the numeraire currency of the LINK system, the change represents an appreciation of the yen against all world currencies. A one-for-one price pass-through would be an increase of 7.4%, since an 8% increase in the exchange value of the yen is equivalent to a 7.4% appreciation of the reciprocal yen/dollar exchange rates.

3. The specification of Japanese export equations and a table of exchange rate

elasticities are given below.

4. The expected change in prices of U.S. imports from Japan, if there is no change in the yen export prices, is not 8%, but 5.6% This number arises from comparing across simulations price changes, which are determined through time. U.S. import prices from Japan *(USPM$_s$)* are linked to Japan export prices by equations of the form:

$$\%\Delta \ (USPM_s) \ = \ \%\Delta \ (JAPE_Y) \ - \ \%\Delta \ (JAREXL)$$

When the yen/dollar exchange rate *(JAREXL)* is reduced 7.4% (see note 2), the change in USPM relative to the base simulation depends on the absolute magnitudes of *JAREXL*, *JAPE*, and *USPM* in the base and scenario simulations.

5. Recall that four of these five categories (industrial chemicals, other nonferrous metals, aircraft, and other transportation equipment) also exhibit rather extreme responses to a fiscal policy shock, so some caution should be used in interpreting these results.

6. In fact, for iron ore and crude petroleum, the gross output price depends only on the import price.

7. The weights used, from baseline forecast U.S. nominal dollar imports in 1988, are: Japan 28.7%; Canada 17.5%, France 2.5%; West Germany 6.5%; Italy 2.7%; United Kingdom 4.7%; rest of world 47.4%.

8. Second-year results are reported, rather than first-year results, since some pass-through coefficients incorporate one-year lags. Because of this, peculiar spikes in dollar prices occur for some industries in year one, before the offsetting yen price reductions are fully effective.

9. The "perverse" movements in export prices in tobacco, natural textiles, wood products, iron and steel, other nonferrous metals, and instruments reflect the "positive" pass-through elasticities estimated for these industries.

CHAPTER 6

1. In reality, these hopeful assumptions have been outpaced by events. In view of the Gulf War and the recession, actual deficits remain much higher than assumed here.

2. Because of solution problems, value-added prices and corporate profits were exogenized in the Japanese model.

3. For the purpose of these simulations, U.S. high-tech industries include electrical and nonelectrical machinery, instruments, nonautomobile transportation equipment, chemicals, and miscellaneous manufactures.

4. The tariff rates are taken from Table 9.2 (pp. 162-163) of Whalley (1985). Other simulations using similar data from Deardorff and Stern (1986) are reported in Gangnes (1990).

5. In fact, since the model system did not initially incorporate a tariff structure, tariff reductions were introduced by adding negative tariff rates of the appropriate magnitude. An accounting framework for tariff revenues was also introduced.

6. For this reason, U.S. imports of nonmanufactures are not modeled at the industry level. See Chapter 2.

7. Not to mention interindustry effects via the input-output system, discussed briefly

below.

8. Price and income elasticities were given in Tables 2.3 and 2.5 of Chapter 2.

9. Compare the Japan and Overall tariff reductions in Table 6.20. Because changes in prices exclusive of tariffs are small, the changes in tariff-inclusive prices are essentially equal to the tariff reductions.

10. The very large (in percentage terms) increases in industrial chemicals, aircraft (by 1999), and "other transportation equipment" are partly the result of rather peculiar functional forms for these equations. The industrial chemicals category was fitted with a negative income elasticity, so that as activity falls, imports rise. The other two industries are among several fitted with a lagged dependent variable, causing prolonged increases after an initial shock.

11. Imports of agricultural goods are not up by as much as might be expected given the magnitude of the tariff declines, since elasticities in these industries are rather small.

12. Japanese imports of agricultural goods are protected by quotas in many cases, so that the modeled effects of tariff reductions may overestimate the actual increases in these categories.

13. Japanese tariffs on tobacco products were reduced considerably in 1987.

14. Although not shown, U.S. imports of nonmanufactures do change at the industrial level, but by "fixed" shares of imports in the broader LINK trade categories. In this case, nonmanufacturing imports are below base.

15. Of course, significant trade does occur in many service industries, but it is not modeled here.

CHAPTER 7

1. A recent application for Japanese auto investment in the United States is Adams, Gangnes, and Huang (1991).

BIBLIOGRAPHY

Adams, F. Gerard. *Industrial Policies for Growth and Competitiveness: Volume II, Empirical Studies.* Lexington: D.C. Heath, 1985.

_____. "Eliminating the Federal Budget Deficit Without Recession?" *Annals of the American Academy of Political and Social Sciences* 500 (November, 1988).

_____, and Byron Gangnes. "Macroeconomic Impacts of U.S.-Japan Trade Linkages with Linked Econometric Models." Economics Research Unit Working Paper, University of Pennsylvania, 1987.

_____, Byron Gangnes, and Gene Huang. "Impact of Japanese Investment in US Automobile Production." *Journal of Policy Modeling* 13, no. 4 (Winter, 1991).

_____, Byron Gangnes, and Shuntaro Shishido. *Structure of Trade and Industry in the U.S.-Japan Economy: Phase II. Integration with Project LINK and Simulation Applications.* NIRA Research Output 3, no. 1. Tokyo: National Institute for Research Advancement, 1990.

_____, and Lawrence R. Klein. *Industrial Policies for Growth and Competitiveness: Volume I.* Lexington: D.C. Heath, 1983.

_____, and Lawrence R. Klein. "Performance of Quarterly Econometric Models of the United States: A New Round of Model Comparisons." In L.R. Klein (ed.), *Comparative Performance of U.S. Econometric Models.* New York: Oxford University Press, 1991.

_____, and Shuntaro Shishido. *Structure of Trade and Industry in the U.S.-Japan Economy.* NIRA Output, NRS-85-1. Tokyo: National Institute for Research Advancement, February, 1987.

Armington, Paul S. "A Theory of Products Distinguished by Place of Production." *IMF Staff Papers* 16 (1969): 159-177.

Baldwin, Richard. "Some Empirical Evidence of Hysteresis in Aggregate US Import Prices." NBER Working Paper no. 2483 (January, 1988).

Ball, R. J., ed. *The International Linkage of National Economic Models*. Amsterdam: North-Holland, 1973.

Bergsten, C. Fred, and William R. Cline. *The United States-Japan Economic Problem*. Policy Analyses in International Economics no. 13. Washington: Institute for International Economics, 1985.

Bodkin, Ronald G., Lawrence R. Klein, and Kanta Marwah. *A History of Macroeconometric Model-Building*. Aldershot: Edward Elgar, 1991.

Bryant, Ralph C. et al., eds. *Empirical Macroeconomics for Interdependent Economies*, Supplemental Volume. Washington, D.C.: The Brookings Institution, 1988.

Deardorff, Alan V., and Robert M. Stern. *The Michigan Model of World Production and Trade: Theory and Applications*. Cambridge: MIT Press, 1986.

Dornbusch, Rudiger. "Exchange Rates and Prices." *American Economic Review* 77, no. 1 (March, 1987): 93-106.

Economic Planning Agency. *Multi-Sectoral Economic Models for Medium and Long Term Analysis, Summary of the Seventh Report of the Committee for Econometric Model Analysis*. Tokyo: Economic Planning Agency, 1985.

Ethier, Wilfred. *Modern International Economics*. 2d ed. New York: W. W. Norton, 1988.

Foster, Harry. "The Relationship Between U.S. Import Prices and the Exchange Rate: An Empirical Investigation." Mimeo, MIT (December, 1986).

Gangnes, Byron. "U.S.-Japan Interdependence in a Detailed Econometric Model of Trade and Industry," unpublished Ph.D. dissertation. Philadelphia: University of Pennsylvania, 1990.

Haynes, S. E., and J. A. Stone. "Secular and Cyclical Responses of U.S. Trade to Income: An Evaluation of Traditional Models." *Review of Economics and Statistics* 65 (1983): 87-95.

Helliwell, John F. "The Effects of Fiscal Policy on International Imbalances: Japan and the United States." NBER Working Paper no. 2650 (July, 1988).

Hickman, Bert, Lawrence R. Klein, and Peter Pauly. *Interdependence in the Global Economy: Recent Advances in Project LINK*.   Amsterdam: North-Holland, forthcoming.

Hickman, Bert, and L. Lau. "Elasticities of Substitution and Export Demands in a World Trade Model." *European Economic Review* 4 (1973): 347-380.

Houthakker, H. S., and S. P. Magee. "Income and Price Elasticities in World Trade." *Review of Economics and Statistics* 51 (1969): 111-125.

Ishii, Naoko, W. McKibbin, and J. Sachs. "Macroeconomic Interdependence of Japan and the United States: Some Simulation Results." NBER Working Paper no. 1637 (June, 1985).

Kendrick, David. *Stochastic Control for Economic Models*. New York: McGraw-Hill, 1981.

Kinoshita, S., et al. *Development and Application for International Industry-Trade Model*. Series no. 38, Economic Research Institute. Tokyo: Economic Planning Agency (in Japanese), 1982.

Klein, Lawrence R. "The LINK Model and Its Use in International Scenario Analysis." In Homa Motamen (ed.), *Economic Modelling in the OECD Countries*, pp. 1-10. London: Chapman and Hall, 1988.

_____. "The Case for International Coordination of Economic Policy". *Business in the Contemporary World* 1 (Spring, 1989): 11-16.

_____, A. Bollino, and S. Fardoust. "International Interactions of Industrial Policy: Simulations of the World Economy, 1982-1990." In F. G. Adams (ed.), *Industrial Policies for Growth and Competitiveness: Volume II: Empirical Studies*, pp. 15-21. Lexington, Mass.: Lexington Books, 1985.

_____, J. Duesenberry, G. Fromm, and E. Kuh. *The Brookings Quarterly Econometric Model of the United States*. Chicago: Rand McNally, 1965.

_____, P. Pauly, and C. Petersen. "Empirical Aspects of Protectionism: Results from Project LINK." In D. Salvatore (ed.), *The New Protectionist Threat to World Trade*, pp. 69-94. Amsterdam: North-Holland, 1987.

_____, P. Pauly and P. Voisin. "The World Economy: A Global Model." *Perspectives in Computing* 2, no. 2 (May, 1982): 4-17.

Krugman, Paul R. "Pricing to Market When the Exchange Rate Changes." In S. W. Arndt and J. D. Richardson (eds.), *Real-Financial Linkages Among Open Economies*. Cambridge: MIT Press, 1986.

Mann, Catherine L. "Prices, Profit Margins, and Exchange Rates." *Federal Reserve Bulletin* (June, 1986).

Marquez, Jaime. "Income and Price Elasticities of Foreign Trade Flows." International Finance Discussion Paper no. 324. Washington: Federal Reserve Board, 1988.

_____. "Bilateral Trade Elasticities." *Review of Economics and Statistics* 72 (1990): 70-77.

_____. "The Econometrics of Elasticities or the Elasticity of Econometrics." International Finance Discussion Paper no. 396. Washington: Federal Reserve Board, 1991.

Oudiz, Gilles, and Jeffrey Sachs. "Macroeconomic Policy Coordination Among the Industrial Economies." *Brookings Papers on Economic Activity*, no. 1 (1984): 1-75.

Petersen, Christian. "Dynamic Bilateral Tariff Games: An Econometric Analysis." Ph.D. dissertation. Philadelphia: University of Pennsylvania, 1988.

Petri, Peter A. *Modeling Japanese-American Trade: A Study of Asymmetric Interdependence*. Cambridge: Harvard University Press, 1984.

Preston, Ross S. *The Wharton Annual and Industry Forecasting Model*. Studies in Quantitative Economics, no. 7. Philadelphia: University of Pennsylvania, 1972.

Sawyer, J. *Modeling the International Transmission Mechanism*. Amsterdam: North-Holland, 1979.

Shishido, S., K. Harada, and Y. Matsumura. "Technical Progress in an Input-Output Framework with Special Reference to Japan's High Technology Industries." In W. Peterson (ed.), *Advances in Input-Output Analysis: Technology, Development and Planning,* Proceedings of the Eighth International Conference on Input-Output Techniques. Oxford University Press, forthcoming.

_____, et al. *Studies on Long-Term International Impacts of Japan's High-Technology Industries.* NRS-84-13. Tokyo: Foundation for the Advancement of International Science, 1986.

Stern, R.M., J. Francis, and B. Schumacher. *Price Elasticities in International Trade*. London: Macmillan, 1976.

Ueno, Hiroya and Hiroichi Muto. "A Multisectoral Model on the Japanese Economy." In H. Ueno and Y. Murakami (eds.), *Econometric Studies on the Japanese Economy*. Tokyo: Iwanami Inc. (in Japanese), 1975.

Waelbroeck, J., ed. *The Models of Project LINK.* Amsterdam: North-Holland, 1976.

The WEFA Group. *US Long-Term Outlook.* Bala Cynwyd, Pennsylvania: The WEFA Group, 1989.

Whalley, John. *Trade Liberalization Among Major World Trading Areas.* Cambridge: MIT Press, 1985.

Wharton Econometric Forecasting Associates. *Wharton Long-Term Model Structure and Specification.* Bala Cynwyd, Pennsylvania: The WEFA Group, 1982.

INDEX

About the Authors

F. GERARD ADAMS is Professor of Economics and Finance and Director of the Economic Research Unit at the University of Pennsylvania.

BYRON GANGNES is Assistant Professor of Economics at the University of Hawaii at Manoa.

SHUNTARO SHISHIDO is President of the International University of Japan.